THE FATHERS
OF THE CHURCH

A NEW TRANSLATION

VOLUME 88

THE FATHERS
OF THE CHURCH

A NEW TRANSLATION

ST. AUGUSTINE

TRACTATES ON THE
GOSPEL OF JOHN
28–54

Translated by

JOHN W. RETTIG
Xavier University
Cincinnati, Ohio

THE CATHOLIC UNIVERSITY OF AMERICA PRESS
Washington, D.C.

The paper used in this publication meets the minimum requirements of
American National Standards for Information Sciences—Permanence of
Paper for Printed Library Materials. ANSI Z39–48–1984
∞

LIBRARY OF CONGRESS CATALOGING-IN-PUBLICATION DATA
(Revised for vol. 3)
Augustine, Saint, Bishop of Hippo.
    Tractates on the Gospel of John.
    (The Fathers of the church ; v. 78–   )
    Translation of: In Evangelium Iohannis
tractatus.
    Bibliography: v. 1, p. ix–xiii.
    Includes indexes.
    Contents: [1] 1–10 — [2] 11–27 — [3] 28–54
    1. Bible. N.T. John—Sermons—Early works
to 1800. 2. Sermons, Latin—Translations into
English—Early works to 1800. 3. Sermons,
English—Translations from Latin—Early works to 1800.
I. Title.   II. Series: Fathers of the church ; v. 78, etc.
BR60.F3A8246   [BS2615]   270 s 226'.506   87–18387
ISBN 0–8132–0078–4 (v. 1)
ISBN 0–8132–0079–2 (v. 2)
ISBN 0–8132–0088–1 (v. 3)

CONTENTS

CONTENTS

ABBREVIATIONS

Works of Augustine

DCD	*De Civitate Dei*
DDC	*De Doctrina Christiana*
DDQ	*De Diversis Questionibus* LXXXIII
En in Ps	*Enarrationes in Psalmos*
Tr in Io Ep	*Tractatus in Primam Epistulam Johannis*

SELECT BIBLIOGRAPHY

[See FOTC 78, pp. ix–xiii; 79, pp. ix–xiv]

Texts and Translations

Berrouard, M.-F. *Homélies sur l'évangile de saint Jean*, I–XVI, BA 71 (1969), XVII–XXXIII, BA 72 (1977), XXXIV–XLIII, BA 73A (1988), XLIV–LIV, BA 73B (1989).

Browne, H. *Homilies on the Gospel According to St. John, and His First Epistle by St. Augustine, Bishop of Hippo*, LFC 26 (1848), 29 (1849).

Caillau, A., et al. (edd.) *A. Aur. Augustini Hipponensis Episcopi In Joannis Evangelium Tractatus CXXIV*, *Patres Ecclesiae* 121, 122, 123. *Augustinus* 14, 15, 16. Paris, 1842.

Gibb, J. *Lectures of Tractates on the Gospel According to St. John*. Vol. 1, Tractates 1–37. The Works of Aurelius Augustine. Vol 10. Edinburgh, 1873.

Gibb, J., Innes, J. *St. Augustine: Lectures or Tractates on the Gospel According to St. John*. LNPF 7, series 1, 1888. Reprint. Grand Rapids, Michigan: Wm. B. Eerdmans, 1983.

Migne, J.-P. *In Joannis Evangelium Tractatus CXXIV*, PL 35.1375–1970. This edition is a reprint of the edition of the Benedictines of St. Maur, *S. Aurelii Augustini Operum*, ed. J. Blampin, P. Coustan, et al., vol. 3, pars altera. Paris, 1680.

Willems, R., ed. *Sancti Aurelii Augustini In Johannis Evangelium Tractatus CXXIV*. CCL 36 (1954).

Secondary Sources

Bardy, G. "Tractare, Tractatus," RSR 33 (1946) 211–35.

Burkitt, F. *The Religion of the Manichees*. Cambridge, 1896.

Burnaby, J. *Amor Dei: A Study of the Religion of St. Augustine*. London, 1938.

Comeau, M. *Saint Augustin, exégète du quatrième évangile*. Paris, 1930.

Decret, F. *Aspects du Manichéisme dans l'Afrique romaine*. Paris, 1970.

De Plinval, G. *Pélage. Ses écrite, sa vie et sa réforme*. Lausanne, 1943.

Dölger, F. "Konstantin der Grosse und der Manichaismus, Sonne und Christus in Manichaismus," AC 2 (1930) 301–14.

Fairweather, E. "Saint Augustine's Interpretation of Infant Baptism." *Augustinus Magister* II (Paris, 1954) 897–903.

Frend, W. *The Donatist Church*. Oxford, 1952.

Gallay, J. *L'Église dans l'empire romain (iv–v siécles)*. Paris, 1958.

Gilson, E. *The Christian Philosophy of Saint Augustine*, tr. L. Lynch. New York, 1960.

Kelly, J. *Early Christian Creeds*, 3d ed. New York, 1981.

———. *Early Christian Doctrines*, 5th ed. New York, 1976.

ix

Koenen, L. "Augustine and Manicheism in light of the Cologne Mani Codex," *Illinois Classical Studies* 3 (1978) 154–95.

Mohrmann, C. *Die Altchristlishe Sondersprache in den Sermones des hl. Augustin.* 2d ed. Amsterdam, 1965.

Moon, A. *The De Natura Boni of Augustine,* Catholic University of America, Patristic Studies 88. Washington, D.C., 1955.

Pétré, H. *Caritas: Étude sur le Vocabulaire de la charité chrétienne. Specilegium Sacrum Lovaniense Études et Documents* 22. Louvain, 1948.

Pontet, M. *L'exégèse de s. Augustin prédicateur.* Paris, 1945.

Portalié, E. *A Guide to the Thought of Saint Augustine,* tr. R. Bastian. Chicago, 1960.

Prestige, G. *God in Patristic Thought.* London, 1949.

Raven, C. *Apollinarianism.* Cambridge, 1923.

Reardon, B. "The Relation of Philosophy to Faith in the Teaching of St. Augustine," *Studia Patristica* 2 (1957) 288–94.

Schumacher, W. *Spiritus and Spiritualis: a Study in the Sermons of St. Augustine.* Mundelein, Ill., 1957.

TeSelle, E. *Augustine the Theologian.* New York, 1970.

Testard, M. *Saint Augustin et Cicéron.* Paris, 1958.

Widengren, G. *Mani and Manichaeism.* Tr. C. Kessler. London, 1965.

Wright, D. F. "The Manuscripts of the *Tractatus in Evangelium Johannis:* A Supplementary List," RechAug 16 (1981) 59–100.

Van der Meer, F. *Augustine the Bishop,* tr. B. Battershaw and G. Lamb. New York, 1961.

TRACTATES
28–54

TRACTATE 28*

On John 7.1–13

I N THIS section of the Gospel, brothers, our Lord Jesus Christ has very much commended himself to our faith according to his humanness. For he always in his words and works effects this, that he be believed as God and man, God who made us, man who sought after us, God with the Father forever, man with us in time. For he would not seek after that which he had made unless he himself became what he had made. But remember this and do not dismiss it from your hearts: that Christ was made man in such a way that he did not cease to be God. Remaining God, he who made man received the man.

(2) Therefore, when he hid as a man, he must not be thought to have lost his power, but to have offered an example to weakness.[1] For when he wished it, he was arrested; when he wished it, he was put to death. But since there would be his members, that is, his faithful, who would not have that power which our God himself had, by hiding, by concealing himself as if [he were doing this] that he might not be killed, he indicated that his members, among whom, of course, he himself was, would do this. For Christ is not in the head *or* in the body, but Christ is wholly in the head *and* in the body. Therefore, what his members are, he is; but what he is, his members are not necessarily. For if he were not his members, he would not have said, "Saul, why do you persecute me?"[2] For Saul was not persecuting him, but his members, that is, his

---

*[Ed. note: The translation has been checked against the text in BA 72, 73A, 73B, and the paragraphing has been adopted throughout.]

1. Cf. *Tractate* 15.2.
2. Acts 9.4; cf. *Tractate* 21.7.

faithful on earth. Yet he did not want to say, my saints, my servants, or the more honorable, my brothers, but "me", that is, my members for whom I am the head.

2. With these preliminary remarks, I think we shall not labor over the section that has just been read; for often what was to be in the body has been signified in the head. [The Gospel] says, "After these things Jesus walked in Galilee, for he did not wish to walk in Judaea because the Jews were seeking to kill him." This is what I meant: he offered an example for our weakness. For he had not himself lost his power, but was comforting our frailness. For it was to be, as I have said, that some believer of his would hide himself that he might not be found by persecutors; and that his hiding place might not be thrown in his face as a crime, that which would be confirmed in the member preceded in the head. For so it was said, "He did not wish to walk in Judaea because the Jews were seeking to kill him," as if Christ could not walk among the Jews and not be killed by the Jews. For when he wanted, he showed this power. When they wanted to arrest him, then, when he was going to suffer, "He said to them, 'Whom do you seek?' They answered, 'Jesus.' And he said, 'I am he,'"[3] not hiding, but manifesting himself. Yet they did not stand firm at this manifestation, but "they drew back and fell."[4] And yet because he had come to suffer, they got up, arrested him, took him before the judge, and slew him. But what did they do? What a certain Scripture says: "The earth has been given into the hands of the wicked."[5] His flesh was given to the Jews, into their power. And this was done for the reason that, like a money sack, he might be torn that the price for us might pour out of there.

3. "Now on the next day was the Jews' feast of Scenopegia." They who have read the Scriptures know what Scenopegia is. On this feast day they make tents,[6] in the likeness of the tents

3. Jn 18.4–5.   4. Jn 18.6.
5. Cf. Jb 9.24.
6. The Latin word is *tabernaculum* which is richer in meaning than the English word tent since it could include huts and booths as well as simple tents, and since it also suggests the lavish tent that housed the Ark of the

in which they dwelt when they were led out of Egypt and were traveling in the desert. This was a feast day, a great solemn celebration. For the Jews kept this festival, they who were going to kill the Lord, as if they were recalling the benefits of the Lord.

(2) Therefore, on this feast day (there were several feast days, for a feast day was so called among the Jews that it was not one day, but several) "his brothers" spoke to the Lord Christ. Accept "his brothers" in the way you know; for this is not a strange thing that you hear. The relatives of the Virgin Mary were called the Lord's brothers. For it was the usual practice in the Scriptures to call any relatives or near relatives brothers;[7] this is outside our usage and not in the manner in which we speak. For who would call his mother's brother or his sister's son brothers? Yet Scripture calls even relatives of this sort brothers. For Abraham and Lot were called brothers, although Abraham was the paternal uncle of Lot;[8] and Laban and Jacob were called brothers although Laban was the maternal uncle of Jacob.[9] When, therefore, you hear of the Lord's brothers, think of kinship to Mary, not any progeny from her bearing again. For as in the tomb where the body of Christ was placed, no dead man was laid either before or afterwards, so the womb of Mary did not conceive anything mortal either before or afterwards.

4. We have said who his brothers were; let us hear what they said. "Leave here and go into Judaea that your disciples also may see your works which you do." The works of the Lord were not unknown to the disciples, but were unknown to these men. For these brothers, that is, relatives, were able to have Christ as a relative, but they were loathe to believe in him because of that very relationship. It was said in the Gospel; for we do not dare to conjecture this ourselves; you just heard it.

Covenant. But the English tabernacle has an inappropriate range of meanings for this context. Berrouard BA 72.572 points out that in *Sermo* 133.1 (PL 38.737) Augustine states that the North African Jews in his time kept this feast and built huts (*casae*).

7. Cf. *Tractate* 10.2.   8. Cf. Gn 11.27, 31; 13.8; and 14.14.
9. Cf. Gn 28.2 and 29.10–15.

[To this] they add and advise: "For no man does anything in secret, and he himself seeks to be known openly. If you do these things, manifest yourself to the world." And immediately, "For neither did his brothers believe in him." Why did they not believe in him? Because they were looking for human glory. For even in what his brothers seemed to advise him, they had regard for his glory. You do miraculous things; become known. That is, appear before all, that you can be praised by all. Flesh was speaking to flesh, but flesh without God to flesh with God. For the practical wisdom of the flesh[10] was speaking to the Word which was made flesh and dwelt among us.[11]

5. What did the Lord [reply] to these words? "Then Jesus said to them, 'My time has not yet come, but your time is always ready.'" What is this? Had Christ's time not yet come? Then why had Christ come, if his time had not yet come? Have we not heard the Apostle saying, "But when the fullness of time came, God sent his Son"?[12] Therefore, if he was sent in the fullness of time, he was sent when he ought to have been, he came when it was necessary. What does "My time has not yet come" mean? Understand, brothers, with what motive they who seem to advise him as their brother were speaking. They were giving him advice to pursue glory, advising him as if in a worldly manner and with an earthly disposition, that he might not be unknown and hidden. The Lord's words, "My time has not yet come," therefore, were his answer to those who were giving him advice about glory: The time of my glory has not yet come.

(2) See how profound it is. They were advising him about glory; but he intended to precede loftiness with humility and, through humility, to pave the way for loftiness itself. For, of course, even those disciples who wanted to sit, the one on his right, the other on his left, were looking to glory.[13] They observed where, but they did not see by what way; the Lord, so that they might come to their homeland in proper order,

10. Cf. Rom 8.6.   11. Cf. Jn 1.14.
12. Gal 4.4.   13. Cf. Mt 20.20–23; Mk 10.35–40.

called them back to the way.[14] For the homeland is on high; the way is low. The homeland is the life of Christ; the way is the death of Christ. The homeland is the dwelling of Christ;[15] the way is the suffering of Christ. He who rejects the way, why does he seek the homeland? Finally, to those seeking loftiness, he also answered this: "Can you drink the cup which I shall drink?"[16] See how one comes to the loftiness which you desire. He meant, of course, the cup of humility and suffering.

6. And so also here: "My time has not yet come; but your time," that is, the glory of the world, "is always ready." This is the time about which Christ, that is, the body of Christ, speaks in prophecy: "When I shall take a time, I shall judge justices."[17] For now is not the time of judging, but of enduring the wicked. Let the body of Christ, therefore, now bear and endure the wickedness of those who live evilly. Yet let it have justice now, before it has judgment; for through justice it will come to judgment.

(2) What indeed does holy Scripture say in a psalm to those members who endure the wickedness of this age? "The Lord will not cast off his people."[18] His people, in truth, toil among the unworthy, among the wicked, among blasphemers, among murmurers, detractors, persecutors, and, if it be allowed, killers. It toils indeed, but "the Lord will not cast off his people, and he will not forsake his own inheritance until justice is turned to judgment."[19] "Until justice," which is now in the saints, "is turned to judgment," when what was said to them will be fulfilled, "You will sit upon twelve seats judging the twelve tribes of Israel."[20] The Apostle had justice, but not yet that judgment about which he says, "Do you not know that we shall judge angels?"[21]

(3) Therefore, let it now be the time of living justly; afterwards there will be the time for judging those who have lived

14. Cf. *Tractate* 25.3.
15. By the dwelling (*mansio*) of Christ Augustine means his divinity. See *Tractate* 42.8, *mansio eius, divinitas eius:* his dwelling is his divinity.
16. Mt 20.22.
17. Ps 74 (75).3 (some texts have this as verse 2).

18. Ps 93 (94).14.   19. Ps 93 (94).14–15 (LXX).
20. Mt 19.28; cf. Lk 22.30.   21. 1 Cor 6.3.

evilly. "Until justice," it says, "is turned to judgment." This will be the time of judgment about which the Lord has now said, "My time has not yet come." For there will be a time of glory, that he who came in humility may come in loftiness. He who came to be judged will come to judge. He who came to be killed by the dead will come to judge the living and the dead. The psalm says, "God will come manifest, and our God will not keep silence."[22] What does "will come manifest" mean? That he came hidden. Then, he will not keep silence; for when he came hidden, he was led like a sheep to the slaughter, and like a lamb before the shearer he did not open his mouth.[23] He will come and he will not keep silence. "I have kept silent," he says, "will I always keep silent?"[24]

7. But what is necessary now for those who have justice? That which is read in that same psalm: "Until justice is turned to judgment; and all who have it are upright of heart."[25] Do you ask, perhaps, who the upright of heart are? In Scripture we find that those who endure the evils of this age and do not find fault with God are upright of heart. See, brothers; this is a rare bird[26] of which I speak. For I know not how, when some evil happens to a man, he runs to find fault with God, although he ought to find fault with himself. When you do something good, you praise yourself; when you suffer some evil, you find fault with God. This, then, is a warped heart, not an upright one. If you should be corrected from that distortion and depravity, what you were doing will be turned to the opposite. For what were you doing before? You were praising yourself in the goods of God, you were finding fault with God

---

22. Ps 49 (50).3 (LXX).   23. Cf. Is 53.7.
24. Is 42.14 (LXX).   25. Ps 93 (94).15 (LXX).
26. The phrase *rara avis* is perhaps colloquial; it designates something unusual or uncommon, a marvel, not, however, the phoenix as the scholiast to Persius 1.46 states. The phrase is found in Juvenal 6.165 and is cited four times for Jerome: *Adversus Jovinianum* 1.47 (PL 23.290), which F. Haase, *L. Annaei Senecae Opera Supplementum* (Leipzig, 1902) 26–32, considers extracted from Seneca's *De Matrimonio; Contra Pelagianos* 2.11 (PL 23.572); *De Perpetua Virginitate Beatae Mariae* 20 (PL 23.214); and *In Osee*, prologue (PL 25.820). See TLL 2.1441 and A. Otto, *Die Sprichwörten und Sprichwörtlichen Redensart der Römer* (New York, 1971, originally Leipzig, 1890) 51–52; neither source cites this occurrence.

in your own evils; when your heart is turned and put aright, you will praise God in his goods and find fault with yourself in your evils. These are the upright of heart.

(2) That man, not yet of upright heart, for whom the good fortune of the evil and the labor of the good were displeasing, when corrected, said, "How good is the God of Israel to the upright of heart! But my feet," when I was not of upright heart, "were almost moved, my steps slipped a little." Why? "For I was envious of sinners, seeing the peace of sinners."[27] I saw, he said, that evil men were fortunate, and God displeased me. For my desire was that God not allow evil men to be fortunate. Let man understand. God never allows this; but an evil man is thought to be fortunate precisely because it is not known what good fortune is.[28]

(3) Therefore, let us be upright of heart; the time of our glory has not yet come. Let it be said to the lovers of this age, such as were the brothers of the Lord, "Your time is always ready." Our "time has not yet come." Let us dare to say this also ourselves. And because we are the body of our Lord Jesus Christ, because we are his members, because we acknowledge our head with joy, let us say it straight on; for he himself also thought it good to say this for our sakes. When the lovers of this age taunt us, let us say to them: "Your time is always ready." Our "time has not yet come." For the Apostle said to us: "For you have died and your life is hidden with Christ in God." When will our time come? "When Christ," he said, "your life, shall appear, then you too will appear with him in glory."[29]

8. What then does he add? "The world cannot hate you." What does this mean except that the world cannot hate its lovers, false witnesses? For you call what is evil good and what is good evil.[30] "But it hates me, because I bear witness concerning it, that its works are evil. As for you, go up to this festival day." What does "this" mean? Where you seek human glory. What does "this" mean? Where you want to increase carnal joys, not think about eternal ones. "I do not go up to this

---

27. Ps 72 (73).1–3 (LXX).　　28. Cf. *Tractate* 25.17.
29. Col 3.3–4.　　30. Cf. Is 5.20.

festival day, because my time is not yet fulfilled." In this festival day you seek human glory, but my time, that is, the time of my glory, has not yet come. This will be my festival day, not preceding and extending over these days, but lasting through eternity. It will be festivity, pure joy without end, eternity without blemish, serenity without a cloud.

(2) "When he had said these things, he himself stayed in Galilee. But as soon as his brothers went up, then he also went up to the festival day, not openly, but, as it were, in secret." And so "not to this festival day" because he desired not to glorify himself in time, but to teach something profitably, to correct men, to instruct about the eternal festival day, to turn love away from this age and to turn it to God. But what does it mean, "as it were, in secret he went up to the festival day"? This act of the Lord, too, is not without meaning. For it seems to me, brothers, that even by the fact that he went up as if in secret, he wanted to signify something; for thus the following words will show that he went up when the feast was half over, that is, when those days were half passed, so that he might even teach openly. But it said, "as it were, in secret" that he might not show himself to men. It is not without meaning that Christ went up to the festival day in secret, because he himself was concealed in that festival day. What I have said is also still in secret. Let it be made more manifest, therefore; let the veil be taken away, and let what was secret be made clear.

9. All the things which were said to the ancient people of Israel in the extensive Scriptures of the Holy Law, what they were to do, whether in sacrifices or in priesthoods or in feast days and in any of the things at all by which they worshipped God, whatever was said to or enjoined upon them, were shadows of future things. Of what future things? Those which are fulfilled in Christ. Whence the Apostle says, "For all the promises of God are in him, indeed,"[31] that is, they have been fulfilled in him. Then in another place he says, "All things happened to them in figure, and they were written for us, upon whom the end of the ages has come."[32] And elsewhere

31. 2 Cor 1.20.
32. 1 Cor 10.11.

he said, "For the end of the Law is Christ."[33] Likewise in another place, "Let no man judge you in food or in drink as in regard to a festival day or the new moon of the Sabbaths, that which is a shadow of things to come."[34] Therefore, if all those things were shadows of things to come, the Scenopegia was also a shadow of things to come. Therefore, let us inquire of what thing to come this festival day is a shadow.

(2) I have explained what the Scenopegia was;[35] it was the celebration of the tents, for this reason: because the people, freed from Egypt, travelling through the desert to the land of promise, dwelt in tents. Let us consider what it is, and we shall be [it], we, I say, who are members of Christ, if we are; but we are if he deigns, not because we deserve to be. Let us consider, then, brothers. We have been led out of Egypt where we were serving the devil as a pharoah, where we were doing works of clay amid earthly desires, and we were laboring much in them.[36] For Christ cried out to us, as if we were making bricks, "Come to me, all you who labor and are burdened."[37] Led out of here, we were led over through baptism as through the Red Sea—red for this reason, because consecrated by the blood of Christ—when all our enemies who were assailing us were dead, that is, when our sins have been wiped out.[38]

(3) Now, therefore, before our arrival at the country of promise, that is, the eternal kingdom, we are in the tents in the desert. They who acknowledge these things are in the tents; for it was to be that some would acknowledge this. For he is in the tents who understands that he is an alien in the world; he understands that he is traveling abroad who sees himself sighing for the homeland. But when the body of Christ is in the tents, Christ is in the tents. But then not openly, but in secret. For a shadow still darkened the light; when the light came, the shadow was removed. Christ was in secret, Christ was at the Scenopegia, but a hiding Christ.

(4) Now when these things have been made manifest, we recognize that we are taking a trip in a wasteland; for if we

33. Cf. Rom 10.4.   34. Col 2.16–17.
35. Section 3.   36. Cf. Ex 1.8–14.
37. Mt 11.28.   38. Cf. *Tractate* 11.4.

should recognize it, we are in a wasteland. What does it mean, in a wasteland? In a desert. Why in a desert? Because in this world, where one thirsts on a waterless road. But let us thirst that we may be filled. For "Blessed are they who hunger and thirst for justice; for they shall have their fill."[39] And our thirst is filled from a rock in the wasteland. For "the rock was Christ."[40] And it was struck with a rod that water might flow.[41] But that it might flow, it was struck twice; for there are the two pieces of wood on the cross.[42] Therefore, all these things that happened in figure are manifested in us. And what was said about the Lord is not without meaning: "He went up to the festival day, not openly, but, as it were, in secret." For the fact had been prefigured in secret, because Christ was hidden in this festival day, because the very festival day signified that the members of Christ would be aliens.

10. "The Jews therefore sought him on the festival day," before he went up. For the brothers went up first and he did not go up then when they were thinking and wanting it, so that his words "not to this" might be fulfilled, that is, not to [the day] which you wish, the first or second day. But he went up afterwards, as the Gospel says, "when the feast was half over," that is, when as many days of that feast had already passed as remained. For they celebrated that festivity, as one must understand, for several days.

11. "Therefore they were saying, 'Where is he?' And there was much murmuring among the crowd concerning him." Whence came the murmuring? From a dispute. What was the dispute? "For some were saying, 'He is a good man.' But others were saying, 'No, but he seduces the crowds.'" This must be understood about all his servants; it is said now. For whoever has excelled in some spiritual grace, some do indeed say, "He is a good man"; others say, "No, but he seduces the crowds." Why is this? Because "our life is hidden with Christ in God."[43] And so men may say during the winter: "This tree is dead," a fig tree, for example, or a pear tree, or fruit trees of this sort; it is like a dried-out tree. And as long as it is winter, it

39. Mt. 5.6.
41. Cf. Nm 20.11.
43. Cf. Col 3.3.

40. 1 Cor 10.4.
42. Cf. *Tractate* 26.12.

does not show itself. Summer proves it; judgment proves it. Our summer is the revelation of Christ. "God will come manifest; and our God will not keep silence."[44] "Before him will go a fire"; this fire "will burn his enemies."[45] The fire will seize hold of the dried out trees. For then the trees will appear dried out when it will be said to them: "I was hungry and you did not give me to eat."[46] But on the other side, that is, on the right, the abundance of fruits and the comeliness of leaves will appear; [their] greenness will be eternity. Therefore, it will be said to those, as if they were dried out: "Go into everlasting fire."[47] "For, behold," he[48] said, "the axe is laid to the root of the trees; every tree therefore that does not bring forth good fruit will be cut down and cast into the fire."[49] Therefore, let them say about you, if you advance in Christ, let men say, "He seduces the crowds." This is said about him, about the whole body of Christ. Think about the body of Christ still in the world; think about the body of Christ still on the threshing floor; see how it is blasphemed by the chaff. They are threshed together, it is true, but the chaff is rubbed off, the grain is cleansed.[50] What was said about the Lord, therefore, can produce consolation for any Christian about whom this was said.

12. "Yet no one spoke openly of him for fear of the Jews." But who was not speaking of him for fear of the Jews? They, of course, who said, "He is a good man"; not they who said, "He seduces the crowds." Of those who said, "He seduces the crowds," their voice was heard like that of dry leaves. "He seduces the crowds," they shouted quite loudly; "He is a good man," they whispered with voices quite subdued. But now, brothers, although that glory of Christ, which will make us eternal, has not yet come, still now his Church grows so much, he has deigned to spread it through all places to such an extent, that now it is whispered, "He seduces the crowds," and resounds quite loudly, "He is a good man."

44. Ps 49 (50).3.
45. Ps 96 (97).3.
47. Mt 25.41.
49. Mt 3.10; cf. Lk 3.9.

46. Mt 25.42.
48. That is, John the Baptist.
50. Cf. *Tractate* 27.11, note 30.

TRACTATE 29

On John 7.14–18

ET US also look next at what follows in the Gospel and was read today, and from it let us say what God has bestowed. Yesterday it had been read up to this point: that, although they had not seen the Lord Jesus in the temple during the festival day, they still were talking about him. "And some were saying, 'He is a good man.' But others were saying, 'No, but he seduces the crowds.'"[1] For this was said for the solace of those who, later on, preaching the word of God, would be as seducers and yet truthful men.[2] For if to seduce[3] is to deceive, neither was Christ a seducer nor were his Apostles, nor ought any Christian be a seducer; but if to seduce is to lead someone from one position to another by persuasion, it must be asked from what and to what. If from evil to good, the seducer is good; if from good to evil, the seducer is evil. Therefore, on this side, where men are seduced from evil to good, may all of us both be called and be seducers!

2. Afterwards, therefore, the Lord "went up" to the festival day, "when the feast was half over, and taught. And the Jews wondered, saying, 'How does this man know letters since he has not learned?'" He who was hiding taught and spoke openly, and he was not seized. For that act, his hiding, was for the sake of example; this one [served to show his] power. But when he taught, "the Jews wondered." All of them indeed, I think, wondered, but not all were converted. And why this

1. Jn 7.12.
2. Cf. 2 Cor 6.8.
3. The Latin verb *seducere* has several connotations, including the neutral "to lead aside" and the pejorative "to lead astray." The English "seduce" seems entirely pejorative, but no synonym occurred to the translator which adequately expresses Augustine's point.

14

wondering? Because many knew where he was born, and how
he had been raised; for they had never seen him learning, but
they heard him discussing the Law, putting forward testimonies to the Law, which no one could put forward unless he
had read the Law, and no one could read the Law unless he
had learned letters—and so they wondered. But this wondering became an opportunity for the Teacher to inculcate the
truth more deeply. From their wondering and words, as one
might expect, the Lord said something profound, and worthy
of being examined and discussed quite carefully. And because
of this, I assume that you are intent, my beloved people, not
only on hearing for yourselves but also on praying for us.

3. What, then, did the Lord answer to those who were wondering how he knew letters which he had not learned? He
said, "My doctrine is not my own, but his who sent me." This is
the first profound truth; for in a few words it seems as if he
has spoken a contradiction. For he did not say, *This* doctrine is
not mine, but "My doctrine is not my own." If it is not yours,
how is it yours? If it is yours, how is it not yours? For you say
both "My doctrine" and "not my own." If he had said, *This*
doctrine is not my own, there would be no problem. But now,
brothers, in the first place pay attention to the problem and so
in proper order look for its solution. For he who does not see
the problem which is proposed, how does he understand what
is explained? His words "My own is not my own" are under
question; this seems to be a contradiction. How is it "My own,"
how is it "not my own"?

(2) If we would examine carefully what the holy Evangelist
himself says in the opening chapter, "In the beginning was the
Word, and the Word was with God, and the Word was God,"[4]
on that the solution of the problem depends. Therefore, what
is the doctrine of the Father except the Word of the Father?
Christ himself is the doctrine of the Father if he is the Word of
the Father.[5] But because the Word cannot be of no one but
[must be] of someone, he said both that it was his doctrine,
[that is,] himself, and not his, because he is the Word of the

4. Jn 1.1.
5. Cf. *Tractate* 14.7.

Father. For what is so much yours as yourself? And what is so much not yours as you, if what you are is someone else's?

4. He is, therefore, the Word and God, and he is the Word of enduring doctrine, not that which sounds through syllables and is fleeting, but that which abides with the Father; and let us turn to this abiding teaching, counseled by the transitory sounds. For what is transitory counsels us, but not in such a way as to call us to what is transitory. We are counseled to love God.[6] All of what I have said was syllables; they struck and smote the air that they might reach the perception of your ears, and, sounding, they passed away. Yet that which I counseled you ought not to pass away because he whom I have counseled you to love does not pass away. And when, counseled by syllables which pass away, you will have been converted to him, neither will you pass away, but you will abide with him who abides. This, therefore, is the important thing in doctrine, the deep and eternal thing which abides; it is to this that all things which pass away in time call, when they signify well and are not offered falsely. For all the signs which we make known by sounds signify something which is not the sound. God is not the two brief syllables [De-us], nor do we worship the two brief syllables, nor adore the two brief syllables, nor desire to attain to the two brief syllables, which cease to be almost before they have begun, nor is there in them a place for the second unless the first has passed away.[7] Something great which is called God remains, even though the sound which is called God does not remain. So direct your attention to the doctrine of Christ, and you will come to the Word of God; but when you come to the Word of God, direct your attention to "The Word was God,"[8] and you will see that "My doctrine" was truly said; direct your attention also to him of whom he is the Word and you will see that "is not my own" was rightly said.

6. I have taken the *ut* clause as a substantive clause, a normal construction with this type of verb. However it could be taken to express purpose, i.e., we are given counsel in order that we may love God. A few lines later he uses the infinitive "to love" with the same verb; hence the normal substantive construction seems preferable here.

7. Cf. *Tractate* 1.8.

8. Jn 1.1

5. Therefore, I say briefly to you, my beloved people, the Lord Jesus Christ seems to me to have said this, "My doctrine is not my own," as if he had said, I am not of myself. For although we say and believe that the Son is equal to the Father, that there is not any difference of nature and substance in them, that there was not any interval of time between the Begetter and the Begotten, nevertheless, we say these things, but with this preserved and guarded, that the one is the Father, the other the Son.[9] Moreover, he is not the Father if he does not have a Son; and he is not the Son if he does not have a Father. But still, the Son is God from the Father; and indeed, the Father is God, but not from the Son. He is the Father of the Son but not God from the Son; but he is the Son of the Father and God from the Father. For the Lord Christ is called Light from Light.[10] Therefore, the Light that is not from Light and the equal Light that is from Light are together one Light, not two Lights.

6. If we have understood, thanks be to God! But if anyone has understood anything insufficiently, man has done as much as he could; as for the rest, let him see in what he may place hope. For, like workmen, we can plant and water from without, but it belongs to God to give growth.[11] He said, "My doctrine is not my own but his who sent me." Let him who says, I have not yet understood, hear advice.

(2) Since an important and profound thing has been said, the Lord Christ himself, in fact, has seen that not all will understand something so profound as this, and in what follows he has given advice. Do you want to understand? Believe. For God said through the prophet, "Unless you believe, you will not understand."[12] What the Lord continued and also added here pertains to this: "If anyone chooses to do his will,

9. This anti-Arian theme is very common in these tractates; the Gospel of John lends itself by its very nature to a discussion of the Trinity. See, e.g., *Tractates* 17.16, 19.13, and 21.3.

10. This credal phrase is undoubtedly from the creed formulated at Nicaea in A.D 325 and Constantinople in A.D. 381 as it appears in no other creed that Augustine is likely to have known. See J. Kelly, *Early Christian Creeds.*

11. Cf. 1 Cor 3.6–7.

12. Is 7.9 (LXX).

he will know of the doctrine, whether it is from God or whether I speak on my own." What does this mean, "If anyone choose to do his will"? But I had said, If anyone believes, and I had given this advice. If you have not understood, I say, believe. For understanding is the recompense of faith.[13] Therefore, seek not to understand so that you may believe, but believe so that you may understand; for "unless you believe, you will not understand." Therefore, since I have given as advice for the possibility of understanding the obedience of believing, and since I have said that the Lord Jesus Christ had added this very thing in the following sentence, we find that he said, "If anyone chooses to do his will, he will know of the doctrine." What does "he will know" mean? It means "he will understand." But what does "if anyone chooses to do his will" mean? This means to believe. All understand that "he will know" is the same as "he will understand"; but, so that it might be more carefully understood that his words, "if anyone chooses to do his will," pertain to believing, we need our Lord himself as interpreter, to inform us whether to do the will of his Father actually pertains to believing.

(3) Who would not know that to do the will of God is to work his work, that is, that which pleases him? Moreover, the Lord himself, in another place, clearly says, "This is the work of God, that you believe in him whom he has sent."[14] "That you believe in him," not that you believe him. For if you believe in him, you believe him; but he who believes him does not as an immediate consequence believe in him. For even the demons believe him, but did not believe in him. Again we can also say about his Apostles, "We believe Paul," but not, "We believe in Paul," "We believe Peter," but not, "We believe in Peter." For "to him who believes in him who justifies the ungodly, his faith is credited as justice."[15] What, then, is it to believe in him? By believing to love, by believing to cherish, by believing to go to him and to be embodied in his members. Therefore, it is faith itself which God demands of us; and he does not find what he

13. Cf. *Tractates* 8.6–7, 15.24, 18.1, 22.2, and 27.29.
14. Jn 6.29.
15. Rom 4.5.

demands unless he gives what he would find. What is faith, except what the Apostle, speaking more fully in another place, has defined? He said, "Neither is circumcision of any avail, nor uncircumcision, but faith which works through love."[16] Not any faith whatsoever, but "faith which works through love." Let this faith be in you and you will understand about the doctrine. What will you understand? That this "doctrine is not my own, but his who sent me," that is, you will understand that Christ, the Son of God, who is the Doctrine of the Father, is not of himself, but is the Son of the Father.

7. This sentence demolishes the Sabellian heresy.[17] For the Sabellians dared to say that the Son is he who is also the Father; that there are two names but one reality. If there were two names and one reality, it would not be said, "My doctrine is not my own." Indeed, if your doctrine is not your own, O Lord, whose is it, if there should not be another whose it is? What you have said, the Sabellians do not understand; for they have not seen the Trinity but have followed the error of their heart. But we, the worshippers of the Trinity and the unity of the Father and the Son and the Holy Spirit, and of one God, let us understand about the doctrine of Christ, that it is not his. And therefore, he said that he did not speak on his own, because Christ is the Son of the Father, and the Father of Christ is the Father, and the Son is God from God the Father, but God the Father is God not from God the Son.

8. "He who speaks on his own seeks his own glory." This will be that one who is called the Antichrist, "exalting himself," as the Apostle says, "above all that is called God and that is worshipped."[18] Indeed, the Lord, announcing that he [i.e., the

16. Gal 5.6.
17. Sabellianism was a Trinitarian heresy named for a Sabellius, fl. c. A.D. 220, who perhaps came from Cyrenaica and taught at Rome. He seems to have provided the heretical doctrine its metaphysical base. The Sabellians emphasized the Divine Unity in such a way as to deny that the Son had either subsistence or personality distinct from the Father; the "persons" of the Trinity were modes, aspects, energies, or phases of the one, divine being. The heresy is also called monarchianism or modalism. See P. Lebeau, "Sabellianism," NCE 12.783; P. Hamell, "Modalism," and "Monarchianism," NCE, 9.988–89, 1019–20; and Berrouard BA 72.845.
18. 2 Thes 2.4.

Antichrist] would seek his own glory, not the glory of the Father, said to the Jews, "I have come in the name of my Father, and you have not received me; another will come in his own name, this one you will receive."[19] He signified that they would receive the Antichrist, who would seek the glory of his own name, puffed up, not solid, and so not enduring, but in fact ruinous.

(2) But our Lord Jesus Christ offered us a great example of humility; certainly he is equal to the Father, certainly "in the beginning was the Word, and the Word was with God, and the Word was God,"[20] certainly he himself said, and he said most truly, "Have I been so long a time with you, and you have not known me? Philip, he who sees me sees also the Father."[21] Certainly he said, and he said most truly, "I and the Father are one."[22] Therefore, if he is one[23] with the Father, equal to the Father, God from God, God with God, coeternal, immortal, equally immutable, equally without time, equally creator and disposer of times, yet if because he came in time and received the form of the servant and was found as a man in appearance,[24] he seeks the glory of the Father, not his own, what ought you, man, to do, who, when you do something good, seek your own glory, but when you do something evil, consider slander against God?

19. Jn 5.43.   20. Jn 1.1.
21. Jn 14.9   22. Jn 10.30.
23. The Latin has a neuter substantive here and in Jn 10.30, that is, "if he is *one thing* with the Father," and "I and the Father, we are *one thing*." Augustine, under the influence of Neoplatonism, emphasizes that the nature of God is absolute Simplicity, total Oneness, perfect Being; he prefers to use the term *essentia* (essence) rather than substance or nature because the latter two have misleading connotations (especially the perplexing confusion in seeing substance as the Greek ὑπόστασις which properly is equivalent to the Latin *persona*). God is *Essentia*, Being itself (i.e., *esse ipsum* in classical Latin philosophical terminology); hence Augustine's use of this term differs from later philosophy. For Augustine the analysis begins with *Essentia* and leads to persons, an emphasis opposite to that of the Greek Fathers. See, e.g., *De Trinitate* 5.2, 8–9; 6.2; 7.5–6 (CCL 50.207–08, 215–17, 229–31, 260–67, or FOTC 45.177, 185–88, 201–03, 234–41); E. Gilson, *The Christian Philosophy of Saint Augustine*, 21–23, 200–205; E. Portalié, *A Guide to the Thought of St. Augustine*, 99–100, 127–32; E. TeSelle, *Augustine the Theologian*, 138–40, 294–99; G. Prestige, *God in Patristic Thought*, 235–37.
24 Cf. Phil 2.7.

(3) Look at yourself; you are a creature; acknowledge the Creator. You are a servant; do not despise the Lord. You have been adopted, but not for your own merits. Seek his glory from whom you, an adopted man, have this grace, whose glory he sought who was the only-begotten from him. "But he who seeks the glory of the one who sent him is truthful, and there is no injustice in him." But there is injustice in the Antichrist and he is not truthful because he will seek his own glory, not that of the one by whom he was sent; in fact he was not sent but allowed to come. Therefore, all of us belonging to the body of Christ, that we may not be tricked into the snares of the Antichrist, let us not seek our own glory. But if he sought the glory of him who sent him, how much more [ought] we [to seek the glory] of him who made us?

TRACTATE 30

On John 7.19–24

ODAY'S READING, which has just been read, follows the reading of the holy Gospel about which we spoke to you, my beloved people, a few days ago. Both the disciples and the Jews were listening to the Lord speaking; both the truthful and the lying were listening to the Truth speaking. Both friends and enemies were listening to Love speaking; both the good and the evil were listening to the Good speaking. They were listening, but he was distinguishing [among them]; and he saw and foresaw to whom his sermon was and would be profitable. He saw it among those who were then there; he foresaw it among us who were yet to be.

(2) And so let us listen to the Gospel just as if to the Lord if he were present; and let us not say, "Oh, those happy men who were able to see him!" For there were many among them who saw him and killed him; but there are many among us who have not seen him, and yet have believed. And the fact is, the preciousness which sounded forth from the Lord's mouth was also written down for our sakes, and preserved for us and recited for our sakes and will also be recited for the sake of our descendants even until this age comes to its end. The Lord is on high, but the Lord, the Truth, is also here. For the body of the Lord in which he arose can be in one place; but his truth is spread out everywhere. Therefore, let us listen to the Lord and let us also say what he has bestowed concerning his words.

2. He said, "Did not Moses give you the Law, and none of you keeps the Law? Why do you seek to kill me?" You seek to kill me precisely because none of you keeps the Law; for if you kept the Law, you would recognize Christ in its very letters and you would not kill him who is present. And they an-

swered: "The crowd answered him." The crowd answered, as
it were, not what pertained to order but to their disquiet; now
see what the disquieted crowd answered. "You have a demon.
Who seeks to kill you?" As if it were not a worse thing to say,
"You have a demon," than to kill him. Why, it was said to him
that he who exorcises demons had a demon! What else could
the disturbed crowd say? What other odor could stirred-up
mire give off? The crowd was disquieted. By what? By the
Truth. The brightness of the light disquieted the crowd of the
bleary-eyed. For eyes lacking good health cannot stand the
brightness of light.[1]

3. But the Lord, obviously not disquieted, rather, tranquil
in his truth, did not render evil for evil, nor abuse for abuse.[2]
And if he were to say to them, You have a demon, of course he
would say the truth. For they would not have said such things
to that Truth unless the falsehood of the demon had provoked them.

(2) What then did he reply? Let us listen tranquilly and
drink the tranquil. "One work I have done and you all
wonder." As if saying, What if you saw all my works? For all
the things which they saw in the world were his and they did
not see him who made all things. He did one thing and they
were disquieted, because he made a man well on the Sabbath.
Just as though, indeed, if some sick man were returned to
health on the Sabbath, someone else had made him well
rather than he who scandalized them because he had made
one man well on the Sabbath. For what other man made other
men well except Health himself, who gives that health which
he gave to this man also to animals? For it was the health of the
body. The health of the flesh both is restored and dies; and
when it is restored, death is delayed, not taken away.

(3) Nevertheless, brothers, even this health, through
whomever it is given, is from the Lord. Although it is im-
parted through someone who takes care and ministers, it is
given by him from whom is all health, to whom it is said in the
psalm, "Men and beasts you will make well, O Lord, as you

1. Cf. *Tractate* 18.11.
2. Cf. 1 Pt 3.9.

have multiplied your mercy, O God."[3] For because you are God, your mercy has been multiplied and pertains even to the health of the human flesh, it pertains even to the health of dumb animals. But you who give the health of the flesh, common to men and animals, is there no health which you reserve for men?

(4) There certainly is another which not only is not common to men and animals but is not even common to good and bad men. Then, too, when he[4] had spoken there about this health which animals and men receive in common, concerning that health for which men (but good men) ought to hope, he continued and added, "But the children of men will hope under the covering of your wings; they will be inebriated with the bounteousness of your house, and you will give them to drink of the torrent of your pleasure. For with you is the fountain of life, and in your light we shall see light."[5] This is the health which pertains to the good, whom he called the children of men, when he said above, "Men and beasts you will make well." Well now, were not those men children of men, so that when he said, "Men," he continued and said, "but the children of men" as if "men" were something other than "children of men"? Nevertheless I do not think that the Holy Spirit has said this without some intentional expression of difference. "Men" to the first Adam, "children of men" to Christ.[6] For perhaps "men" pertains to the first man; but "children of men" pertains to the Son of Man.[7]

3. Ps 35 (36).7–8.

4. I.e., David, the author of the psalm, although near the end of this section, he ascribes the psalm, as is customary, to the Holy Spirit.

5. Ps 35 (36).8–10.

6. The Maurist edition questions the genuineness of this sentence, seeing it as redundant; it has the look of a scholium about it. This note is not reprinted in the PL or CCL texts but is found in *Patres Ecclesiae* 122, edd., A. Caillau, et al. *Augustinus* 15.343.

7. This distinction is explained in more detail in *En in Ps* 8.10–11. Man is the old man carrying the image of the earthly man alone, namely, Adam or the unrepentant person who belongs to Adam; the child of man is the new man carrying the image of the heavenly man, namely, Christ or the repentant Christian who belongs to Christ. See also *En in Ps* 35.12 and 48.1.3. A similar idea is expressed in *Tractate* 3.12 and *Tr in Io Ep* 4.11. See Browne LFC 26.447, and Berrouard BA 72.845–47.

4. "One work I have done and you all wonder." And immediately he added, "Therefore Moses gave you circumcision." It was beneficial that you received the circumcision from Moses. "Not because it is from Moses, but from the fathers." Abraham, of course, was the first to receive the circumcision from the Lord.[8] "And on the sabbath day you circumcise." Moses has refuted you. In the Law you have received that you circumcise on the eighth day;[9] you have received in the Law that you are to be free from labor on the seventh day.[10] If the eighth day of one who was born occurs on the seventh day of a week, what will you do? Will you be free from labor that you may keep the Sabbath, or will you circumcise that you may fulfill the ritual[11] of the eighth day? But I know, he says, what you do. "You circumcise a man." Why? Because circumcision pertains to a sign of salvation[12] and men ought not be exempt from salvation on the Sabbath. Therefore, do not "be angry with me because I made a whole man well on the Sabbath, if a man receives circumcision," he said, "on the Sabbath so that the Law of Moses may not be broken" (for through Moses, in that institution of circumcision, something health-giving was established). Why are you indignant with me if I produce health on the Sabbath?

5. Perhaps that circumcision signified the Lord himself, with whom those men were indignant because he healed and cured. For circumcision was ordered to be administered on the eighth day, and what is circumcision except the stripping off of flesh?[13] Therefore, this circumcision signifies the stripping off of carnal desires from the heart. Therefore not without reason was it given and commanded to be done in that member, because through that member the offspring of mortals are procreated. And by one "man [came] death," so by one

---

8. Cf. Gn 17.9–14.   9. Cf. Gn 17.12 and Lv 12.3.
10. Cf. Ex 20.10.
11. The Latin word is *sacramentum*; see *Tractate* 20.2, note 4.
12. There is at work here a connotation of *salvus* and *salus* in Christian Latin where they connote "salvation" and also the secular denotations of health and well-being.
13. Cf. Col 2.11.

"man [came] the resurrection of the dead;"[14] and "by one man sin entered into the world, and by sin death."[15] And thus each man is born with the foreskin, because every man is born with the fault of the race. And God does not cleanse us either of the fault with which we are born or of the faults which we add by living evilly, except through the stone knife, the Lord Christ. For "the rock was Christ."[16] They used to circumcise with stone knives[17] and by the name of stone they represented Christ in figure; and they did not recognize him when present, but, what is worse, they desired to kill him.

(2) But why on the eighth day, except that the Lord arose in the Lord's day after the seventh day of the Sabbath? Therefore, the resurrection of Christ, which happened on the third day, indeed, of the passion, but on the eighth day in the days of the week, itself circumcises us. Hear that you have been circumcised by the True Rock, when the Apostle instructs: "Therefore, if you have risen with Christ, seek the things which are above, where Christ is, sitting at the right hand of God. Mind the things that are above, not the things that are in earth."[18] He is speaking to the circumcised: Christ has arisen, he has taken carnal desires away from you, he has taken away evil concupiscences, he has taken away the excess with which you were born and, what is much worse, that which you have added by living evilly. Why do you, though circumcised by the Rock, still savor the earth?

(3) And finally, because Moses gave the Law and you circumcise a man on the Sabbath, understand that by this is signified the good work in which I made a whole man well on the Sabbath; for he was cured that he might be healthy in body and he believed that he might be healthy in soul.

6. "Do not judge as to the person but judge just judgment." What does this mean? You who circumcise on the Sabbath by the Law of Moses are not angry at Moses; and yet, because I

14. 1 Cor 15.21.
15. Rom 5.12; observe that the "one man" of this quotation has influenced Augustine's citation of the previous quotation. See Berrouard BA 72.624–25.
16. 1 Cor 10.4.   17. Cf. Jos 5.2–3.
18. Col 3.1–2.

made a man well on the day of Sabbath, you are angry with me. You judge as to the person; attend to the truth. I do not put myself before Moses, said the Lord, who was also the Lord of Moses himself. So observe us as two men; as if [we were] both men, judge between us, but judge a true judgment. Do not condemn him and honor me; but understand him and then honor me. For he said this to them in another place, "If you believed Moses, you would certainly believe me also, for he wrote of me."[19] But in this place he did not wish to say this, as though he and Moses were placed before them.

(2) You circumcise according to the Law of Moses even when the Sabbath has occurred; and do you not wish that I display the beneficence of performing cures during the Sabbath? Because the Lord of circumcision and the Lord of the Sabbath is the source of health, and you have been prohibited from doing servile works on the Sabbath, if you understand servile works truly, you do not sin. For "he who commits a sin is the slave of sin."[20] Is it a servile work to heal a man during the Sabbath? You eat and you drink (to say something in accord with the teaching of our Lord Jesus Christ, and in accord with his words) at any rate; why do you eat and drink on the Sabbath except that what you do pertains to health? By this you show that works of health are not in any way to be omitted on the day of Sabbath. Therefore, "do not judge as to the person, but judge just judgment." Observe me as a man; observe Moses as a man. If you should judge according to the truth, you will condemn neither Moses nor me; and when you know the truth, you will know me because I am the Truth.[21]

7. To escape this fault, brothers, which the Lord has noted in this place is a task requiring great effort in this age, that is, not to judge as a person but to maintain just judgment. The Lord did indeed admonish the Jews, but he also advised us; he convicted them, but instructed us; he refuted them, but excited us. Let us not think that this was not said to us just because we were not there then. It was written down, it is

19. Jn 5.46.
20. Jn 8.34; see also *Tractate* 3.19.
21. Cf. Jn 14.6.

read; we have listened to it when it was recited, but we listened
to it as if it were said to the Jews. Let us not put ourselves
behind ourselves, as if we were both looking at him scolding
enemies and ourselves doing what Truth itself may scold in
us.

(2) For the Jews judged as to the person, and thus they do
not belong to the New Testament, thus they do not have the
kingdom of heaven in Christ, thus they are not joined to the
society of holy angels. They were seeking earthly things from
the Lord; namely, the land of promise, victory over enemies,
fruitfulness in childbearing, multiplication of sons, abundance of fruits, and all of these things from the true and good
God, indeed, yet as they were promised to carnal men, all of
these things made the Old Testament for them. What is the
Old Testament? It is like an inheritance belonging to an old
man.

(3) We have been renewed, we have been made a new man,
because that New Man has also come.[22] For what is so new as to
be born of a virgin?[23] Therefore, because there was nothing
that teaching might renew in him, because he had no sin, a
new birth was given. In him a new birth, in us a new man.
What is the new man? Renewed from the old. Renewed for
what purpose? For desiring heavenly things, for coveting the
eternal, for desiring the homeland which is on high and where
he fears not the enemy, where we lose not a friend, fear not an
enemy; where we live with good disposition, without any deficiency; where no one is born, because no one dies; where no
one any longer progresses and no one fails; where there is no
hunger and no thirst, but immortality is satiety, and truth is
food. Having these promises and belonging to the New Testament, having become heirs of a new inheritance and coheirs
of the Lord himself,[24] we certainly have a different hope. Let
us not judge as to the person, but keep just judgment.

8. Who is it who does not judge as to the person? He who

22. Cf. Eph 4.22–24; Col 3.9–11; and perhaps 2 Cor 5.17; see also *Tractate*
25.12.
23. Cf. Is 7.14; Mt 1.18–25; Lk 1.26–34.
24. Cf. Rom 8.17.

loves equally. Equal love causes persons not to be received with partiality. When we do not honor men in a different way in accord with their ranks, then do we need fear that we receive persons with partiality. But when we judge between two, it is sometimes even between relatives. Judgment on occasion is made between father and son; father complains of an evil son or a son complains of a harsh father. We preserve the honor for the father which is owed by the son; we do not equate the son with the father in honor, but we put him first if he has a good case. Let us equate the son to the father in truth and so we shall bestow the honor owed, that equality may not destroy merit. Thus we progress by the words of the Lord, and we are helped by his grace to progress.

TRACTATE 31

On John 7.25–36

OU REMEMBER, my beloved people, that in the previous sermons[1] it was both read in the Gospel and discussed by us, as well as we could, that the Lord Jesus went up to the festival day as if secretly, not because he feared that he who had the power not to be arrested, might be arrested, but that he might signify even on the very festival day which was celebrated by the Jews that he was hidden and that the mystery [of it] was his own.

(2) In today's reading what was accounted timidity appeared as power, for he was speaking openly on the festival day so that the crowds wondered and said what we heard when the reading was read: "Is not this the one whom they were seeking to kill? And behold, he speaks openly and they say nothing to him. Can it be that the rulers have really come to know that this is the Christ? They who knew with what ferocity he was sought wondered by what power he was not arrested. Then, not fully understanding his power, they thought that it was the knowledge of the rulers, that they had themselves come to know that he was the Christ, and therefore they spared him whom they had sought so very much to kill.

2. Then those very people, who had said among themselves, "Can it be that the rulers have really come to know that this is the Christ?", proposed to themselves a problem by which it seemed to them that he was not the Christ; for they said in addition, "Yet we know where this man is from; but when the Christ comes, no one knows where he is from."

1. Cf. *Tractate* 28.8–9.

(2) Whence did this opinion, that "when the Christ comes,
no one knows where he is from," arise among the Jews (for it
did not arise vainly)? If we should examine the Scriptures,
we find, brothers, that the holy Scriptures said about Christ,
"He shall be called a Nazarene."[2] Therefore, they predicted
"where he is from." Again if we shoud seek the place of his
birth, as if he would be from where he was born, neither was
this concealed from the Jews, because of the Scriptures which
had predicted these things. For when the Magi, after they saw
the star, sought to adore him, they came to Herod and said
what they sought and what they wanted. But he called together those who knew the Law and asked of them where the
Christ would be born; they said, "In Bethlehem of Juda."[3]
And they even offered the witness of a prophet.

(3) Therefore, if the prophets predicted both the place
from which the origin of his flesh was and the place where his
mother gave birth to him, whence arose this opinion among
the Jews which we have just heard, "when the Christ comes,
no one knows where he is from," except that the Scriptures
had foresaid and foretold both? The Scriptures had predicted
where he was from according to his humanness; according to
his divinity he was concealed from the ungodly and was seeking to win the devout. For this reason, they also said this,
"when the Christ comes, no one knows where he is from,"
because what was said by Isaiah, "But who shall declare his
generation?"[4] generated this opinion for them.

(4) Finally, the Lord himself also answered to each, both
that they knew where he was from and that they did not know,
in order that he might bear witness to the holy prophecy
which was predicted about him before, both according to the
humanness of his weakness and according to the divinity of
his majesty.

3. Therefore, brothers, hear the Word of the Lord; see
how he confirmed for them both their words, "We know
where this man is from," and their words, "When the Christ

2. Mt 2.23.
3. Mt 2.6, quoting Mi 5.2; Cf. Mt 2.1–6.
4. Is 53.8 (LXX).

comes, no one knows where he is from." "Jesus therefore, while teaching in the temple, cried out, 'You both know me and know where I am from. And yet I have not come of myself, but he is true who has sent me, whom you do not know.'" That is to say, You both know me, and you do not know me. That is to say, You both know where I am from and you do not know where I am from. You know where I am from, Jesus from Nazareth, whose parents you also know. For in this situation only the birth from a virgin was concealed, to which nevertheless the husband was a witness;[5] for he who could love ardently as a husband could also reveal this faithfully. Therefore, with the exception of the virgin birth, they knew everything about Jesus which had to do with the man. His appearance was known, his homeland was known, his family was known, where he was born was known. Therefore, he said rightly, "You both know me and know where I am from," according to the flesh and form of the man which he was bearing; but according to the divinity, "And yet I have not come of myself, but he is true who has sent me, whom you do not know." But that you may know him, believe in him whom he sent, and you will know. For "no one has seen God at any time, except the only-begotten Son, who is in the bosom of the Father, he has declared him."[6] And, "no one knows the Father except the Son and he to whom the Son wishes to reveal him."[7]

4. Next when he had said, "but he is true who has sent me, whom you do not know," to show them from whom they could know what they did not know, he added, "I know him." Therefore, inquire of me that you may know him. But how do I know him? "Because I am from him, and he has sent me." Splendidly has he shown each. "I am from him," he said, because the Son is from the Father and whatever is the Son is from him of whom he is the Son. Therefore, we call the Lord Jesus God from God, we do not call the Father God from God but only God; and we call the Lord Jesus Light from Light; we do not call the Father Light from Light, but only Light.[8] His

---

5. Cf. Mt 1.18–25.   6. Jn 1.18.
7. Mt 11.27.   8. Cf. *Tractate* 29.5.

words, "I am from him," therefore, pertain to this. But that you see me in the flesh, "He has sent me." Where you hear, "He has sent me," do not understand a dissimilarity of nature, but the authorization[9] of the Begetter.

5. "They sought therefore to seize him, and no one laid hands on him because his hour had not yet come," that is, because he was unwilling. For what does it mean, "His hour had not yet come"? The Lord was not born subject to fate. This must not even be believed about yourself, much less about him through whom you were made.[10] If your hour is his will, what is his hour except his own will? Therefore, he did not mean an hour in which he would be forced to die, but in which he would deign to die.

(2) He was waiting for the time when he would die, because he also waited for the time when he was to be born. The Apostle, speaking about this time, said, "But when the fullness of time came, God sent his Son."[11] That is why many ask: Why did not the Christ come before?[12] To them it must be answered that the fullness of time had not yet come, inasmuch as he, through whom times were made, regulates [them]; for he knew when he ought to come. First he had to be predicted through a long series of times and years; for it was no small thing that was to come. He had to be predicted for a long time,

9. The Latin *auctoritas* here has its connotation of a right of an originator or source to authorize or command, relative to what was originated or derived, or the right to authorize or command based on prestige or influence stemming from an office or function or from respect for the person authorizing or commanding; it does not have a connotation of superiority based on power since this would imply an inequality in the Trinity.

10. Cf. *Tractate* 8.10.

11. Gal 4.4.

12. Augustine gives a different answer to this question to *DDQ* 44 where he says that Christ came in the youth of mankind since the propriety and beauty that attaches to the varied ages of a person apply to the ages of mankind also, and youth is the appropriate time for teaching and learning. But if John the Baptist inaugurated the sixth age of mankind (see *Tractates* 9.6 and 15.9), then mankind is in its old age. Augustine is aware of this inconsistency which he resolves in *Retractationes* 1.26.107–120 (CCL 57.79–80 or FOTC 60.109–11) by suggesting that a person has mental ages as well as physical ages and can be both youthful (lively and teachable) and elderly (serious) at the same time.

who was to be held onto for always. The greater the Judge
who was coming, the longer the line of heralds who preceded.

(3) Finally, when the fullness of time came, he who was to
free us from time also came. For, freed from time, we shall
come to that eternity where time is not. And there it is not
asked, when will the hour come? For the day is everlasting and
is not preceded by a yesterday nor closed out by a tomorrow.
But in this age the days turn, and some pass away, and some
come. No day remains, and the moments in which we are
speaking drive one another away, and the first syllable stays
not, so that the second syllable may be able to make its sound.
Since we began to speak, we have grown a little older,[13] and
without any doubt, I am now older than this morning; thus
nothing stays still, nothing remains fixed in time. And so we
ought to love him through whom times were made, that we
may be freed from time and fixed in eternity where there is no
longer any alteration of time. Therefore, great is the mercy of
our Lord Jesus Christ that he through whom all things were
made was made among all things; that he was made what he
made. For he was made what he had made; he who had made
man was made man, so that what he had made might not
perish. By this economy[14] the hour of his nativity had come
and he was born; but the hour of his passion had not yet come,
and so he had not yet suffered.

6. Then, that you may know not the necessity but the
power of the one dying,[15]—I say this because of some who,
when they have heard "His hour has not yet come," are confirmed in their belief in the fates and their hearts become
fatuous—therefore, that you may know the power of the one
dying, recall the passion itself, look upon him crucified.

(2) Hanging on the cross, he said, "I thirst."[16] When they
heard this, they offered him on the cross vinegar by a sponge
on a reed. He took it and said, "'It is consummated.' And

13. See Horace, Odes 1.11.7–8: Dum loquimur, fugerit invida aetas. Even
while we are speaking, envious time already has fled away.
14. The Latin word is dispensatio; see Tractate 19.10, note 11.
15. Cf. Tractate 8.10–12.
16. Jn 19.28.

bowing his head, he gave up his spirit."[17] You see the power of
the one dying, because he waited for this, until all things concerning him that were predicted to happen before his death
were completed. For the prophet had said, "They put gall in
my food, and in my thirst they gave me vinegar to drink."[18] He
waited so that all these things might be accomplished; after
they were accomplished, he said, "It is consummated," and he
departed by his power; for he had not come by necessity.

(3) And so some marveled more at this power [of his] of
dying than at his power of performing miracles. For they
came to the cross so that the bodies might be taken down from
the wood, because the Sabbath was dawning, and the robbers
were found alive. For the punishment of the cross was quite
harsh for the reason that it tormented excruciatingly for quite
a long time, and all who were crucified were killed by a long
death. But they, that they might not remain on the cross, were
forced to die by having their legs broken, so that they might be
taken down from there. But the Lord was found dead, and
the men were astonished.[19] And they who despised him when
he was alive were so astonished at him dead that some said,
"Truly he was the Son of God."[20]

(4) From this source[21] also occurred that [incident],
brothers, where he said to those who were seeking him, "I am
he," and they all drew back and fell down.[22] There was in him,
therefore, the greatest power. He was not forced by the hour
to die, but he awaited the hour at which his will was suitably
done, not at which the necessity of one unwilling was fulfilled.

7. "Many of the crowd, however, believed in him." The
Lord saved the humble and the poor. The rulers were in a
mad rage, and therefore they not only did not recognize the
Physician, but they also wanted to kill him. There was a certain
crowd who quickly saw their own sickness, and without delay
recognized his medicine. See what the crowd itself, stirred by
his miracles, said to one another, "When the Christ comes, will

17. Jn 19.30.
18. Ps 68 (69).22.
19. Cf. Jn 19.31–35.
20. Mt 27.54; cf. Mk 15.39.
21. I.e., from his power of dying.
22. Cf. Jn 18.5–6.

he do more signs?" Assuredly, if there will not be two, this is
he. Therefore, saying these things, they believed in him.

8. But those leaders, when they heard the faith of the multitude and the murmuring in which Christ was being glorified,
"sent attendants to arrest him." Whom were they to arrest?
Him who was, at this time, unwilling. Therefore, because they
could not arrest him, since he was unwilling, they were sent
that they might hear him teaching. Teaching what? "Jesus
therefore said, 'Yet a little while I am with you.'" What you
now wish to do, you will do, but not now, because I do not will
it now. Why do I not yet will it now? Because "yet a little while
I am with you, and then I go to him who sent me." I am bound
to fulfill my dispensation[23] and so attain my Passion.

9. "You will seek me and will not find me; and where I am,
you cannot come." Here he has now predicted his own resurrection; for they were unwilling to acknowledge him when he
was present, and afterwards, when they saw the crowd now
believing in him, they sought him. For important signs occurred even when the Lord arose and ascended into heaven.
Then great things were done through the disciples, but he
[worked] through them as he also [had] through himself. For
in fact he himself had said to them, "Without me you can do
nothing."[24] When that lame man who was sitting at the gate
rose up at the voice of Peter and walked on his own feet so that
men marveled, Peter addressed them thus, that he did not do
these things by his own power, but by the strength of him
whom they themselves had killed.[25] Many felt remorse and
said, "What shall we do?"[26] For they saw that they were impli-
cated in an enormous crime of impiety, since they had killed
him whom they ought to have venerated and adored; and
they thought this crime was inexpiable. For it was a great
crime, a consideration of which would make them despair.
But they did not need to despair; for the Lord, hanging on the

23. Cf. section 5 and note 14; but here I have translated it as dispensation
rather than economy because the focus is on the particular part of the divine
plan set down for this particular Person rather than the plan itself.
24. Jn 15.5.   25. Cf. Acts 3.1–16.
26. Acts 2.37.

cross, deigned to pray for them. For he had said, "Father, forgive them, for they know not what they do."[27] Among the many hostile people he saw some of his own; for them, from whom he was still receiving injury, he now was seeking pardon. For he did not consider that he was dying because of them, but that he was dying for them. For it was a great thing which was granted to them, [i.e., he was dying] both because of them and for them, that no one may despair of forgiveness for his sin, when those who killed Christ obtained pardon. Christ died for us; but can it be because of us? They saw Christ dying by their crime and they believed in Christ forgiving their crime. Until the time they would drink the blood which they had poured out, they despaired of their own salvation. Therefore, he said this, "You will seek me and will not find me; and where I am you cannot come," because after his resurrection they would feel remorse and seek him.

(2) He did not say, where I shall be but "where I am." For Christ was always there where he was going to return; for he came in such a way that he did not withdraw. Wherefore, in another place he said, "No one has ascended into heaven except he who has descended from heaven, the Son of Man who is in heaven."[28] He did not say, who was in heaven. He was speaking on earth and he was saying that he was in heaven.[29] He came in such a way that he did not depart from there; he has returned in such a way that he has not abandoned us. Why are you amazed? God does this. For man is in a place on account of his body, and he goes away from that place; and when he has come to another place, he will not be in that place from which he came. But God fills all places and he is wholly everywhere; he is not held in places according to dimensions. Nevertheless, the Lord Christ was on earth according to his visible flesh; according to his invisible majesty he was in heaven and on earth. And so he said, "Where I am you cannot come."

27. Lk 23.34. NAB brackets this verse; C. Stuhlmeyer, JBC 2.161, however, argues for its authenticity.
28. Jn 3.13.
29. Cf. *Tractate* 12.8 and 27.4.

(3) He did not say, you will not be able but "you are not able." For they were then of such character that they could not. But, that you may know that this was not said to cause despair, he also said some such thing to his disciples, "Where I go you can not come,"[30] although, praying for them, he said, "Father, I will that where I am, they also may be with me."[31] Finally, he explained this to Peter, and said to him, "Where I am going you cannot follow me now, but you shall follow later on."[32]

10. "The Jews therefore said" not to him but "among themselves, 'Where will he go that we shall not find him? Will he go to those dispersed among the Gentiles, and teach the Gentiles?'" They did not know what they said; but because he wished it, they prophesied. For the Lord was going to go to the Gentiles, not by the presence of his body but rather by his feet. Who were his feet? Saul wanted to trample upon those feet by persecution when the Head cried out to him, "Saul, Saul, why do you persecute me?"[33]

(2) "What is this saying that he has said, 'You will seek me and you will not find me, and where I am you cannot come'?" They did not know why the Lord said this; and yet, unknowingly, they predicted something that was going to be. For the Lord said this because they did not know the place, if it is nonetheless to be called a place, that is, the bosom of the Father, from which the only-begotten Son never departed. Nor were they ready to think about where Christ was, from where Christ had not withdrawn, where Christ could return, where Christ remained. What means does the human heart have to think about this, much less explain it with the tongue? Therefore, in no way did they understand this; and yet, as this occasion provided, they foretold our salvation, that the Lord would go to those dispersed among the Gentiles and fulfill what they read but did not understand, "A people I knew not has served me; at the hearing of the ear, it obeyed me."[34]

30. Jn 13.33.
31. Jn 17.24, without the clause: *quos dedisti mihi.*
32. Jn 13.36.   33. Acts 9.4.
34. Ps 17.45 (NAB 18.44–45).

They, before whose eyes he was, did not hear; they, in whose ears he sounded, heard.

11. The woman who was suffering a hemorrhage exhibited a type of that Church which was to come from the Gentiles; she touched and was not seen, she was not known and was healed.[35] Of course, it was in figure that the Lord asked, "Who touched me?" As if he, unknowing, healed her who was unknown; so he did also to the Gentiles. We have not come to know him in the flesh, yet we have deserved to eat his flesh and to be members in his flesh. Why? Because he sent to us. Whom? His heralds, his disciples, his servants, his own redeemed whom he created, but his brothers whom he also redeemed; I have said altogether too little, his members, himself. For he sent his members to us and made us his members.

(2) Yet according to the appearance of the body which the Jews saw and despised, Christ has not been among us, because this also had been said about him as the Apostle says, "For I say that Christ Jesus has been a minister of the circumcision for the truth of God to confirm the promises made to the fathers."[36] He ought to have come to those by whose fathers and to whose fathers he had been promised; and thus he also said, "I was not sent except to the sheep that are lost of the house of Israel."[37] But what did the Apostle say in the words that follow [the quotation above]? "But that the Gentiles glorify God because of his mercy."[38] What did the Lord himself also say? "And other sheep I have that are not of this fold."[39] How does he who had said, "I was not sent except to the sheep that are lost of the house of Israel," have other sheep to which he was not sent, except that he signified that he had been sent to manifest his bodily presence only to the Jews, who saw and killed [him]? And yet many of them believed both before and afterwards. The first harvest was winnowed from the cross that there might be seed from which another harvest might arise. But now, when his faithful in all the nations, excited by the fame of the Gospel and by its good odor,[40] believe, the

35. Cf. Lk 8.43–48.   36. Rom 15.8.
37. Mt 15.24.   38. Rom 15.9.
39. Jn 10.16.   40. Perhaps he has 2 Cor 2.15 in mind.

expectation of nations will be: when is he to come who has already come?[41] when is he to be seen by all who then was not seen by some [and] was seen by some? when is he to come to judge who came to be judged, when is he to come to separate who came that he might not be separated? For Christ was not separated from the ungodly, but was judged with the ungodly; for it was said about him, "He was counted among the wicked."[42] The bandit escaped; Christ was condemned.[43] The one guilty of many crimes received a pardon; he who had remitted the crimes of all who confess was condemned. And yet the cross itself also, if you reflect upon it, was a tribunal; for in the middle of it, a Judge was found, and one robber who believed was freed, the other who insulted him was condemned.[44] He was then signifying what he would do concerning the living and the dead; he would put some on his right and some on his left.[45] The one robber was like to those who would be on the left; the other, to those who would be on the right. He was being judged, and he was threatening judgment.

41. Cf. Gn 49.10 (LXX).
42. Is 53.12.
43. Cf. Mt. 27.26; Mk 15.15; Lk 23.25; Jn 18.40.
44. Cf. Lk 23.39–43.
45. Cf. Mt 25.31–33.

TRACTATE 32

On John 7.37–39

MID THE disputes and doubts of the Jews about the Lord Jesus Christ among the other things that he said by which some were confounded [and] others were taught, on that "last day of the festivity" (for these things were being done then) which is called Scenopegia, that is, the building of tents—and you remember, my beloved people, this festivity has previously been discussed[1]—the Lord Jesus Christ calls, and this not merely by speaking, but by crying out, that he who thirsts may come to him. If we thirst, let us come, and not on foot,[2] but in our feelings; let us come not by traveling but by loving. Though, according to the interior man, he who loves also travels. To travel by the body is one thing, by the heart another. He who changes place by movement of the body travels by the body; he who changes his feeling by the movement of his heart travels by the heart. If you love one thing, [but] you were loving another, you are not there where you were.

2. Therefore, the Lord cries out to us. "He stood and cried out, 'If anyone thirsts, let him come to me and drink. He who believes in me, as the Scripture says, out of his belly there shall flow rivers of living water.'"[3] Since the Evangelist has ex-

---

1. Cf. *Tractate* 28.3, 9.
2. Berrouard BA 72.664 notes here a reminiscence of Plotinus *Enneads* 1.6.8. Reality exists not in the external, physical world but in our true homeland where our Father is and which we can reach only internally, through the soul.
3. The reference to the Old Testament is not at all clear; R. E. Brown, *The Anchor Bible* 29.321–23, discusses the various possible sources. It should also be pointed out that Augustine does not deal with a punctuation problem here, undoubtedly because Augustine only knows this punctuation, as the lengthy

plained what this means, we ought not to tarry. For the Evangelist explained next why the Lord said, "If anyone thirsts, let him come to me and drink," and "he who believes in me, out of his belly there shall flow rivers of living water," saying, "He said this, however, of the Spirit whom they who believed in him were to receive; for the Spirit had not yet been given, since Jesus had not yet been glorified."

(2) There is, therefore, an inner thirst and an inner belly because there is an inner man. And that inner man is indeed invisible; the outer man, however, is visible; but the inner man is better than the outer man. And what is not seen, this is loved more; for it is agreed upon that the inner man is loved more than the outer man. Upon what grounds is this agreed? Let each one prove it in himself. For even though those who live evilly surrender their minds to the body, yet they still desire to live—a phenomenon that is characteristic only of the mind; and they who rule reveal themselves more than those things which are ruled. And in fact minds rule, bodies are ruled. Each one delights in pleasure and takes pleasure from the body; but take away the mind, nothing remains in the body which may delight. And if there is delight from the body, the mind delights. If it has delight from its house,[4] ought it not have delight from itself? And if the mind has something from which it may be delighted from the outside, does it remain without delights on the inside?[5] It is quite well established that a man loves his soul more than his body.

(3) But even in another man, a man loves the soul more than the body. For what is loved in a friend where the love is

---

discussion in Berrouard BA 72.852–54 shows. Some texts attach "who believes in me" to the previous sentence, modifying "him," as in Cyprian, *Testimonia* 1.22 (CSEL 3.58) and *Epistula* 63.8 (CSEL 3.206), and Ambrose, *De Spiritu Sancto* 3.20.153–54 (PL 161.812). This would cause the Scriptural quotation to refer to Christ; but as Augustine punctuates, it refers to the believer. Cf. Comeau, *Saint Augustine*, 77–78; B. Vawter, JBC 2.440; R. E. Brown, *The Anchor Bible* 29.320–21.

4. Cf. *Tractate* 8.2 where the soul is called the "inhabitant" (*habitatrix*) of the body.

5. Cf. *Tractate* 26.4.

quite genuine and chaste? What is loved in a friend, the mind or the body? If loyalty is loved, the mind is loved; if good will is loved, the seat of good will is the mind. If you love this in another, that he also loves you, you love his mind, because it is the mind that loves, not the flesh. You love for the very reason that he loves you; seek the source from which he loves you, and see what you love. Therefore, [the mind] is loved more, and is not seen.

3. I also want to say something wherein it may be clearer to you, my beloved people, how much the mind is loved and how it is preferred to the body. Those lascivious lovers themselves who are delighted by beauty of body and inflamed by the shape of limbs, love more when they are loved. For if one should love and feel that he is hated, he is more angry than affectionate. Why is he more angry than affectionate? Because what he invests is not paid back to him.

(2) Therefore, if these very lovers of the body want to be loved in return and it delights them more if they should be loved, what are lovers of minds like? And if lovers of minds are great, what are lovers of God, who makes minds beautiful, like? For as the mind effects comeliness in the body, so does God effect comeliness in the mind. For nothing effects for the body that by which it is loved except the mind; and when the mind has gone away, you shudder at the corpse, and however much you loved those beautiful limbs, you hasten to bury them. Therefore, the comeliness of the body is the mind; the comeliness of the mind is God.

4. Therefore, the Lord cries out that we should come and drink if we thirst within; and he says that when we drink, rivers of living water shall flow out of our belly. The belly of the inner man is the conscience of the heart. Therefore, when this liquid has been drunk, the cleansed conscience gains life; and drawing [the water] out, it will have a fountain; it will itself even be a fountain.

(2) What is the fountain and what is the river which flows out of the belly of the inner man? Good will by which he wishes to look after his neighbor's interests. For if he should think that what he drinks ought to suffice for himself alone,

living water does not flow out of his belly; but if he hastens to look after the interests of his neighbor, then he is not dry because he flows.

(3) Now we shall see what it is that they drink who believe in the Lord; for, of course, we are Christians, and if we believe, we drink. And each one ought to recognize in himself if he drinks and if he lives on what he drinks; for the fountain does not desert us if we do not desert the fountain.

5. The Evangelist has explained, as I have said, why the Lord had cried out, to what drink he had invited, what he had offered the drinkers to drink, saying, "He said this, however, of the Spirit whom they who believed in him were to receive; for the Spirit had not yet been given, since Jesus had not yet been glorified." What spirit did he mean except the Holy Spirit? For each man has within himself his own spirit about which I was speaking when I mentioned the mind. For the mind of each man is his own proper spirit, about which the Apostle Paul said, "For who among men knows the things that are of a man but the spirit of a man which is in him?" Then he added, "So the things also that are of God no one knows but the Spirit of God."[6] No one knows our things except our spirit. For I do not know what you are thinking or you what I am thinking; for these are our own proper things which we think within, and the spirit of each man himself is the witness of his thoughts. "So the things also that are of God no one knows but the Spirit of God." We with our spirit, God with his, yet in such a way that God with his Spirit knows even what is done in us, but we without his Spirit cannot know what is done in God. But God knows in us even what we ourselves do not know in ourselves. For Peter did not know his weakness when he heard from the Lord that he would deny him three times,[7] and, though, sick, he did not know himself; the Physician knew the sick man. Therefore, there are certain things which God knows in us although we ourselves do not know them. Nevertheless, as far as pertains to men, no one knows

6. 1 Cor 2.11.
7. Cf. Mt 26.33–35, Mk 14.29–31, Lk 22.31–34, Jn 13.36–38.

himself so well as the man himself; another does not know what is done in him, but his spirit knows.

(2) But when the Spirit of God has been received, we learn also what is done in God, but not everything because we have not received everything. We know much about the pledge; for we have received the pledge,[8] but the fullness of the pledge will be given later. Meanwhile, on this journey, let the pledge comfort us, because he who deigned to give the pledge to us is ready to give much. If the bond is such, what is he whose bond it is?

6. But what do his words mean: "For the Spirit had not yet been given because Jesus had not yet been glorified"? The meaning is quite clear. For it was not that the Spirit of God who was with God did not exist; but he was not yet in those who had believed in Jesus. For the Lord Jesus had ordained not to give them this Spirit about whom we are speaking until after his resurrection; and this not without reason. And perhaps if we should ask, he will grant that we may find; and if we should knock, he will open that we may enter.[9] Devotion knocks, not the hand, although the hand also knocks if the hand ceases not from the works of mercy. What, then, is the reason why the Lord Jesus Christ decided to give the Holy Spirit only when he has been glorified?

(2) But before we say this as best as we can, it must first be asked, in case it should trouble anyone, how the Spirit was not yet in holy men, since it was read in the Gospel about the Lord himself, just after his birth, that Simeon recognized him in the Holy Spirit.[10] The prophetess, the widow Anna, also recognized him;[11] John himself, who baptized him recognized him;[12] Zacharias, filled with the Holy Spirit, said many things;[13] Mary herself received the Holy Spirit that she might conceive the Lord.[14] Therefore, we have several prior indications of the Holy Spirit before the Lord was glorified by the

8. The sending of the Holy Spirit as a pledge. See *Tractate* 8.4; 2 Cor 1.22 and 5.5; Eph 1.14.
9. Cf. Mt 7.7–8, Lk 11.9–10.   10. Cf. Lk 2.25–27.
11. Cf. Lk 2.36–38.   12. Cf. Jn 1.26–34.
13. Cf. Lk 1.67–79.   14. Cf. Lk 1.35.

resurrection of his flesh. Again, neither did the prophets who predicted that Christ would come have another Spirit.[15]

(3) But of this giving, there was to be a certain mode which had not at all appeared before; about this there is a question here. For nowhere before have we read that men, having been gathered together, after the Holy Spirit was received, had spoken in the languages of all nations.[16] But after his resurrection, when he first appeared to his disciples, he said to them, "Receive the Holy Spirit."[17] About this giving, then, it was said, "The Spirit had not yet been given because Jesus had not yet been glorified." "And he breathed upon their face"[18]—he who first gave life to man by breathing,[19] and raised him up from the mire, and by breathing gave a soul to his members, signifying that he was the one who breathed upon their face that they might rise up from the slime and renounce filthy works. Then first after his resurrection, which the Evangelist calls his glorification,[20] he gave his disciples the Holy Spirit. Then, staying with them for forty days, as the book of the Acts of the Apostles shows, while they were watching and accompanying him by watching, he ascended into heaven.[21] There, when ten days had passed, on the day of Pentecost, he sent down the Holy Spirit,[22] and, as I said, when they who had been gathered together in one place received him and were filled with him, they spoke the tongues of all nations.

7. Well now, brothers, because he who is baptized in Christ and believes in Christ does not now speak in the languages of all nations, must it be believed that he has not received the Holy Spirit? Far be it that our hearts be tempted by this perfidy. We are certain that every man receives him; but as big a vessel of faith as he shall bring to the fountain, so much does he fill.

(2) Therefore, since also now he is received, someone might ask, Why does no one speak in the languages of all nations?

---

15. Cf. *DDQ* 83.62.　　　　16. Cf. Acts 2.1–4.
17. Jn 20.22.　　　　18. Jn 20.22.
19. Cf. Gn 2.7.
20. Perhaps a reference to Jn 7.39; cf. Lk 24.26.
21. Cf. Acts 1.3, 9.
22. Cf. Acts 2.1–4.

Because now the Church herself speaks in the languages of all nations. Before the Church was in one nation, when it was speaking in the languages of all. By speaking in the languages of all it signified the future, that, by growing through the nations, it might speak in the languages of all.

(3) He who is not in this Church neither does he now receive the Holy Spirit.[23] For cut off and separated from the unity of the members, a unity which speaks in the languages of all, let him retract [his claim] if he does not have [him].[24] For if he has [him], let him give the sign which was given then. What do I mean, let him give the sign which was given then? Let him speak in all languages.

(4) He replies to me, Well now, do you speak in all languages? I say plainly that every language is mine, that is, every language belongs to this body among whose members I am. The Church, spread through the nations, speaks in all languages; the Church is the body of Christ, in this body you are a member. Therefore, since you are a member of this body, which speaks in all languages, believe that you speak in all languages. For the unity of the members is made into its oneness of heart by love; and this unity speaks as then one man spoke.

8. Therefore, we also receive the Holy Spirit if we love the Church, if we are joined together by love,[25] if we rejoice in the Catholic name and faith. Let us believe, brothers, that as much as each one loves Christ's Church, so much does he have the Holy Spirit. For the Spirit was given, as the Apostle says, "For

23. Cf. *Tractate* 27.6.
24. I.e., the Holy Spirit.
25. On Augustine's use of the various Latin words for love, see *Tractate* 3.5, note 20. In a very detailed study, not mentioned in the earlier note, H. Pétré, *Caritas* 22.1–100, demonstrates that Augustine, whatever earlier practice was in Christian Latin, uses *dilectio, caritas,* and *amor,* and *amare* and *diligere,* both as exact synonyms and with *amor* having a pejorative connotation when the context so requires. She also shows that Augustine is primarily responsible for raising *amor* to this coequal ameliorative sense. See especially pp. 28, 78, 80–81, and 90–96. See also J. Burnaby, *Amor Dei* 92–100. 114–15, 221–23. *Sermo* 349 (PL 39.1529–33) is a good example of Augustine's usage of the three Latin words for love; cf. also *Tractate* 123.5; *Tr in Io Ep* 8.5; and *En in Ps* 31.2.5.

manifestation." What manifestation? As he likewise says, "To one by the Spirit is given the word of wisdom; to another the word of knowledge, according to the same Spirit; to another faith, in the same Spirit; to another, the gift of healings, in the one Spirit; to another the working of miracles, in the same Spirit."[26] For many things are given for manifestation, but perhaps you have none of all these things which I have mentioned. If you love, you do not have nothing; for if you love unity, whoever in it has anything has it also for you. Take away envy, and what I have is yours; let me take away envy, and what you have is mine. Jealousy separates, right reason joins.[27] In the body, only the eye sees; but does the eye see only for itself? It also sees for the hand, and it sees for the foot, and it sees for the other members; for if some blow should come against the foot, the eye does not turn itself away from it so that it may not forewarn. Again, in the body, only the hand works; but does it work only for itself? It also worked for the eye; for if some blow were coming and not going against the hand but only against the face, does the hand say, "I do not move myself because it is not aiming at me"? So the foot by walking serves for all the members; the rest of the members are silent, the tongue speaks for all.

(2) Therefore, we have the Holy Spirit if we love the Church; but we love if we are within its unity and love. For the Apostle himself, when he had said that various gifts were given to various men, like the functions of each of the members, said, "And I show you a yet more excellent way,"[28] and he began to speak about love.[29] He set it above the tongues of men and angels; he set it above the miracles of faith. He set it above knowledge and prophecy; he set it above even that great work of mercy by which each man distributes what he possesses to the poor. And finally, he set it above even the

---

26. 1 Cor 12.7–10.
27. There is a word play here. The Latin *livor* means both a black and blue bruise and jealousy; *sanitas* means the healthy condition either of body or of mind.
28. 1 Cor 12.31.
29. Cf. 1 Cor 13.

suffering of the body; he set love above all such great things as these. Have love, and you have everything, because without it, whatever you could have profits you nothing.[30] But because the love about which we are speaking belongs to the Holy Spirit (for now the problem in the Gospel about the Holy Spirit is taken up again), hear the Apostle speaking, "The love of God has been poured forth in our hearts through the Holy Spirit who has been given to us."[31]

9. Why, therefore, did the Lord want to give the Spirit, whose greatest benefits are in us because "the love of God has been poured forth in our hearts" through him [i.e. the Holy Spirit] after his resurrection. What did he signify? That our love may be on fire in our resurrection, and may separate [us] from the love of [this] age, that all our love may run to God. For we are born and we die here; let us not love this age. Let us journey by love, let us dwell on high by love, by that love with which we love[32] God. In this journey, which is our life, let us meditate upon nothing else except that we shall not always be here and we shall there, by living well, prepare a place for ourselves from which we shall never go. For our Lord Jesus Christ, after he arose, "dies now no more; death shall no more," as the Apostle says, "have dominion over him."[33] Look at what we should love. If we live, if we believe in him who has risen, he will give us not what men who do not love God love here, or the more they love that,[34] the less they love him, but the more they love him, the less they love it.

(2) But let us see what he promised us—not earthly and temporal riches, not honors and powers in this age; for you see that all these things are also given to evil men, so that they may not be highly esteemed by the good. And, furthermore, not even bodily health, not because he does not give that, but because, as you see, he also gives it to brute animals. Not long

30. A theme many times repeated in these tractates, e.g., 6.4, 7.3, 9.8.
31. Rom 5.5.
32. In the opening sentences of this section, Augustine uses all three Latin words for love, cf. note 24.
33. Rom 6.9.
34. I.e., what men love here.

life. For what is long which is at some time ended?[35] He did not promise to us who believe longevity as a great thing, or decrepit old age, which all desire before it comes, but all murmur about when it has come. Not beauty of body, which either a disease of the body or the very old age which is desired puts to an end. One wishes to be beautiful and wishes to be old; these two desires cannot accord with one another. If you will be old, you will not be beautiful; when old age comes, beauty will flee; the vigor of beauty and the moaning of old age cannot dwell in one person. Therefore, none of these things did he who said, "He who believes in me, let him come and drink, and out of his belly there will flow rivers of living water," promise us.

(3) He promised eternal life where we are to fear nothing, where we are to be untroubled, from where we are not to travel, where we are not to die, where neither a predecessor is to be mourned nor a successor is to be hoped for. Therefore, because such it is that he has promised to us who love and are ablaze with the love of the Holy Spirit, he did not wish to give the Holy Spirit himself, except when he had been glorified, so that he might show in his body the life which we do not now have but hope for in the resurrection.

35. For this sentiment similarly expressed, cf. Cicero, *De Senectute* 16.69 and *Pro Marcello* 9.27. M. Testard, *Saint Augustin et Cicéron* does not cite either of these references.

TRACTATE 33

On John 7.40–53: 8.1–11

YOU REMEMBER, my beloved people, that in the previous sermon, as a result of the circumstances presented in the reading of the Gospel, we spoke to you about the Holy Spirit. When the Lord had invited those who believed in him to this drinking, speaking among those who were thinking about laying hold of him, and who desired to kill him but were unable because he did not will it, when, therefore, he had said these things, a disagreement about him sprang up in the crowd, since some thought that he was the very Christ and others said that the Christ will not arise from Galilee.

(2) Those who had been sent to lay hold on him returned, free of crime and filled with admiration. For they also bore witness of his divine teaching, when they by whom they had been sent asked, "Why have you not brought him?" They answered that they had never heard a man speaking in such a way: "For not any man speaks in such a way." Now, he spoke thus because he was God and man.

(3) Yet the Pharisees, rejecting their witness, said to them, "Have you also been seduced?" For we see that you have been delighted with his discourses. "Has any one of the rulers believed in him, or of the Pharisees? But this crowd, who know not the Law, are accursed." They who did not know the Law, these believed in him who had sent the Law; and they who were teaching the Law despised him who had sent the Law so that what the Lord himself had said might be fulfilled, "I have come that they who do not see may see and they who see may become blind."[1] For the Pharisees, the teachers, became blind;

---

1. Jn 9.39.

and the people, now knowing the Law, and yet believing in the
Author of the Law, were enlightened.

2. Nevertheless, "Nicodemus, the one of the Pharisees who
had come to him at night,"[2] was also himself, indeed, not
unbelieving, but timid. For he had come to the Light at night
precisely because he wanted to be enlightened but was afraid
to be known. He replied to the Jews, "Does our Law judge a
man unless it first listen to him and know what he does?" For,
perversely, they wanted to be condemners before they were
judges. Nicodemus knew, or rather believed, that if only they
were willing to listen patiently to him, perhaps they would be
like those who were sent to lay hold on him but chose rather to
believe. "They answered," from the prejudice of their heart,
as they also had to those men,[3] "Are you also a Galilean?" That
is, as if seduced by the Galilean. For the Lord was called a
Galilean because his parents were from the town of Nazareth.
I said parents according to Mary, not according to the male
seed; for he, who already had a Father above, sought nought
but a mother on earth. For both births of his were miraculous,
the divine without a mother, the human without a father.[4]
What then did they, the so-called teachers of the Law, say to
Nicodemus? "Search the Scriptures and see that out of Galilee
a prophet arises not." But the Lord of prophets arose from
there. "They returned, each one to his own house."[5]

3. "From there Jesus went up to the mountain," but to the
mountain "of Olives," to the fruitful mountain, to the mountain of ointment, to the mountain of chrism.[6] For where was it

2. The entire account of Nicodemus in Jn 3.1–21 is discussed in *Tractate*
11.3–15 and *Tractate* 12.

3. That is, those who had been sent to arrest Jesus; see Jn 7.44–47.

4. Augustine repeats this teaching frequently; cf. *Tractates* 8.8, 12.8, 14.2,
26.10.

5. There is no mention of the textual problem concerning Jn 7.53 and
8.1–11; this story of the adulteress is not found in the early Greek manuscripts but was widely preserved in the West. Augustine, in the *De Adulterinis
Coniugiis* 2.7.6. (CSEL 41.387–88), does note that its genuineness is questioned. Cf. B. Vawter, JBC, 2.441; R. E. Brown, *The Anchor Bible* 29.335–36;
Berrouard 72.857–60.

6. Located east of Jerusalem, this mountain was of great importance in the
cultic and political history of Jerusalem as well as for Christians. The name

fitting for Christ to teach, if not on the Mount of Olives? For the name Christ is derived from chrism; what is called χρῖσμα in Greek is called *unctio* (ointment) in Latin.[7] Now he has anointed us for the reason that he has made us wrestlers against the devil.[8] "And at daybreak he came again into the temple, and all the people came to him; and sitting down he taught them." And he was not arrested because he did not yet deign to suffer.

4. Observe now how the gentleness of the Lord was tested by his enemies. "Now the Scribes and Pharisees brought to him a woman caught in adultery, and they set her in the midst, and said to him. 'Master, this woman has just now been caught in adultery. Now in the Law, Moses commanded us to stone such a one. What, therefore, do you say?' Now they were saying this testing him, that they might be able to accuse him." To accuse him of what? Had they caught him in any crime or was that woman said to have pertained to him in any way? What, then, does it mean, "testing him, that they might be able to accuse him?"

(2) We shall understand, brothers, that an admirable gentleness was conspicuous in the Lord. They noticed that he was extremely kind, that he was extremely gentle; this, to be sure, had been predicted about him before: "Gird your sword upon your thigh, most mighty one; in your comeliness and beauty exert yourself, proceed prosperously, and reign because of truth and gentleness and justice."[9] He brought truth as a

---

Mount of Olives first appears in Zec 14.4 and the common Hebrew name seems to have been the Mount of Anointing. On its western slope was Gethsemane, the site of an olive grove; Gethsemane means either "oil press" or "oil valley" with Jerome preferring the latter (*Liber Interpretationis Hebraicorum Nominum,* s.v., CCL 72.136). Augustine's use of several names, then, refers to actuality, not interpretation only. See J. McKenzie, JBC 2.109; C. Stuhlmueller, JBC 2.159; *Encyclopedia Iudaica* (Jerusalem 1971) 481–85.

7. Cf. *Tractates* 7.13 and 15.27.

8. Ancient athletes used to rub down with olive oil for muscle conditioning.

9. Cf. Ps 44 (45).4–5. The text of these verses is problematical and many commentators and translators see dittography in verse five and omit some of the words herein included. The Latin *intende* is especially difficult and is

teacher, gentleness as a deliverer, justice as a defender.[10] Because of these things the prophet predicted that he would reign in the Holy Spirit.[11] When he spoke, truth was recognized; when he was not aroused against his enemies, gentleness was praised. Therefore, since his enemies were tormented by jealousy and envy over these two things, that is, his truth and gentleness, in the third, that is, justice, they put up a stumbling block.

(3) Why? Because the Law had ordered adulterers to be stoned, and, of course, the Law could not order what was unjust; if anyone said something other than the Law had ordered, he would be detected as unjust. Therefore, they said to one another: He is considered truthful, he seems gentle; slander must be sought against him on the grounds of justice. Let us present to him a woman caught in adultery; let us say what has been prescribed about her in the Law. If he orders her to be stoned, he will not have gentleness; if he judges that she be pardoned, he will not keep justice. But, they say, so as not to lose his gentleness in which he has now become beloved to the people, without doubt, he will say that she ought to be pardoned. From this we find an opportunity for accusing him and we make him guilty as a transgressor of the Law, saying to him, You are an enemy of the Law; you answer against Moses, nay, rather against him who gave the Law through Moses. You are guilty of death and you ought yourself to be stoned with her.

(4) By these words and these thoughts envy could be inflamed, and accusation agitated, condemnation demanded.

---

taken variously; hence Innes has "urge on," Browne has "go thy way," Douay has "set out," and NAB omits. The LXX has ἔντεινον usually translated "bend your bow." I base my translation on the verses as they appear and are interpreted in *En in Ps* 44.14.

10. As a legal technical term, *cognitor* can be either a defender or a judge; see TLL 3.1487–88 and A. Berger, *Encyclopedic Dictionary of Roman Law* (Philadelphia 1953) 394. As a defender, the *cognitor* was appointed by the court to investigate the case and defend one of the contending parties as though the suit were his own.

11. Cf. Is 11.1–4.

For to whom [was] this [to be done]? Perversity to uprightness, falsehood to truth, a corrupt heart to an upright heart, stupidity to wisdom. When would they prepare snares into which they would not first stick their heads? Look, the Lord, in answering, was going to maintain justice and was not going to depart from gentleness. For he for whom [the net] was stretched was not caught, but rather were they caught who were stretching [the net], because they did not believe in him who could pluck them out of the snares.

5. What, then did the Lord Jesus answer? What did Truth answer? What did Wisdom answer? What did Justice itself, against whom a slander was being readied, answer? He did not say, "Let her not be stoned!" so that he might not seem to speak contrary to the Law. But far be it from him to say, "Let her be stoned!" For he came not to destroy what he had found but to seek out what had been lost.[12] What, then, did he answer? See how his reply is filled with justice, filled with gentleness and truth. He said, "Let him who is without sin among you be the first to cast a stone at her." Oh, response of Wisdom! How he did send them into themselves! For they were slandering without, not examining themselves within. They saw an adulteress; they did not look closely at themselves. Transgressors of the Law, they desired the Law to be fulfilled, and this by slander, not truly, as by condemning adulteries with chastity.

(2) O Jews, you heard, O Pharisees, you heard, O teachers of the Law, you heard the guardian of the Law; but you have not yet understood the Law-maker. What else did he signify to you when he wrote on the ground with his finger? For the Law was written by the finger of God; but because they were hard men, it was written on stone.[13] Now the Lord was writing on the ground, because he sought for fruit.

(3) You have heard; let the Law be fulfilled, let the adulteress be stoned, but in punishing her is the Law to be fulfilled by those who ought to be punished? Let each one of you reflect upon himself, let him enter into himself, let him go up

12. Lk 19.10.
13. Cf. Ex 31.18.

to the tribunal of his mind, let him compel himself to confess. For he knows who he is, because "no one among men knows the things of a man save the spirit of man which is in him."[14] Each one, gazing upon himself, found himself a sinner. Yes, indeed. Therefore, either pardon her or accept the punishment of the Law together with her. If he had said, "Let the adulteress not be stoned!" he would have been proved an unjust man; if he had said, "Let her be stoned!" he would not have seemed gentle. Let him say what he ought to say, [and he is] both gentle and just: "Let him who is without sin among you be the first to cast a stone at her." This is the voice of Justice. Let the woman who has sinned be punished, but not by sinners; let the Law be fulfilled, but not by transgressors of the Law. This is certainly the voice of Justice. And when they were struck by this Justice as if by a spear the size of a beam, looking into themselves and finding themselves guilty, "they went away, all of them, one by one."

(4) There were left [but] two, the pitiable woman and Pity. But when the Lord had struck them with that shaft of justice, he deigned not to watch them collapse, but with his view turned away from them, "Again he wrote with his finger on the ground."

6. Now when that woman was the only one left and everybody was going away, he raised his eyes to the woman. We heard the voice of Justice; let us also hear that of Gentleness. For, I believe, that woman had been more frightened when she heard it said by the Lord, "Let him who is without sin be the first to cast a stone at her." They, turning their thoughts to themselves and having confessed about themselves by their very departure, had left the woman with her huge sin to him who was without sin. And because she had heard this, "Let him who is without sin be the first to cast a stone at her," she expected to be punished by him in whom no sin could be found. But he, who had repulsed his adversaries with the tongue of justice, raising the eyes of gentleness to her, asked her, "Has no man condemned you?" She answered, "Lord, no

14. 1 Cor 2.11; cf. *Tractate* 32.5.

man." And he, "Neither will I condemn you"—I, by whom perhaps you feared to be condemned because you have found no sin in me. "Neither will I condemn you." What does it mean, O Lord? Do you, therefore, countenance sins? Certainly not. Mark what follows: "Go, and from now on, sin no more." Therefore, the Lord also condemned, but the sin, not the person. For if he favored sins, he would say, Neither will I condemn you; go, live as you will. Be without anxiety as regards my liberation. However much you sin, I shall free you from all the punishment of Gehenna and the tortures of Hell. He did not say this.

7. Therefore, let those who love the gentleness in the Lord and fear the truth pay attention. For "sweet and righteous is the Lord."[15] You love [him] because he is sweet. Fear [him] because he is righteous. As a gentle man, he said, "I have kept silence." But as a just man, "Shall I always be silent?"[16] "A Lord compassionate and merciful."[17] Yes, indeed. Yet add, patient; yet add, and very compassionate. But fear what comes last, and truthful. For those whom he now endures as sinners he will judge as despisers. "Or do you despise the riches of his forebearance and gentleness, not knowing that the patience of God leads you to repentance? But according to the hardness of your heart and your unrepentant heart, you do treasure up to yourself wrath on the day of wrath and of the revelation of the just judgment of God who will render to every man according to his works."[18] He is a gentle Lord, a patient Lord, a merciful Lord, but also a just Lord and a truthful Lord. A period of time for correction is bestowed on you; but you love procrastination more than amendment. Were you evil yesterday? Be good today. And have you spent this day in wickedness? At least change tomorrow. You are always waiting, and you promise yourself very much from the mercy of God, as if he who promised you forgiveness through your repentence[19] also promised you a longer life. How do you know what to-

15. Ps 24 (25).8.   16. Is 42.14 (LXX).
17. Ps 85 (86).15.   18. Rom 2.4–6.
19. So one codex, the Maurist edition and some other editions; the other codices have *per patientiam,* through his forebearance.

morrow may bring forth? You say rightly in your heart, "When I correct myself, God will forgive all my sins." We cannot deny that God promised forgiveness to those who have been amended and converted. But in whichever prophet you read to me that he promised forgiveness to one who has been amended, you do not read to me that God has promised you a long life.[20]

8. Therefore, men are endangered by two things, both hoping and despairing, contrary things, contrary feelings. Who is deceived by hoping? He who says, God is good, God is merciful; let me do what I please, what I feel like; let me relax the reins on my desires; let me fulfill the cravings of my soul. Why this? Because God is merciful, God is good, God is gentle. These men are imperiled by hope.

(2) But by despair, they who, when they have fallen into grave sins, think to themselves that they cannot be forgiven even though they are repentent, decide that they are without a doubt destined for damnation, and say to themselves, Now we must be damned: why not do what we want?—with the attitude of gladiators doomed by the sword. And so the desperate are troublesome; for they do not now have anything to fear, and they must be very much feared.

(3) Despair kills these; hope, those. The mind fluctuates between hope and despair. It must be feared lest hope slays you; and when you hope for too much from mercy, you fall into judgment. Again, it must be feared lest despair slays you; and when you think that you cannot now be forgiven for grave sins you have committed, you do no penance and you encounter the Judge, Wisdom, which says, "And I will laugh at your doom."[21]

(4) What, then, has the Lord to do with those endangered by these diseases? To those who are endangered by hope, he says this: "Delay not to be converted to the Lord; and put it not off from day to day; for suddenly his wrath will come, and in the time of vengeance he will destroy you."[22] To those who

---

20. Cf. Is 40–45 with its emphasis on the promise of salvation or Ez 18.23–32; see section 8, notes 22 and 23.

21. Prv 1.26.

22. Ecclus (Sir) 5.8–9.

are endangered by despair, what does he say? "On whatever day the wicked man is converted, I shall forget all his iniquities."[23] Therefore, because of those who are endangered by despair, he has proposed the harbor of forgiveness; because of those who are endangered by hope and deluded by delays, he has made the day of death uncertain. You do not know when the last day may come. Are you ungrateful because you have today, in which you may be corrected?

(5) So therefore, [he said] to that woman, "Neither will I condemn you"; but, made secure about the past, beware the future. "Neither will I condemn you." I have erased what you committed; observe what I commanded that you may find what I promised.

23. Cf. Ez 18.21–22, 33.14–15.

TRACTATE 34

On John 8.12

DO NOT doubt that we all tried also to understand what we have just now heard and attentively received when the Holy Gospel was read; and each of us took what he could according to his own capacity from so great a matter which has been read. And when the bread of the word has been served, there is no one who complains that he has tasted nothing. But again I do not doubt that there is rarely anyone who has understood the whole. Nevertheless, even if there is someone who understands well all the words of our Lord Jesus Christ just recited from the Gospel, let him endure our ministry, until, if we can, with his help, we enable, by our discussion, all or many to understand what the few are delighted to have understood.

2. I think that what the Lord said, "I am the Light of the world," is clear to those who have eyes with which they may become partakers of this Light. But they who do not have eyes except in the flesh alone wonder at what was said by the Lord Jesus Christ: "I am the Light of the world." And perhaps there may even be present someone who would say to himself, Is the Lord Christ perhaps this sun which brings to pass a day by its rising and setting? For there have actually been heretics who have held these opinions.

(2) The Manichees thought that Christ the Lord was this sun, visible to the eyes of the flesh, open and public not only to men but also to brute animals to see.[1] But the orthodox faith

1. In the complex syncretic religion founded by Mani, A.D. 216–c. 277, Jesus held a special and unique position. As a particular emanation of the Divine Light, Jesus the Brilliant came as the Third Messenger to bring the knowledge of salvation to Adam. He is variously syncretized with the histori-

of the Catholic Church condemns such a fabrication and recognizes that it is a diabolical doctrine; not only does it recognize it by believing, but also by reasoning it out, it refutes it in
the case of those for whom it can. And so let us repudiate an
error of this kind which the holy Church has made anathema
from the beginning. Let us not think that the Lord Jesus
Christ is this sun which we see rising from the east, setting in
the west, whose passing night follows, whose rays are darkened by a cloud, which journeys by fixed motion from place to
place. The Lord Christ is not this thing. The Lord Christ is
not the sun [which was] made, but it is he through whom the
sun was made. For "all things were made through him and
without him was made nothing."[2]

3. Therefore, there is a Light which made this light [that we
see]. Let us love this Light, let us desire to understand this
Light. Let us thirst for it that under its guidance, we may
sometime come to it itself and may so live in it that we may

---

cal Jesus who is human in appearance only; sometimes, Jesus Patibilis, the
historical Jesus, is rejected as a false representation of the Darkness, a work of
the devil, though sometimes, and particularly in North Africa, he is a lower
element of Jesus the Brilliant, crucified in the realm of matter and mingled in
the corporeal world, an individual moment in the cosmic drama of passion
and redemption. Jesus the Brilliant "dwells in" the sun. Since God, the Divine
Light, is to the Manichees a substance, not a person, he is the Light, he is what
he dwells in; hence Jesus is the sun. Both the mythical Jesus and the sun are
particular emanations of the one Divine Light. Augustine, of course, points
out that Christ is light not in the physical sense, not the light of nature, but the
light of Divine Wisdom; Augustine frequently mentions the Manichaean
identification of Jesus with the sun, as, e.g., *En in Ps* 25.2.3 and 93.5; *Sermo*
4.5, 12.11–12, and 50.7 (Pl 38.36, 105–106, and 329); *Contra Faustum* 16.10,
20.2 and 5–8, and 21.4 (PL 42.320–21, 369, 371–74, and 391); and *De Genesi
contra Manichaeos* 1.6 and 2.38 (PL 34.176 and 216–17). See F. Dolgen, "Konstantin der Grosse und der Manichaismus, Sonne und Christus in Manichaismus," AC 2 (1930) 301–14; F. Burkitt, *The Religion of the Manichees*
(Cambridge 1925) esp. 37–43, 49–52, 92–93; G. Widengren, *Mani and Manichaeism* (London 1961); G. Bardy, "Manichéisme," *Dictionnaire de théologie
catholique* (Paris 1927) 9.2.1841–95; J. Ries, "Manichaeism," NCE 9.153–60;
A. Moon, *The De Natura Boni of Saint Augustine*, esp. 141, 202–204, 224–28;
Augustine, *De Haeresibus* 46 (CCL 46.312–20). However, F. Decret, *Aspects du
Manichéisme dans l'Afrique romaine* (Paris 1970) 229–31, questions Augustine's
accuracy on this point.
2. Jn 1.3.

never at all die. For it is this Light about which long ago
prophecy set forth and sang in the psalm as follows: "You will
save men and beasts, O Lord, as your mercy has been multiplied, O God."³ These are the words of the holy psalm; notice
what the ancient utterance of the holy men of God has announced in advance about such a Light. It said, "You will save
men and beasts, O Lord, as your mercy has been multiplied, O
God." For, because you are God and have multiple mercy, the
same multiplicity of your mercy has come not only to men,
whom you created in your image, but also to brute animals,
which you have made subject to men. For the well-being⁴ of
the brute animal is also from that one from whom is the well-
being of man.⁵ You would not blush to think this about the
Lord, your God; nay, rather you would take it for granted and
count on it, and take care that you not think otherwise. The
very one who saves you also saves your horse, your ewe—and
let us come to the absolutely least of things—your hen. "Salvation is the Lord's."⁶ And God saves these things. It disturbs
you; you ask. I wonder why you doubt. Will he who deigned to
create disdain to save? Salvation of angels, of men, of brute
animals is the Lord's; "Salvation is the Lord's." As no one is of
himself, so no one is saved of himself. Accordingly, most truly
and excellently did the psalm say, "You will save men and
beasts, O Lord." Why? "As Your mercy has been multiplied, O
God." For you are God, you created, you save; you have given
that one exists, you give that one is well.

4. Therefore if, as God's mercy has been multiplied, men
and beasts are saved by him, do not men have something else
which God the creator may present to them which he does not
present to the beasts? Is there no distinction between the animal made in the image of God and the animal subjected to the
image of God? Certainly there is! Besides this salvation com-

3. Ps 35 (36).7–8.
4. Throughout this passage there is a double connotation of the Latin
words *salus* and *salvus*, health or salvation and healthy or saved, which cannot
be adequately reflected in the translation. See *Tractates* 7.9, note 55; 17.12,
note 37; 30.4, note 12.
5. Cf. *Tractate* 30.3.
6. Ps 3.9.

mon to us and the dumb animals there is something which God may present to us but does not present to them. What is this? Continue in the same psalm, "But the children of men will hope under the covering of your wings."[7] Having now salvation in common with their brute animals, "the children of men will hope under the covering of your wings." They have one salvation in present reality, another in hope. The salvation in the present is common to both men and beasts, but the other is that for which men hope. And they who hope receive it; they who despair do not. For it says, "the sons of men will hope under the covering of your wings." But they who hope perseveringly are protected by you that they be not downcast from their hope by the devil: "they will hope under the covering of your wings." Therefore, if they will hope, for what will they hope, except what the brute animals will not have? "They will be inebriated by the richness of your house, and you will give them to drink of the torrent of your pleasure."[8] What kind of wine is it from which it is praiseworthy to be inebriated? What kind of wine is it which does not confuse, but guides the mind? What kind of wine is it which makes a man forever sane and does not by inebriation make him insane? "They will be inebriated." By what? "By the richness of your house, and you will give them to drink of the torrent of your pleasure." Why? "Because with you is the fountain of life."[9] The very Fountain of life himself walked upon the earth. He said, "Let him who thirsts come to me."[10] Behold, the Fountain.

(2) But we had begun to speak about light, and we were dealing with a problem proposed from the Gospel about light. In the words of the Lord it was read to us, "I am the light of the world." From this arose the problem that no one, thinking in carnal terms, should suppose that he be understood as this sun; from there we came to the psalm in the consideration of which we again found the Lord as the Fountain of life. Drink and live. "With you," it says, "is the fountain of life." And so

7. Ps 35 (36).8.
9. Ps 35 (36).10.
8. Ps 35 (36).9.
10. Jn 7.37.

the children of men hope under the bower of your wings, seeking to be inebriated by this Fountain. But we were speaking of light. Continue therefore; for when the prophet had said, "with you is the fountain of life," he continued and added, "In your light we shall see light"[11]—God from God, Light from Light. Through this Light, the light of the sun was made; and the Light which made the sun, under which he also made us, was made under the sun for our sakes. The Light which made the sun, I say, was made for our sakes under the sun. Do not despise the cloud of the flesh; he is covered with a cloud not that he may be darkened, but that [his brightness] may be rendered endurable.

5. Speaking, therefore, through the cloud of the flesh, the unfailing Light, the Light of Wisdom, said to men: "I am the Light of the world. He who follows me will not walk in darkness but will have the light of life." How did he withdraw you from the eyes of the flesh and recall you to the eyes of the heart? It was not enough to say, "He who follows me will not walk in darkness but will have the light"; he added, "of life," as it was said there.[12] "Because with you is the fountain of life." See, therefore, my brothers, how the words of the Lord concur with the truth of that psalm; there, light was placed with the fountain of life, and by the Lord "light of life" was said. But in these physical experiences light is one thing, a fountain is another. Mouths seek a fountain; eyes, light. When we thirst, we seek a fountain; when we are in darkness, we seek a light. And if perchance we should be thirsty at night, we kindle a light so that we may come to the fountain. Not so with God; light is the same thing as fountain; he who shines for you that you may see also himself flows for you that you may drink.[13]

6. Therefore, you see, my brothers, you see, if you see

11. Ps 35 (36).10. The psalm uses the Latin word *lumen* for light, whereas Jn 8.12 has *lux*. In association with the fountain (*fons*) as a source one might expect the Latin *lux* as a source of light (see *Tractate* 21.4, note 15); but Augustine here makes no distinction between *lumen* and *lux*.

12. I.e., in Ps 35 (36).10.

13. Cf. *Tractate* 13.5.

within, what kind of light this is about which the Lord says, "He who follows me will not walk in darkness." Follow this sun; let us see if you will not walk in darkness. Look, by rising, it comes out for you. That [sun] in its passage goes to the west. You are, perhaps, setting out for the east. Unless you were to go in the opposite direction and not where it is heading, by following it you will really make a mistake and you will reach the west instead of the east. If you follow it on land, you will make a mistake; if a sailor follows it at sea, he will make a mistake. Finally, it seems to you that the sun must be followed and you yourself are going west where it, too, is heading. Let us see when it has set, if you will not walk in darkness. See how, even if you do not wish to desert it, it will desert you, completing the day by the necessity of its servitude. But in the meantime our Lord Jesus Christ, even when he was not appearing to all through the cloud of the flesh, was controlling all things through the power of his wisdom. Your God, the whole [of him], is everywhere; if you should not fall from him he never sets on you.

7. Therefore, he said, "He who follows me will not walk in darkness, but will have the light of life." What he promised, he put in a verb of the future tense; he did not say, He has, but he said, "he will have the light of life." Yet neither did he say, Who will follow me, but "who follows me." That which we ought to do, he has put in the present tense; but what he promised to those who do it he has signified by a verb of the future tense. "He who follows will have." Now he follows, later he will have, now he follows by faith, later he will have by sight. For the Apostle says, "while we are in the body, we are absent from the Lord, for we walk by faith and not by sight."[14] At what time by sight? When we shall have had the light of life, when we shall have come to that vision, when this night will have passed. In fact, about that day which will rise, it has been said, "In the morning I shall stand before you, and I shall see."[15] What does "in the morning" mean? When the night of

14. 2 Cor 5.6–7.
15. Ps 5.5 (NAB 5.4).

this age has passed, when the terrors of temptations have been
traversed, when that lion has been overcome which "goes
about at night, roaring, seeking someone to devour."[16] "In the
morning I shall stand before you, and I shall see."

(2) But now what do we think, brothers, is suited to this time
except what is said again in a psalm: "Every night I shall wash
my bed; I shall water my couch with my tears."[17] Every night,
it says, I shall weep; I shall burn with desire for the light. The
Lord sees my desire; for another psalm says to him, "Before
you is all my desire, and my groaning has not been hidden
from you."[18] Do you desire gold? You can be seen; for in
seeking gold, you will be apparent to men. Do you desire
grain? You ask who has it and to him also you announce your
desire to attain that for which you long. Do you desire God?
Who sees it except God? From whom do you seek God, as you
seek bread, water, gold, silver, grain? From whom do you seek
God except from God? He himself is sought from himself who
promises himself. Let your soul expand its desire, and with a
bosom capable of holding more, let it seek to grasp what eye
has not seen, nor ear heard, nor has it entered into the heart
of man.[19] For that, one can desire, one can long, one can sigh;
but one cannot worthily reflect upon it and explain it in words.

8. Therefore, my brothers, because the Lord said briefly, "I
am the light of the world. He who follows me will not walk in
darkness but will have the light of life," and in these words
what he commanded is different from what he promised, let
us do what he commanded that we may not desire what he
promised with shameless face. Let him not say to us in his
judgment: Have you done in fact what I commanded, that you
may seek after what I promised? What, then, did you command, O Lord our God? He says to you, That you should
follow me. You sought the counsel of life. Of what life except
that about which it was said, "With you is the fountain of
life"?[20] A certain man heard, "Go, sell all that you have, and
give to the poor, and you shall have treasure in heaven; and

16. 1 Pt 5.8.   17. Ps 6.7.
18. Ps 37 (38).10.
19. Cf. 1 Cor 2.9, quoting Is 64.4 (NAB 64.3).
20. Ps 35 (36).10.

come, follow me." "He went away sad,"[21] he did not follow. He
sought a good master, he questioned a teacher, and scorned
him when he was teaching. "He went away sad," bound up in
his desires. "He went away sad," carrying a huge pack of greed
upon his shoulders. He labored; he felt anxiety;[22] and he who
wanted to put his pack away from him was considered one
who was not to be followed, but deserted. But after the Lord
cried out through the Gospel, "Come to me, all you who labor
and are burdened, and I will refresh you. Take my yoke upon
you, and learn from me, for I am meek and humble of
heart,"[23] how many, when they heard the Gospel did what the
rich man, when he heard it from the Lord's own mouth, did
not do? Therefore, let us now do it, let us follow the Lord. Let
us loose the shackles by which we are prevented from following. And who is suited to loose such knots, if that one should
not help to whom it was said, "You have broken my bonds"?[24]
And about him another psalm says, "The Lord releases those
that were fettered, the Lord raises up those that were bowed
down."[25]

9. And what do those released and raised up follow except
the Light from whom they hear, "I am the light of the world.
He who follows me will not walk in darkness"? For the Lord
enlightens the blind.[26] Therefore we are now enlightened,
brothers, having the eye-salve of faith. For his saliva together
with earth, with which he who was blind from birth was
smeared,[27] came first.[28] And we were born blind from Adam,
and we have need of him who enlightens. He mixed saliva
with earth: "The Word was made flesh and dwelt among us."[29]
He mixed saliva with earth; and so it was predicted: "Truth
has sprung out of the earth."[30] But he himself said, "I am the
way, the truth, and the life."[31]

21. Mt 19.21–22, Cf. Mk 10.21–22, Lk 18.22–23.
22. Or simply, as Browne translates, he was hot.
23. Mt 11.28–29.   24. Ps 115 (116).16.
25. Ps 145 (146).7–8.   26. Cf. Ps 145 (146).8.
27. Cf. Jn 9.6.
28. I.e., before faith. As usual, all the elements in the miraculous event are
taken in a figurative sense.
29. Jn 1.14.   30. Ps 84 (85).12.
31. Jn 14.6.

(2) We shall fully enjoy the truth when we have seen him face to face, because this, too, is promised to us. For who could dare to hope for what God had not deigned either to promise or to give? We shall see him face to face. The Apostle says, "Now I know in part, now in a dark manner through a mirror, but then face to face."[32] And John the Apostle says in his epistle, "Beloved, now we are the children of God, and it has not yet appeared what we shall be. We know that, when he shall appear, we shall be like to him, for we shall see him as he is."[33] This is a great promise; if you love, follow.

(3) I love, you say, but by what way do I follow? If the Lord your God had said to you, "I am the truth and the life," longing for truth, desiring life, you would immediately ask the way by which you could come to these things, and you would say to yourself, A great thing is truth, a great thing is life; if only there were some way by which my soul might come to these! Do you seek by what way? Hear him saying first, "I am the way." Before he said to you where, he gave the way by which: "I am," he said, "the way." The way where? "And the truth and the life." He first said by what way you were to come, then he said where you were to come. I am the way, I am the truth, I the life. Abiding with the Father, the truth and the life; clothing himself with flesh, he became the way. It is not said to you: Labor in seeking the way that you might attain the truth and the life. This is not said to you. Lazy man, rise up! The way himself has come to you, and he has roused you who were sleeping from your sleep—if he has really roused you up: "Rise and walk."[34] Perhaps you are trying to walk and cannot because your feet hurt. From what do your feet hurt? Is it that they have run through rough places at the bidding of greed? But the Word of God has healed even the lame. Look, you say, I have healthy feet, but I do not see the way. He has enlightened the blind, too.

10. All of this is through faith while we are exiled from the Lord and remain in body.[35] But when we have walked throughout the way and come to the homeland itself, what will

32. I Cor 13.12.
34. Jn 5.8.

33. I Jn 3.2.
35. Cf. 2 Cor 5.6–7.

be more joyful to us? What will be more blessed for us? For there will be nothing more tranquil: for nothing will rebel against man.

(2) But now, brothers, we are scarcely without quarrel. We have indeed been called to concord; we are commanded to have peace among ourselves. This must be attempted and striven for with all our strength, that one day we may come to the most perfect peace. But now very often we quarrel with those whose interests we want to look after. That man goes astray; you want to lead him to the way. He resists you; you quarrel. A pagan resists; you argue against the errors of idols and demons. A heretic resists; you argue against other doctrines of demons. An evil Catholic does not wish to live well; you reproach even your inner brother. He remains in the house with you, and he seeks profligate ways. You seethe as to how you may correct him that you may render a good accounting about him to the Lord of both of you. How great are the necessities for quarrels everywhere! Very often a man, feeling weariness, says to himself, What good does it do me to endure opponents, to endure those who return evil for good? I wish to work in their interests; they want to perish. I consume my life in quarreling; I have no peace. What's more, I make those my enemies whom I ought to have as friends, if they would observe the good will of one working in their interest. What good does it do me to suffer these things? Let me return to myself. I shall be with myself; I shall call upon my God.

(3) Return to yourself; there you find a quarrel. If you have begun to follow God, there you find a quarrel. What quarrel, you say, do I find? "Flesh lusts against spirit, and spirit against flesh."[36] Look, you are yourself. Look, you are alone. Look, you are with yourself. Look, you suffer no other man. But you see another law in your members, fighting against the law of your mind, and imprisoning you in the law of sin which is in your members.[37] Therefore, cry out, and from your inner quarrel shout to God, that he may pacify you for yourself:

36. Gal 5.17.
37. Cf. Rom 7.23.

"Unhappy man that I am, who will deliver me from the body of this death? The grace of God through Jesus Christ our Lord."[38] For he said "He who follows me will not walk in darkness, but will have the light of life."

(4) When all quarreling has been ended, immortality will follow, because "the enemy death will be destroyed last."[39] And what kind of peace will there be? "This corruptible must put on incorruption, and this mortal must put on immortality."[40] That we may come there, because then it will be in reality, let us now follow in hope him who said, "I am the light of the world. He who follows me will not walk in darkness, but will have the light of life."

38. Cf. Rom 7.24–25.
39. 1 Cor 15.26.
40. 1 Cor 15.53.

TRACTATE 35

On John 8.13–14

YOU WHO were present yesterday remember that we discussed for some time the words of our Lord Jesus Christ, where he says, "I am the light of the world. He who follows me will not walk in darkness, but will have the light of life."[1] And if we should still desire to discuss that light, we can speak at length; for we cannot explain it in brief. And so, my brothers, let us follow Christ, the Light of the world, that we may not walk in darkness. Darkness must be feared— of character, not of eyes, and if of eyes, not of external ones, but of the inner ones with which are distinguished, not the white and the black, but the just and the unjust.

2. Therefore, when our Lord Jesus Christ had said these [words], the Jews replied, "You give testimony about yourself. Your testimony is not true." Before our Lord Jesus Christ came, he kindled many prophetic lamps before him and sent them. From among these, there was also John the Baptist,[2] to whom the very great Light itself which is the Lord Christ bore testimony such as to no one of men; for he said, "Among those born of women there has not arisen a greater than John the Baptist."[3] Yet this man, than whom no one among those born of women was greater, says of the Lord, Jesus Christ, "I indeed baptize you with water; but he who is coming is mightier than I, whose shoe I am not worthy to loose."[4] See how the lamp abases himself before the Day. In fact, the Lord himself attests that John was himself a lamp. He says, "He was a lamp,

---

1. Jn 8.12.
2. On John the Baptist as a lamp, see *Tractate* 2.8–9, 5.14–15, and 23.2.
3. Mt 11.11.
4. Cf. Jn 1.26–27; Mt 3.11.

burning and shining; and you were willing for a while to rejoice in his light."[5]

(2) But when the Jews said to the Lord, "Tell us, by what
authority do you do these things?,"[6] the Lord, knowing that
they valued John the Baptist highly and that he himself whom
they valued highly had born testimony to them about the
Lord, answered them, "I also will ask you one question. Tell
me, whence is the baptism of John? from heaven, or from
men?"[7] They were troubled and were thinking among themselves that if they should say, from men, they might be stoned
by the crowd which believed that John was a prophet; if they
should say, from heaven, he would answer them, He whom
you admit to have had prophecy from heaven bore testimony
to me; and you heard from him by what authority I do these
things. Therefore, they saw that whichever of these answers
they gave, they would fall into a trap; and they said, "We do
not know." And the Lord said to them, "Neither do I tell you
by what authority I do these things."[8] I do not tell you what I
know because you do not wish to admit what you know. Most
justly repulsed, undoubtedly they departed in confusion, and
there was fulfilled what God the Father had said through the
prophet in a psalm, "I have made ready a lamp for my Christ,"
that is, John himself; "His enemies I shall clothe with confusion."[9]

3. Therefore, the Lord Jesus Christ had the testimony of
the prophets sent before him, of the heralds preceding the
Judge; he had the testimony of John. But he was himself a
greater testimony which he bore to himself. But they with
their weak eyes were seeking lamps because they could not
bear the day. For the same John the Apostle himself, whose
Gospel we are dealing with, at the very beginning of his Gospel said of John, "There was a man sent from God, whose
name was John. This man came for a witness, to bear testi-

5. Jn 5.35.
6. Mt 21.23; cf. Mk 11.28; Lk 20.2.
7. Lk 20.3–4; cf. Mt 21.24–25; Mk 11.29–30.
8. Mt 21.27; Mk 11.33; Lk 20.7–8.
9. Ps 131 (132).17–18.

mony concerning the light, that all men might believe through him. He was not the light, but was to bear testimony about the light. It was the true light which enlightens every man who comes into the world."[10] If "every man," then John also. From this John himself also says, "And of his fulness we have all received."[11]

(2) Therefore, make these distinctions, that your mind may advance in the faith of Christ, that you might not always be infants seeking breasts and recoiling from solid food. You ought to be nourished and weaned under the care of holy Mother, the Church of Christ, and to approach more solid food with your mind, not your stomach. Therefore, make this distinction: the light which enlightens is one thing, the light which is enlightened is another. For our eyes too are called lights, and each one swears by his lights, touching his eyes, thus: So may my lights live. It is a usual oath. And if these lights are lights, let a light be lacking in your closed bedroom; let them open and shine for you—of course, they cannot. Therefore, just as we also call these things which we have on our face lights, both when they are healthy and when they are open, they need the help of a light from without, and if this light was taken away or not brought, they are healthy, they are open, and yet they do not see[12]—so our mind, which is the eye of the soul, unless it be irradiated by the light of truth and unless it be miraculously lighted by him who enlightens and is not enlightened, it will be able to attain neither wisdom nor justice. For this is our way to live justly. How would he for whom the light does not shine not stumble on the way? And for this reason, on such a way it is necessary to see, on such a way it is a great thing to see. For Tobias had the eyes of his face closed up and the son gave his hand to the father; the father showed the way to the son by teaching him.[13]

4. The Jews therefore answered, "You give testimony about yourself. Your testimony is not true." Let us see what

10. Jn 1.6–9.
11. Jn 1.16.
12. Cf. *Tractate* 2.6, 14.1, and 19.11.
13. Cf. Tb 2.11 and 4; also *Tractate* 13.3.

they hear; let us also hear, but not as they. They [hear], despising; we, believing. They [hear], wanting to kill Christ; we, desiring to live through Christ. Meanwhile, let this difference distinguish our ears and minds,[14] and let us hear what the Lord answered to the Jews. "Jesus answered and said to them, 'Although I bear testimony about myself, my testimony is true, because I know where I came from and where I am going.'"

(2) A light shows both itself and other things. You light a lamp, for example, to look for a tunic, and the burning lamp is responsible for your finding the tunic. Do you light a lamp to see a burning lamp? For, the fact is, a burning lamp is capable both of making visible other things which were covered with darkness and of showing itself to your eyes. So also the Lord Christ distinguished between both his own faithful and his enemies, the Jews, as between light and darkness, as between those whom he has drenched with the ray of faith and those whose closed eyes he has surrounded. For this sun of ours lights up the face both of the one who sees and of the blind; both standing alike and having their face to the sun are lighted up on the flesh, but both are not enlightened in their eyes. One sees, the other does not see; the sun is present to both, but one is absent from the present sun. So, too, the Wisdom of God, the Word of God, the Lord Jesus Christ, is present everywhere; for the truth is everywhere, wisdom is everywhere. One man in the east understands justice; another in the west understands justice. Is the justice which the one understands different from that which the other understands? They are separated in body and yet have the sight of their minds on one thing. The justice which I who am here see, if it is justice, the just man also sees, however many days' journey he is separated from me in body, when he is joined to me in the light of that justice.

(3) Therefore, the light bears testimony to itself; it opens healthy eyes, and is itself a witness to itself that it may be recognized as light. But what do we do about the unbelievers?

14. I.e., from theirs.

Is the light not present to them? It is also present to them; but they do not have the eyes of the heart with which to see it. Hear a sentence quoted from the Gospel itself about them: "And the light shines in the darkness, and the darkness did not comprehend it."[15] Therefore the Lord said, and said truly, "Although I bear testimony about myself, my testimony is true, because I know where I came from and where I am going." He wanted the Father to be understood; the Son was giving glory to the Father. An equal glorifies him by whom he was sent. How much ought man to glorify him by whom he was created?

5. "I know where I came from and where I am going." This one who is present and speaks to you has that which he has not parted with, but still he has come. For he did not withdraw from there by coming, or has he abandoned us by returning. Why are you amazed? He is God. This cannot be done by a man; it cannot be done by the sun itself. When [the sun] goes to the west, it departs from the east; and until it returns to the east to rise again, it is not in the east. But our Lord Jesus Christ both comes and is there, and returns and is here. Hear the Evangelist himself speaking in another place; and if you can, grasp [it]; if you cannot, believe. He says, "No man has seen God at any time, but the only-begotten Son, who is in the bosom of the Father, he has revealed him."[16] He did not say, *was* in the bosom of the Father, as though by coming he had departed from the bosom of the Father. He was speaking here and saying that he was there; and as he was about to depart from here, what did he say? "Behold, I am with you even to the consummation of the world."[17]

6. Therefore, the testimony of the light is true, whether it should show itself or other things; for without light you cannot see light, and without light you cannot see anything else which is not light. If the light is capable of showing the things which are not light, does it fail in itself? Does not that without which other things cannot be exposed reveal itself? The

15. Jn 1.5.   16. Jn 1.18.
17. Mt 28.20.

prophet spoke the truth; but from where would he have it unless he drew from the Fountain of truth? John spoke the truth; but from where he spoke, ask him. He said, "And of his fulness we have all received."[18] Therefore our Lord Jesus Christ is capable of bearing testimony to himself.

(2) But in truth, my brothers, in the night of this world let us also hear prophecy attentively; for now our Lord has wished to come, in humility, to our frailty and the innermost nocturnal darkness of our hearts. He came as a man to be despised and honored; he came to be denied and confessed. Despised and denied by the Jews, honored and confessed by us. To be judged and to judge; to be judged unjustly, to judge justly. As such a one, therefore, he came that it was necessary for a lamp to bear testimony to him. For why was it necessary for John to bear testimony as a lamp to the Day if the Day himself could be seen by our weakness? But we could not see. He became weak for the weak; through weakness he healed weakness, through mortal flesh, he took away the death of flesh. From his body he made a salve for our lights.[19] Therefore, because the Lord has come and we are still in the night of the world, we need to listen also to prophecies.

7. For from prophecy we refute the objecting pagans. Who is Christ? a pagan asks. And to him we answer: He whom the prophets foretold. And he [says], Who are the prophets? We recite [their names], Isaiah, Daniel, Jeremiah, the other holy prophets; we say how long before him they came and by how great a space of time they preceded his coming. Therefore, we answer this: The prophets came before him; they predicted he would come. Someone of them answers, Who are the prophets? We recite [the names of] those who are recited to us daily. And he says, Who are these prophets? We answer, They who also predicted what we see happening. And he says, You have contrived these things for yourselves. You saw things happen; and you have written [them] in the books in which it pleased you as if they had been predicted to be going to come.

18. Jn 1.16.
19. I.e., our eyes; see section 3.

(2) Here against our enemies, the pagans, the testimony of our other enemies presents itself to us. We proffer the books from the Jews and we answer, Assuredly both you and they are enemies of our faith. And they have been scattered through the nations for the very purpose that we may convict some enemies by other enemies. Let the book of Isaiah be brought forth from the Jews; let us see if I do not read there: "as a sheep he was led to the slaughter, and as a lamb before the shearer he was without voice [and] so opened not his mouth. In his lowliness his judgment was taken away; by his bruises we have been healed. Like sheep we have all gone astray, and he was delivered up for our sins."[20] Look, this is one lamp. Let another be brought forth; let the psalm be opened; let the passion of Christ, also predicted therein, be recited. "They have dug my hands and my feet; they have numbered all my bones. And they have looked and stared upon me; they divided my garments among them, and for my vesture they cast lots. My praise with you; in a great church I shall declare you. All the ends of the earth shall remember and shall be converted to the Lord; all the families of the nations shall adore in his sight. For the kingdom is the Lord's, and he shall rule the nations."[21] Let one enemy blush because another enemy provides the book for me.

(3) But see that the other enemy is defeated by the books proferred by the one enemy. Let him who has proferred me the book not be left behind; let that be proferred by him by which he too may be defeated. I read another prophet and I find the Lord speaking to the Jews: "I have no pleasure in you, says the Lord; and I will not receive a sacrifice from your hands. For from the rising of the sun even to its setting, a clean sacrifice is offered to my name."[22] You do not come, O Jew, to a clean sacrifice; I convict you as unclean.

20. Cf. Is 53.5–8 (LXX).
21. Ps 21 (22).17–19, 26, 28–29.
22. Mal 1.10–11. The Latin of the first sentence says, very literally, "There is no favorable disposition for me in the case of you." The connotation "pleasure" for *voluntas* appears to be sound, perhaps a Christian Latin connotation, rather than a confusion of *voluntas* with *voluptas*. While none of the standard Latin dictionaries cite this connotation for secular Latin, it is an easy

8. Look, the lamps bear witness to the day on account of our weakness, because we cannot endure the brightness of the Day and look upon it. For we Christians ourselves also, in comparison with the unbelievers, at any rate, are now light. Whence the Apostle says, "For you were once darkness, but now [you are] light in the Lord. Walk as children of light."[23] And elsewhere he said, "The night is far spent, and the day is at hand. Let us therefore cast off the works of darkness, and put on the armor of light. Let us walk honorably as in the day."[24] Yet because, in comparison with that light to which we shall come, even the day in which we are is still night, hear the Apostle Peter; he tells of a voice that came down to Christ the Lord "from the magnificent Power: 'You are my beloved Son in whom I am well pleased.' This voice," he says, "we ourselves heard borne from heaven when we were with him on the holy mount."[25] But because we were not there and did not then hear this voice from heaven, Peter himself says to us, "And we have the word of prophecy, surer still."[26] You did not hear the voice borne from heaven, but you have the still surer voice of prophecy. For the Lord Jesus Christ, foreseeing that there would be certain impious men who would depreciate his miracles by attributing them to magical arts, sent the prophets before him. For if he was a magician and by magical arts

---

development from some of its other connotations and from the base word, the verb *volo*. The Greek text has the word θέλημα. LSJ 788, cites the connotation "pleasure" only for the Septuagint, although the cognate verb ἐθέλω or θέλω (LSJ 479) has meanings that are closely allied to this one. Nonetheless, in Christian Latin and Greek the connotation "pleasure," if not itself a Hebraicism, receives strong support from a similar Hebrew word; see G. Kittel, *Theological Dictionary of the New Testament*, trans. G. Bromiley (Grand Rapids, Michigan, 1965) 3.53–54, s.v. θέλημα. Neither the Hebrew word used in Malachi, *hēphets*, nor its cognate verb have this double connotation but denote pleasure only. See W. Genesius, *A Hebrew and English Lexicon of the Old Testament*, trans. E. Robinson, ed. F. Brown, et al. (Oxford, 1966, reprint with corrections of original from 1907) 343. A similar Hebraic influence on *voluntas* and the Greek εὐδοκία is found in Lk 2.14; see F. Fitzmeyer, 'Peace upon earth among men of His good will' (Lk 2:14), *Essays on the Semitic Background of the New Testament* (London 1974) 101–4.

23. Eph 5.8.   24. Rom 13.12–13.
25. 2 Pt 1.17–18; Cf. Mt 17.5.   26. 2 Pt 1.19.

effected that, even when dead, he be worshipped, was he a magician before he was born? Hear the prophets, O dead man, and becoming the prey of worms because of your calumny, hear the prophets. I read, hear those who have come before the Lord. The Apostle Peter said, "We have the word of prophecy, surer still, to which you do well to attend, as to a lamp in a dark place, until the day dawns and the morning star rises in your hearts."[27]

9. Therefore, when our Lord Jesus Christ has come, and, as the Apostle Paul also says, "has brought to light the things hidden in darkness and has made manifest the thoughts of the heart that everyone may have praise from God,"[28] then when such a day is at hand, lamps will not be necessary. A prophet will not be read to us, the book of the Apostle will not be opened; we shall not seek the testimony of John, we shall not need the Gospel itself. Therefore, all the Scriptures will be taken from our midst which were burning as lamps for us in the night of this world that we might not remain in the darkness. With all these taken away that they may not shine for us as if we were in need and with these men of God, through whom these things were administered, seeing together with us that true and clear light, when these helps have been removed, what shall we see? Upon what will our minds be fed? At what will that sight rejoice? Whence will be that joy which neither eye has seen nor ear has heard nor has it risen up in the heart of man?[29] What shall we see? I beg you, love with me, run with me by believing. Let us long for our celestial homeland, let us sigh for our celestial homeland. Let us believe that we are foreigners here. What shall we see then? Let the Gospel speak now. "In the beginning was the Word, and the Word was with God, and the Word was God."[30] From where the dew has sprinkled upon you, you will come to the fountain; from where the ray has been sent to your shadow-filled heart by a winding and oblique path, you will see the naked light itself; and to see and endure [it] you are being cleansed. John him-

27. 2 Pt 1.19.   28. 1 Cor 4.5.
29. Cf. 1 Cor 2.9, citing Is 64.4.   30. Jn 1.1.

self, as I mentioned yesterday,[31] says, "Beloved, now we are children of God, and it has not yet appeared what we shall be. We know that, when he shall appear, we shall be like to him, for we shall see him as he is."[32] I perceive that your feelings are carried up with me to the celestial; but "the body which is corrupted burdens the soul and the earthen shelter weighs down the mind that has many concerns."[33]

(2) I am about to put down this book and you are about to depart, each one to his own affairs. We have been happy together in the common Light, we have truly rejoiced, we have truly exulted. But, although we depart from one another, let us not depart from him.

31. Cf. *Tractate* 34.9.   32. 1 Jn 3.2.
33. Wis 9.15.

TRACTATE 36

On John 8.15–18

N THE four Gospels, or rather the four books of the one Gospel, the holy Apostle John, not unjustly compared to an eagle[1] because of his spiritual understanding, has elevated his preaching more highly and much more sublimely than the other three. And in this elevation of his, he also wanted our hearts to be elevated. For the three other evangelists, as though they were walking on earth with the Lord, a man, said few things about his divinity; but this [evangelist], as if he loathed to walk upon the earth, as he thundered at the very beginning of his discourse, elevated himself not only above the earth and above all the circuit of air and sky, but also above even the whole host of angels and above the whole hierarchy of invisible powers; and he came to him through whom all things were made, saying, "In the beginning was the Word, and the Word was with God, and the Word was God. He was in the beginning with God. All things were made through him and without him was made nothing."[2] Harmonious to such a sublime beginning as this, he also preached the rest and he spoke about the divinity of the Lord as has no other man. He uttered what he had imbibed.[3] For not without reason is it told about him in this very Gospel that at the supper he reclined upon the Lord's bosom.[4] From that bosom he imbibed secretly; but what he imbibed secretly he has uttered openly that there may come to all nations not only

1. Cf. Introduction, FOTC 78, note 2, and *Tractate* 15.1.
2. Jn 1.1–3.
3. Augustine's language is much more concrete, as is usual in Latin, but the resultant English has a tone of vulgarity that the Latin lacks: he belched out what he had drunk.
4. Cf. Jn 13.23.

81

the incarnation of the Son of God, and his passion and resurrection, but also what was before the incarnation, the only one of the Father, the Word of the Father, coeternal to the Begettor, equal to him by whom he was sent, but in the sending itself, [he] became lesser that the Father might be greater.

2. Therefore, whatever you have heard about the Lord Jesus Christ expressed in terms of lowliness, think of the economy[5] of the Incarnation, what he was made for us, not what he was in order to make us. But whatever you hear or read expressed about him in the Gospel that is sublime and excellent above all created beings, and divine, and equal to the Father, and coeternal, know that you are reading what pertains to the form of God, not to the form of a servant.[6] For if you hold this rule, you who can grasp it—but not all of you can grasp it, but all of you ought to rely on it—if, then, you hold this rule, freed of anxiety, you will do battle against the calumnies of heretical darkness, as if walking in light. For there have not been lacking those who in their reading followed only the gospel testimonies which were expressed about Christ's lowliness and who were deaf to those testimonies which asserted his divinity; they were deaf precisely to be perniciously loquacious. Likewise some men, observing only those things that were said about the Lord's sublimity, did not even themselves believe his mercy by which he became man for us, even if they read it; and they thought that [these things] were introduced by men and were false, maintaining that Christ our Lord was God only, not man also. So some, so others; both are in error.

(2) But the Catholic faith, holding fast to the truth in both and preaching the truth which each believes has understood that Christ is God and has believed that he is man; for each [doctrine] has been written and each is true. If you have said that Christ is God only, you deny the medicine by which you have been healed; if you have said that Christ is man only, you deny the power by which you have been created. Therefore, hold each, faithful soul and Catholic heart, hold each, believe

5. *dispensationem.* See *Tractate* 19.10, note 11, and *Tractate* 31.5 and 8.
6. Cf. Phil 2.5–7.

each, profess each faithfully. Both Christ is God, and Christ is man. What kind of God is Christ? Equal to the Father, one with the Father. What kind of man is Christ? Born of a virgin, drawing from man his mortality, not drawing iniquity.

3. These Jews, then, saw the man; they neither understood nor believed the God. And, among the other [words], you have already heard how they said to him, "You utter testimony about yourself; your testimony is not true."[7] You also heard what he answered when it was read yesterday and discussed to the best of our ability. Today these words of his have been read: "You judge according to the flesh." For this reason he said: you say to me, "You utter testimony about yourself; your witness is not true," because "you judge according to the flesh," because you do not understand the God and you see the man, and by persecuting the man, you offend the hidden God. Therefore, "you judge according to the flesh."

(2) I seem arrogant to you for this reason, that I bear testimony to myself. For every man, when he wishes to bear praiseworthy testimony to himself, seems arrogant and proud. So it has been written: "Let not your own mouth praise you but let the mouth of your neighbor praise you."[8] But this was said to man. For we are weak and we speak among the weak. We can speak the truth and tell lies, although we ought to speak the truth, and yet we can tell lies when we want. The Light cannot lie; far be it that the darkness of untruth be found in the splendor of the Divine Light. He was speaking as light, he was speaking as truth; but "the light shone in the darkness and the darkness did not comprehend it."[9] And so they were judging according to the flesh. "You," he said, "judge according to the flesh."

4. "I do not judge anyone." Does the Lord Jesus Christ then, not judge anyone? Is it not he of whom we profess that he arose on the third day, ascended into heaven, there sits at the right hand of the Father, from there will come to judge the living and the dead? Is this not our faith, about which the

7. Jn 8.13.
8. Prv 27.2.
9. Jn 1.5.

Apostle says, "With the heart one believes unto justice, but
with the mouth confession is made unto salvation"?[10] Therefore, when we confess these things, do we contradict the
Lord? We say that he will come as the judge of the living and
the dead; but he himself says, "I do not judge anyone."

(2) This problem can be solved in two ways: either that you
understand, "I do not judge anyone," that is, *now*, as he says in
another place, "I have not come to judge the world, but to save
the world,"[11] not denying judgment, but delaying it; or, because he said, "You judge according to the flesh," he added
immediately, "I do not judge anyone," so that you supply,
"according to the flesh." Therefore, let no scruple of doubt
remain in our hearts against the faith we hold and proclaim
about Christ the Judge.

(3) Christ has come, but first to save, afterwards to judge, by
adjudging punishment for those who were unwilling to be
saved and by leading those to life, who, by believing, did not
spurn salvation. Thus the first dispensation of our Lord Jesus
Christ is medicinal, not judicial; for if he had come first to
judge, he would have found no one to whom to grant the
rewards of justice. Therefore, because he saw that all were
sinners and that no one at all was free from the death of sin,
his mercy first had to be bestowed and his judgment shown
later. For the psalm had sung about him: "Mercy and judgment I will sing to you, Lord."[12] It does not say judgment and
mercy. For if judgment were first, there would be no mercy;
but mercy first, judgment afterwards.

(4) What is mercy first? The Creator of man deigned to be a
man; he was made what he had made that he whom he had
made might not perish. What can be added to this mercy?
And yet he added. It was not enough for him to be made
man, but he was also rejected by man. It was not enough to
be rejected, but he was also dishonored. It was not enough
to be dishonored, but he was also killed—even this was not
enough—by the death of the cross. For when the Apostle

10. Rom 10.10.   11. Jn 12.47.
12. Ps 100 (101).1.

commended his becoming obedient even to death, it was not enough for him to say, "becoming obedient even to death," for [it was] not any kind of death at all, but he added, "even the death of the cross."[13] Among all the kinds of deaths there was none worse than that death. Indeed, when very severe pains torment one, it is called ex*cruci*ation, from the word *crux* (cross). For those crucified, hanging on the wood, fastened to the wood by nails in the feet and hands, were slain by a long drawn out death. For to be crucified was not to be killed by being struck down; but one was alive on the cross for a long time, not because a longer life was chosen, but because the death itself was being protracted so that the pain would not be ended too quickly. He wanted to die for us. We say too little: he deigned to be crucified, having become obedient even to the death of the cross.

(5) He who would take away all death chose the most extreme and worst kind of death; by the worst death he killed all death. To the Jews, who did not understand, it was the worst; but it had in fact been chosen by the Lord. He would have his cross itself as his sign; he would place the cross itself as a trophy over the defeated devil on the foreheads[14] of his faithful, so that the Apostle might say, "But God forbid that I should glory save in the cross of our Lord Jesus Christ, by whom the world is crucified to me, and I to the world."[15] Then, there was nothing more unbearable in the flesh; now, there is nothing more glorious on the forehead. What did he who gave such honor to his punishment save for his faithful? Indeed now among the punishments of the convicted, it is no longer in use by the Romans; for where the cross of the Lord has been honored, it has been thought that a guilty man would also be honored if he were crucified.

(6) Therefore, he who came judged no one and suffered evil men. He endured unjust judgment that he might give a just one. But, that he endured unjust judgment was a part of his mercy. Indeed, having become so humble that he came to

13. Cf. Phil 2.8.
14. On the sign of the cross on the forehead, see *Tractate* note 4.
15. Gal 6.14.

the cross, he put aside his power but showed the people his mercy. How did he put aside his power? Because he who could rise from the tomb did not wish to come down from the cross. How did he show the people his mercy? Because hanging on the cross, he said, "Father, forgive them, for they know not what they do."[16]

(7) Therefore, either he said, "I do not judge anyone," for the reason that he had not come to judge the world but to save the world; or, as I have mentioned, because he had said, "You judge according to the flesh," he added, "I do not judge anyone," that we may understand that Christ does not judge according to the flesh as he was judged by men.

5. For, that you may know that Christ is even now a judge, hear what follows: "And if I do judge, my judgment is true." Look, you also have a judge; but acknowledge the Savior that you may not meet with the judge. But why did he say that his judgment is true? "Because I am not alone," he said, "but I and he who sent me, the Father."

(2) I have said to you, brothers, that this holy Evangelist, John, flies very high;[17] it is scarcely possible to comprehend him with the mind. But it is necessary to remind you, my beloved people, of the mystery of him who flies higher. Both in the prophet Ezechiel and in the Apocalypse of the same John whose gospel this is, there is mentioned a quadruple beast, having four characteristic faces:[18] a man's, a calf's, a lion's, an eagle's.[19] Very many [of those] who have commented on the mysteries of the holy Scriptures before us have understood the four evangelists in this animal, or rather in these animals. The lion, [they say], has been put for king, because the lion seems to be, in a way, the king of beasts because of his power and terrifying bravery. This character has been attributed to Matthew because he described in proper order the royal line in the generations of the Lord, how the Lord was

16. Lk 23.34; cf. *Tractate* 31.9, note 26.
17. See section 1.
18. The Latin word is *personas,* and I use Gibb's translation of it to connect the word with the Scriptural references and to allow the translation "character" below.
19. Cf. Ez 1.5–10; Apoc (Rv) 4.6–7.

through royal descent from the seed of king David. But Luke, because he began from the priesthood of the priest Zacharias, making mention of the father of John the Baptist, is accounted the calf because the calf was the important victim in the sacrifice of the priests. Christ as a man has rightly been assigned to Mark, because neither did he say anything about his royal power nor did he begin from the priestly, but he simply started with Christ the man. All of these have practically not departed from the earth, that is, from those deeds which the Lord Jesus Christ performed on earth; as if they were walking with him on earth, they said very few things about his divinity. There remains the eagle: it is John, he who preaches the sublime and who gazes with unflinching eyes upon the internal and eternal light. For, as a matter of fact, it is said that baby eagles are tested by their parents as follows: [the fledgling] is suspended, of course, on the claws of the father and held up to the rays of the sun; if it gazes steadily [into the sun,] it is acknowledged as a son; if it quivers at the sight, it is dropped from the claw as a bastard.[20] Now then, see how he who has been compared to an eagle ought to have spoken the sublime; and yet, even we, crawling on the ground, weak, and of scarcely any importance among men, dare to discuss these things and to explain them; and we think either that we can understand them when we reflect upon them or that we can be understood when we speak.

6. Why have I said these things? For perhaps after these words, someone might justly say to me, Well, then, put down the book. Why do you take in your hand what surpasses your limited capacity? Why do you put your tongue to it? To this I answer: Many heretics abound and God has allowed them to abound for this reason, that we may not forever be nourished with milk and remain in unreasoning infancy.[21] For because they did not understand how the divinity of Christ was revealed, they conceived it as they wanted; but by not comprehending aright, they presented very troublesome problems to the Catholic faithful. The hearts of the faithful began to be

20. Cf. *De gestibus Pelagii* 6.18 (CSEL 42; FOTC 86).
21. Cf. 1 Cor 3.1–3.

disturbed and to waver. Then came immediately the need for spiritual men who had not only read in the Gospel something about the divinity of our Lord Jesus Christ but also understood it, to advance the armament of Christ against the armament of the devil and to do battle over the divinity of Christ in open conflict with false and fallacious teachers, with as great strength as possible, that others might not perish because they themselves were quiet.

(2) For whoever thought that our Lord Jesus Christ either was of a different substance from the Father or that there was only Christ, so that he is the Father, he is the Son, he is the Holy Spirit; also whoever wanted to think that he was man alone, not God made man, or God so as to be changeable in his divinity or God so as not also to be man, these have suffered shipwreck from the faith and have been expelled from the harbor of the Church, that they might not break up the ships docked with them by their disquietude. And this fact compels us, too, slight as we are, and as far as pertains to us, utterly unworthy, but as far as pertains to his mercy, set down in the number of his stewards, not to remain silent either about what you may understand and rejoice at with me, or, if you cannot yet understand, you may by believing remain securely in port.

7. I shall say, therefore—let him grasp it who can, let him believe it who cannot—I shall still say what the Lord said, "You judge according to the flesh. I do not judge anyone" either now or according to the flesh. "But even if I do judge, my judgment is true." Why is your judgment true? "Because I am not alone," he said, "but I and he who sent me, the Father."

(2) Well now, Lord Jesus, if you were alone, your judgment would be false; and do you therefore judge truly because you are not alone, but you and he who sent you, the Father? What shall I reply? Let him reply himself. "My judgment," he says, "is true." Why? "Because I am not alone, but I and he who sent me, the Father." If he is with you, how did he send you? Did he both send you and is with you? Have you been sent thus and not departed? And have you been sent to us thus, and yet remained there? How does a man believe this? How does he

grasp it? To these two questions I reply: you say, how does he grasp it? rightly; but not rightly do you say, How does a man believe it? Rather he believes it well precisely because it is not quickly grasped; for if it were quickly grasped, there would be no need for belief, because it would be seen. You believe precisely because you do not grasp; but by believing you become capable of grasping. For if you do not believe, you will never grasp because you will remain incapable. Therefore, let faith cleanse you that understanding may fill you.[22]

(3) He said, "My judgment is true, because I am not alone, but I and he who sent me, the Father." Therefore, O Lord, our God, Jesus Christ, your incarnation is your sending. So I see, so I understand; finally so I believe that it may not belong to arrogance to say, so I understand. Accordingly our Lord Jesus Christ is even here; rather, he was here according to the flesh, now he is here according to his divinity. And he was with the Father and had not withdrawn from the Father. Therefore, as to the fact that it is said that he was sent and came to us, his incarnation is revealed, because the Father did not become incarnate.

8. For certain heretics have been named the Sabellians, who are also called the Patripassianists, who say that the Father himself had suffered.[23] Not you, Catholic! For if you were a Patripassianist, you would not be sane. Therefore, understand that the sending of the Son was called the incarnation of the Son; but you may not believe that the Father became incarnate, and also you may not believe that the Father had withdrawn from the incarnate Son. The Son carried the flesh; the Father was with the Son.

(2) If the Father was in heaven, the Son on earth, how was the Father with the Son? Because both the Father and the Son were everywhere; for God is not in heaven in such a way that

22. Cf. *Tractate* 8.6–7, 18.1, 22.2, 27.9, and 29.6.
23. Cf. *Tractate* 29.7, note 17. Patripassianism was identical with Sabellianism. The Greek Christians called the heretics Sabellians after the founder of the heresy; in the West they were called by the Latin name Patripassianists because, in identifying the Son with the Father, they maintained that the Father himself suffered and died on the cross in the mode of the Son. See P. Legeau, "Patripassianism," NCE 10.1103.

he is not on earth. Hear him who wanted to flee the judgment of God and found not where [to go]. He said, "Where shall I go from your spirit? And from your face where shall I flee? If I ascend into heaven, you are there." The inquiry was about the earth. Hear what follows. "If I descend to hell, you are present."[24] If, therefore, it is said that he is present even in hell, what part of the universe remains where he is not? For it is the voice of God in the prophet: "I fill heaven and earth."[25] Therefore, he who is shut in by no place is everywhere. Turn not aside from him, and he is with you. If you wish to come to him, be not slow to love; for you run not with your feet, but with your feelings.[26] Staying in one place, you come, if you believe and love. Therefore, he is everywhere; if he is everywhere, how is he not with the Son? Is he not thus with the Son, he who, if you believe, is also with you?

9. Therefore, whence is his judgment true, except that the Son is true? For he said this: "And if I judge, my judgment is true, because I am not alone, but I and he who sent me, the Father." As if he were to say, "My judgment is true" because I am the Son of God. Whence do you prove that you are the Son of God? "Because I am not alone, But I and he who sent me, the Father." Blush, Sabellian! You hear Son, you hear Father. The Father is the Father; the Son is the Son. He did not say, "I am the Father, and I myself am the Son." But he said, "I am not alone." Why are you not alone? Because the Father is with me. "I am, and he who sent me, the Father."

(2) You hear, "I am and he who sent me." That you may not destroy a person, distinguish the persons. Distinguish with understanding; do not separate them by faithlessness, that you may not again, in fleeing Charybdis, so to speak, run into Scylla.[27] For the whirlpool of the Sabellians' impiety was swallowing you that you might say that he who is the Son is the Father. Now you have learned, "I am not alone, but I and he

---

24. Ps 138 (139).7–8.   25. Jer 23.24.
26. Cf. *Tractate* 32.1.
27. Here Charybdis is Sabellianism and Scylla Arianism. Cf. *Sermo* 11.4 from the *Codex Guelferbytanus* 4096 where the opposite metaphor occurs, i.e., Scylla is Sabellianism and Charybdis Arianism; see G. Morin, *Miscellanea Agostiniana, Testi e Studi* (Rome 1880) 1.476–477.

who sent me, the Father." You acknowledge that the Father is the Father and the Son is the Son. You acknowledge well. But do not say, The Father is greater, the Son is less. Do not say, The Father is gold, the Son is silver. There is one substance, one divinity, one coeternity, perfect equality, no dissimilarity. For if you believed only that Christ was another, not him who is the Father, and yet you thought that he differed in something according to his nature, you have indeed escaped from Charybdis, but you have shipwrecked on the Scyllaean rocks.

(3) Sail in between; avoid both dangerous sides. The Father is the Father; the Son is the Son. Now you say, The Father is the Father; the Son is the Son. You have definitely avoided the danger of the sucking whirlpool. Why do you want to go to the other side, so as to say, The Father is one thing, the Son another? You say rightly, He is another person. But not rightly, Another thing. For the Son is another person because he is not he who is the Father; and the Father is another person because he is not he who is the Son, yet not another thing but both the Father and the Son are this very thing. What does it mean, are this very thing? There is one God. You have heard, "Because I am not alone, but I and he who sent me, the Father." Hear how you may believe the Father and the Son; hear the Son himself: "I and the Father are one."[28] He did not say, I am the Father, or I and the Father *is* one [person]. But when he said, "I and the Father are one," hear both "one thing" and "we are,"[29] and you will be free of both Charybdis and Scylla. In these two words, the word "one thing" [*unum*] frees you from the Arian, and the word "we are" [*sumus*] frees you from the Sabellian. If "one thing," then not different; if "we are," then both the Father and the Son. For he would not say "we are" about one; but he also would not say "one thing" about [something] different.

(4) Therefore, he says, "My judgment is true," that you may hear briefly that I am the Son of God. But I so persuade you,

28. Jn 10.30.
29. The Latin reads, *Ego et Pater unum sumus,* which very literally means, "I and the Father, we are one thing." Cf. *Tractate* 5.1, 9.8, 10.11, 20.3, and 29.8.

he said, that I am the Son of God, that you may understand that the Father is with me. For I am not the Son so as to have deserted him; I am not here so as not to be with him. He is not there so as not to be with me. I have received the form of the servant but I have not lost the form of God.[30] "I am not alone" therefore, he says, "but I and he who sent me, the Father."

10. He had spoken about judgment; he wishes to speak about testimony. He said, "In your law it has been written that the testimony of two men is true. I am the one who gives testimony of myself, and he who sent me, the Father, gives testimony of me." He has explained the law also to them, if they were not ungrateful. For it is an important problem, my brothers, and the matter seems to me to have been very much propounded in mystery where God said, "In the mouth of two or three witnesses every word shall stand."[31] Is truth sought through two witnesses? Yes, indeed, such is the custom of mankind. And yet it is possible for even two to lie. The chaste Susanna was beset by two false witnesses;[32] because there were two, were they therefore not false witnesses? Are we speaking about two or about three? A whole people lied against Christ.[33] Therefore, if a people, composed of a great multitude, was found a false witness, how must it be understood, "In the mouth of two or three witnesses every word shall stand," except that in this way the Trinity, in which is unending stability of truth, was revealed through a mystery?[34] Do you want to have a good case? Have two or three witnesses, the Father and the Son and the Holy Spirit. Indeed, when Susanna, a chaste woman and a faithful wife, was beset by two false witnesses, the Trinity supported her in her conscience and in secret; that Trinity secretly stirred up one witness, Daniel, and convicted the two.

(2) Therefore, because "in your law it has been written that the testimony of two men is true," receive our testimony that you may not experience judgment. For, he said, "I do not

30. Cf. Phil 2.7.   31. Dt 19.15 (LXX); Mt 18.16.
32. Cf. Dn 13.   33. Cf. Lk 23.1–2.
34. Cf. *Tractate* 9.7 where another Scriptural passage involving the phrase "two or three" is discussed as a reference to the Trinity.

judge anyone" but "I give testimony of myself"; I put off judgment, I do not put off testimony.

11. For ourselves, brothers, let us choose God as judge, God as witness, against the tongues of men, against the pusillanimous suspicions of the human race. For he who is the judge does not disdain to be a witness, or is he advanced when he becomes judge, because he who is witness will himself be judge. Why is he himself a witness? Because he does not seek another from whom he may know who you are. Why is he himself a judge? Because he himself has the power of giving death and life, of condemning and absolving, of hurling down into Hell and lifting up into heaven, of joining to the devil and crowning with the angels. Therefore, since he himself has this power, he is a judge. But because he, who will judge you then and who sees you now, seeks not another witness that he may know you, there is no way in which you may deceive him when he has begun to judge. For you do not use for yourself any false witnesses who can circumvent that judge when he has begun to judge you. God says this to you: When you were despising, I saw it; and when you did not believe, I was not rendering my sentence null and void, I was delaying, not laying aside. You did not want to hear what I instructed; you will perceive what I predicted. Now if you should hear what I instructed, you will not think what I predicted evil, but you will perceive what I predicted as good.

12. Let it certainly not disturb anyone that he said, "My judgment is true, because I am not alone, but I and he who sent me, the Father," when he said elsewhere, "The Father does not judge any man, but all judgment he has given to the Son."[35] We have already discussed these same words of the Gospel,[36] and we now remind [you] that this was said not for the reason that the Father will not be with the Son when he is judging, but because only the Son will appear to the good and evil in the judgment, in that form in which he suffered, arose and ascended into heaven. In fact, to his disciples who were then watching him ascending, an angel's voice sounded: "He

35. Jn 5.22.
36. Cf. *Tractate* 21.11–14.

shall so come as you have seen him going into heaven,"[37] that is, in the form of the man in which he was judged he will judge, in order that that prophecy may also be fulfilled: "They will look upon him whom they have pierced."[38] But, when, as the just are going into eternal life, we shall see him as he is, there will not be that judgment of the living and the dead, but only the reward of the living.

13. Likewise, let it not disturb you that he said, "In your law it has been written that the testimony of two persons is true," and let no one therefore think that that was not the law of God because it was not said, In the law of God. Let him know that it was so said, "in your law," as if he were to say, In the law which was given to you. By whom but by God? As we say, "our daily bread"; and yet we say, "Give us this day."[39]

37. Acts 1.11.   38. Jn 19.37, quoting Zec 12.10.
39. Mt 6.11; Lk 11.3.

TRACTATE 37

On John 8.19–20

HAT IS said briefly in the holy Gospel ought not to be explained briefly, so that what is heard may be understood. For the words of our Lord are few, but great, to be judged not by their number but by their weight; they should not be scorned because they are few, but should be examined precisely because they are great.

(2) You who were present yesterday heard, and we discussed, as well as we could, from what the Lord said: "You judge according to the flesh; I do not judge any one. But even if I do judge, my judgment is true, because I am not alone, but I and he who sent me, the Father. In your law it has been written that the testimony of two persons is true. I am the one who gives testimony of myself, and he who sent me, the Father, gives testimony of me."[1] From these words, as I said, a discourse was delivered to your ears and minds yesterday. When the Lord said these things, those who heard, "You judge according to the flesh," made clear what they heard. For they replied to the Lord who was speaking of God his Father, and they said, "Where is your father?" They understood the father of Christ in a flesh [and blood] sense because they judged the words of Christ according to the flesh. But he who was speaking was flesh openly, the Word secretly, man manifest, God hidden. They saw the clothing and scorned the one clothed; they scorned because they did not know. They did not know because they did not see. They did not see because they were blind. They were blind because they did not believe.

2. Let us also see, then, what the Lord answered to these

1. Jn 8.15–18.

95

things. They say, "Where is your father?" For we heard you say, "I am not alone, but I and he who sent me, the Father." We see only you; we do not see your father with you. How do you say that you are not alone but that you are with your father? Or show us that your father is with you.

(2) And the Lord [says], Do you see me, that I may show you the Father? For this follows, this he himself answers in his words, an explanation of which words we have set as a premise above. For see what he said: "You know neither me nor my Father. If you knew me, perhaps you would know my Father also." Therefore, you say, "Where is your father?" as if you already knew me, as if I were wholly this which you see. Therefore because you do not know me, for that reason I do not show my Father to you. To be sure, you think I am a man; therefore, you seek for my Father as a man, because you judge according to the flesh. But because according to what you see I am one thing, and according to what you do not see I am another, [and because] I, hidden, speak of my Father, hidden, knowing me comes first; then you will know my Father also.

3. For "if you knew me, perhaps you would know my Father also." He who knows all things, when he says "perhaps"[2] does not have doubts, but is chiding. For observe how this "perhaps" which seems to be a word of doubt is said chidingly. For it is a word of doubt when it is said by a man who doubts precisely because he does not know; but when a word of doubt is said by God, since, of course, nothing is hidden from God, by that doubt unbelief is accused, Divinity is not expressing an opinion. For sometimes men doubt chidingly about these things which they hold certain, that is, they employ a word of

2. The Latin word for "perhaps" here is *forsitan* which translates an ἄν in the Greek text where the particle simply makes the imperfect indicative into the conclusion of a present contrary to fact condition. This is a frequent practice in both the Vulgate and the Itala. For examples see TLL 6.1.1138–1139; H. Rönsch, *Itala und Vulgata* (Marburg 1869) 340; and W. Plater and H. White, *A Grammar of the Vulgate* (Oxford 1926) 61. Augustine, however, gives *forsitan* a dubitative sense, which is a common Latin usage (see TLL 6.1.1138), and makes no reference to the Greek meaning at all. LaGrange, *Évangile selon saint Jean*, 235, states that Augustine wrongly insists that the Vulgate *forsitan* is dubitative. Cf. also Comeau, *Saint Augustin*, 66–67.

doubt when they do not doubt in their heart, as for example, if you were indignant at your slave and you should say, You despise me; think, perhaps I am your master." In this way also the Apostle speaks to certain ones who despise him, saying, "I think, however, I also have the Spirit of God."[3] He who says, "I think," seems to have doubt; but he was chiding, not doubting. And the Lord Christ himself, in another place, chiding the future unbelief of the human race, says, "When the Son of Man comes, will he find, do you think, faith on earth?"[4]

4. Now, I think, you have understood how "perhaps" was put. Let no weigher of words and scrutinizer of syllables, as being one who knows how to speak Latin, find fault with a word which the Word of God said, and by reproaching the Word of God, remain not eloquent, but mute. For who speaks in the same way as the Word who[5] in the beginning was with God speaks? Do not consider these words and from these ordinary words seek to measure that Word which is God.

(2) For you hear the Word and you despise [him]; hear God and fear. "In the beginning was the Word."[6] You think back to the use [of the word as you employ it in] your conversation and you say to yourself: What is a word? What great thing is a word? It sounds and it passes away; having smitten the air, it smites the ear, and after that it will not exist. Hear the next part: "The Word was with God." It remained, it did not sound and pass away. Perhaps you still scorn it; "The Word was God."

(3) With you, O man, when a word is in your heart, it is something other than sound; but the word which is with you, that it may pass over to me, seeks sound as its vehicle. Therefore, it puts on sound; it places itself, in a sense, on a vehicle, races across through the air, comes to me, yet does not withdraw from you. But the sound, in order to come to me, withdrew from you, and yet did not persist with me. Did the word, then, which was in your heart, pass away when the

3. 1 Cor 7.40.
4. Lk 18.8.
5. The Latin literally reads "which" since *Verbum* is neuter.
6. Jn 1.1.

sound passed away? You said what you were thinking; and, in order that what was hidden in you might come to me, you sounded out syllables. The sound of the syllables led your thought to my ear; through my ear your thought descended into my heart. The intervening sound flew over. But that word which took on the sound, before you sounded it, was with you; because you sounded it, it is with me, yet has not withdrawn from you. Pay attention to this, you scrutinizer of sounds, whoever you are. You who do not comprehend the word of man, you despise the Word of God!

5. Therefore, he by whom all things were made[7] knows all things, and still chides by doubting: "If you knew me, perhaps you would know my Father also." He chides the unbelievers. For he said such a sentence to his disciples; but there, there is no word of doubt, because there was not a reason for chiding unbelief. For what he said just now to the Jews, "If you knew me, perhaps you would know my Father also," he also said to the disciples when Philip asked, nay, rather demanded of him, and said, "Lord, show us the Father and it is enough for us,"[8] as if he were to say, Even we ourselves now know you; you have appeared to us. We have seen you; you have deigned to choose us. We have followed you, we have seen your miracles, we have heard the words of salvation, we have received your commands, we hope for what was promised. By your presence you have deigned to confer much on us. But still, although we know you, because we do not yet know the Father, we are inflamed with a longing for seeing him whom we do not yet know, and for this reason, because we know you; but it is not enough for us, until we know the Father also. "Show us the Father, and it is enough for us."

(2) And the Lord, that they might know that they did not know what they thought they already knew, said, "Have I been so long a time with you, and you do not know me? Philip, he who has seen me has seen also the Father."[9] Does this sentence have a word of doubt? Did he say, He who has seen me, perhaps also has seen the Father? Why? Because a be-

7. Cf. Jn 1.3.   8. Jn 14.8.
9. Jn 14.9.

liever was listening, not a persecutor of the faith; therefore, the Lord was not a chider, but a teacher.

(3) "He who has seen me has also seen the Father." And here: "If you knew me, you would also know my Father." Let us take away the word by which the unbelief of the listeners was branded, and it is the same sentence.

6. Yesterday, we pointed out to you, my beloved people, and we said that the sentences of John the Evangelist, in which he tells us what he learned from the Lord, would not have to be discussed, if it were possible, if the fabrications of the heretics did not force it.[10]

(2) Briefly, then, yesterday we declared to you, my beloved people, that there are heretics who are called the Patripassianists or, from their founder, Sabellians;[11] these men say that the very one who is the Son is the Father, that there are different names, but one Person. When he wishes, they say, he is the Father; when he wishes, he is the Son, yet he is one. Likewise, there are other heretics who are called Arians.[12] They do indeed profess that our Lord Jesus Christ is the only Son of the Father, that the one is the Father of the Son and the other the Son of the Father, that he who is the Father is not the Son and he who is the Son is not the Father; they profess the begetting, but deny equality.

(3) We, that is, the Catholic faith, coming from the teaching of the Apostles emplanted in us, received through a continuous line of succession a healthy faith to be transmitted to our posterity, has held that truth between both, that is, between each error. In the error of the Sabellians, there is only one; the very same one who is the Son is the Father. In the error of the Arians, the Father is a different person from the Son, but the Son is not only another person but also another thing. You in the middle, what about you? You have excluded the Sabellians; exclude also the Arians. The Father is the Father; the Son is the Son, another person, not another thing. For he said, "I and the Father, we are one thing,"[13] as I taught yester-

10. Cf. *Tractate* 36.5–6.   11. Cf. *Tractate* 29.7 and 36.8.
12. Cf. *Tractate* 1.11, note 27.
13. Jn 10.30, translated literally; cf. *Tractate* 36.9, note 28.

day, as well as I could.[14] When he hears, "we are," let the
Sabellian depart in confusion; when he hears, "one thing," let
the Arian depart in confusion. Let the Catholic pilot the ship
of his faith between each; for one must beware of shipwreck
upon each. Therefore, do you say what the Gospel says: "I
and the Father, we are one thing." Not different, because "one
thing," not one [person], because "we are."

7. A little before, he said, "My judgment is true, because I
am not alone, but I and he who sent me, the Father," as if he
were to say, My judgment is true precisely because I am the
Son of God, because I spoke the truth, because I am the truth
itself. They, understanding carnally, said, "Where is your father?" Listen now, Arian! "You know neither me nor my Father," because "if you knew me, you would also know my
father." What does it mean, "If you knew me, you would also
know my Father," except "I and the Father, we are one
thing"?

(2) When you see someone who resembles someone else
(observe, my beloved people; it is an everyday expression. Let
what you notice to be of familiar usage not be difficult for
you.), when, therefore, you see someone like someone else,
and you know the person to whom he is like, you wonder and
say: How like to that man is this man! You would not say this
unless there were two. Now another, who does not know him
to whom you say this fellow is like, says, Is he so much like
him? And you say to him, What? Don't you know him? But he
says, I do not know him. Now, in order to make known to your
companion from the one present, whom he sees, the man
whom he does not know, you answer and say, If you have seen
this man, you have seen him. You have not, of course, because
you said this, maintained that there was one person and denied that there were two, but because of such close similarity
you gave the answer: If you know this man, you know that one
too; for he is so much alike and not at all different. In this way,
too, the Lord said, "If you knew me, you would also know my
Father," not because the Father is the Son, but because the
Son is like the Father. Let the Arian blush.

14. Cf. *Tractate* 36.9.

(3) Thanks be to the Lord that even the Arian himself has departed from the Sabellian error and is not a Patripassianist; he does not say that the Father himself came to men, clothed in flesh, that he suffered, that he arose, and, in a sense, ascended to himself. He does not say this; with me, he acknowledges that the Father is the Father and the Son is the Son. But, O brother, you have escaped that shipwreck; why do you tend to the other? The Father is the Father, the Son is the Son; why do you say [that they are] not alike? Why [do you say that they are] different? Why [do you say that there is] another substance? If he were not alike, would he say to his disciples, "He who has seen me has also seen the Father"? Would he say to the Jews, "If you know me, you would also know my Father"? How would this be true unless this were also true: "I and the Father, we are one thing"?

8. "These words Jesus spoke in the treasury, teaching in the temple," with great confidence, without fear. For he who would not even have been born if he did not wish it would not suffer what he did not wish. Then what follows? "And no one seized him, because his hour had not yet come." Likewise, when some hear this, they believe that the Lord Christ was subject to fate, and they say, "Look, Christ had a fate!" Oh, if your heart were not fatuous, you would not believe in fate!

(2) If, as some understand, fate is derived from [the Latin verb] *fari*, that is, to speak, how does the Word of God have a fate, since all things which have been created are in the Word himself?[15] For God does not establish something which he did not know before; what has been made was in his Word. The world was made; and it was made and was there. How was it made and was there? Because the house which the builder constructs existed first in his creative knowledge;[16] and there it was better, without age, without collapse. Yet, that he may show his creative knowledge, he builds the house; and a house, in a sense, proceeded from a house. And if the house collapses, the creative knowledge remains. So with the Word

15. Cf. *Tractates* 8.10 and 31.5–6.
16. See *Tractate* 1.17, note 40, for this translation of *in arte*.

of God all things were which were created; because God made all things in wisdom[17] and made all things [already] known [to him]. For he did not learn because he made, but he made because he knew. Because they have been made, they are known to us; but, if they had not been known to him, they would not have been made. Therefore, the Word preceded. And what was before the Word of God? Absolutely nothing. For if there were something before, it would not have been said, "In the beginning was the Word,"[18] but, In the beginning was made the Word. And then what did Moses say about the world? "In the beginning God made heaven and earth."[19] He made what was not; therefore, if he made what was not, what was there before? "In the beginning was the Word." And from what are heaven and earth? "All things were made through him."[20]

(3) Do you, then, place Christ under fate? Where are the fates? In heaven, you say, in the order and changes of the stars. How, then, does he through whom the heaven and the stars were made have a fate, since your will, if you should understand rightly, transcends even the stars? Is it because you know that Christ's flesh was under heaven, that you therefore think that Christ's power was subject to heaven?

9. Listen, fool! "His hour had not yet come," not the hour in which he would be compelled to die, but in which he deigned to be put to death. For he himself knew when he ought to die. He focused his attention on the things which were predicted about him, and he was waiting for all the things to be accomplished which had been predicted to be going to be before his passion, so that when they were fulfilled, then his passion, too, might come, in the order of God's plan for the world,[21] not by the necessity of fate.

(2) Now then, hear, that you may prove it. Among the other things that were prophesied about him, it was also written, "They put gall in my food, and in my thirst they gave me

---

17. Cf. Ps 103 (104).24.   18. Jn 1.1.
19. Gn 1.1.   20. Jn 1.3.
21. *dispositionis ordine;* see Blaise, *Dictionaire latin-français des auteurs chrétiens.* (Turnhout, 1954), 282, s.v. 2.

vinegar to drink."²² We know in the Gospel how these things
happened.²³ First, they gave him gall; he took it, tasted it, and
spit it out. Later, while hanging on the cross, that all predic-
tions might be filled, he said, "I thirst."²⁴ They took a sponge
full of vinegar, fastened it on a reed, and offered it to him as
he hung there. He took it and said, "It is consummated." What
does "It is consummated" mean? All the things which had
been prophesied before my passion have been fulfilled; what
then is there still for me to do? Then, after he said, "It is
consummated," "bowing his head, he gave up the spirit."²⁵
Those robbers crucified next to him, did they breathe their
last when they wanted to? They were held fast by the chains of
the flesh because they were not the creators of the flesh; fastened by nails, they were tormented for a long time because
they were not masters of their infirmity. But the Lord took on
flesh in the Virgin's womb, when he wished it. He came forth
to men, when he wished it. He lived among men, so long as he
wished it. He departed from the flesh, when he wished it. This
is a sign of power, not of necessity.

(3) He was awaiting this hour, not fated, but suitable and
self-chosen that all things might first be fulfilled which should
be fulfilled before his passion. For how had he been put under
the nescessity of fate who in another place said, "I have the
power to lay down my life, and I have the power to take it up
again. No one takes it from me, but I lay it down myself and I
take it up again"?²⁶ He showed this power when the Jews were
looking for him. He said, "Whom do you seek?" And they
said, "Jesus." And he said, "I am he." And when they heard
this, "they went backward and fell to the ground."²⁷

10. Someone says, If this power was in him, why, when the
Jews insulted him as he was hanging there and said, "If he is
the Son of God, let him come down from the cross,"²⁸ why did
he not come down, that by coming down he might show them

22. Ps 68 (69).22.
23. See Mt 27.34, 48–50; Mk 15.23, 36–37; Jn 19.28–30.
24. Jn 19.28.   25. Jn 19.30.
26. Jn 10.18.   27. Cf. Jn 18.4–6.
28. Mt 27.40; cf. *Tractate* 3.3.

his power? Precisely because he was teaching patience, he put aside his power. For if he had come down, as if disturbed at their words, he would have been thought defeated by the pain of their insults. Accordingly, he did not come down; he remained fastened, to depart when he wanted. What great thing was it for him to come down from the cross who could raise up from the tomb? Therefore, let us to whom this has been granted understand that the power of our Lord Jesus Christ [was] hidden then, [but] will be manifest at the judgment about which it has been said, "God will come manifest, our God, and will not keep silence."[29] What does it mean, "will come manifest"? Because he has come hidden, our God, that is, Christ, will come manifest. "And he will not keep silence." What does it mean, "will not keep silence"? Because he had first kept silence. When did he keep silence? When he was judged, that there might be fulfilled this which the prophet had also predicted: "as a sheep he was led to the slaughter, and as a lamb before his shearer, without a voice, so he opened not his mouth."[30] Therefore, if he were unwilling to suffer, he would not suffer. If he did not suffer, his blood would not be poured forth. If his blood were not poured forth, the world would not be redeemed.

(2) Therefore, let us give thanks both to the power of his divinity and the compassion of his weakness: both covering the hidden power which the Jews did not know, of which it has just been said to them, "You know neither me nor my Father," and concerning the assumed flesh which the Jews did know and whose homeland they knew, of which he said to them in another place, "You both know me, and know where I am from."[31] We know both things in Christ, both how he is equal to the Father and how the Father is greater than he. The former is the Word, the latter the flesh; the former God, the latter man. But Christ, God and man, is one person.

29. Ps 49 (50).3.
30. Cf. Is 53.7.
31. Jn 7.28.

TRACTATE 38

On John 8.21–25

HE READING of the holy Gospel which preceded to-day's had concluded thus: "The Lord, teaching in the treasury, spoke" what he wanted and what you heard; "and no one seized him, because his hour had not yet come."[1] From this our discourse which he himself deigned to grant was delivered on the Lord's day. We suggested to you, my beloved people, why it was said, "His hour had not yet come"—so that no impiety would dare wrongfully to suspect that Christ had been put under some necessity of fate. For the hour had not yet come in which, by his own disposition of affairs, according to the things which had been predicted about him, he was not compelled to die against his will but was put to death when he was ready.

2. But now he spoke to the Jews about his passion itself, which had been put not in a necessity for him but in his power, saying, "I go." Death for Christ the Lord was a departure to that place from which he had come and from which he had not withdrawn. He said, "I go, and you will seek me," not out of longing, but out of hatred. For after he had departed from the eyes of men, they searched for him, both they who hated him and they who loved him, the former by persecution, the latter by a desire to have him. In the psalms, the Lord himself says through the prophet, "Flight has failed me; and there is no one who seeks after my soul."[2] And again in another place, in a psalm, he said, "Let them be put to confusion and shame who seek after my soul."[3] He censured those who would not seek; he condemned those who would seek. For it is evil not to

---

1. Jn 8.20.
2. Ps 141 (142).5.
3. Ps 39 (40).15.

seek after the soul of Christ as the disciples sought it; and it is evil to seek the soul of Christ as the Jews sought it. For the former sought to have it; the latter, to destroy it.

(2) Now because these, [i.e. the Jews] thus sought [his soul] in an evil way, with perverse heart, what did he continue and add? "You will seek me, and," that you may not think that you will seek me well, "in your sin you will die." This is to seek Christ badly, to die in one's sin; this is to hate him through whom alone one could be saved. For although men whose hope is in God ought not to return evil for evil,[4] these men returned evil for good. Therefore, the Lord predicted to them and in his foreknowledge declared their sentence, that they would die in their sin.

(3) Then he added, "Where I go, you cannot come." He also said this to the disciples in another place;[5] yet he did not say to them, in your sin you will die. But what did he say? What he said to these men: "Where I go , you cannot come." He did not take away hope, but he foretold delay. For when the Lord said this to his disciples, they were then not able to come where he was going, but they would come later; but these would never come to whom in his foreknowledge he said, "in your sin you will die."

3. But when they heard these words, thinking about things of the flesh, as they were accustomed, and judging according to the flesh, and hearing and understanding completely carnally, they said, "Will he kill himself, since he said, 'Where I go, you cannot come'?" Stupid words, and completely filled with foolishness! Well now, could they not come there where he would go if he killed himself? Were not they themselves going to die? What, then, does it mean, "Will he kill himself, since he said, 'Where I go, you cannot come'?" If he spoke about the death of a man, what man does not die? Therefore, he said, "Where I go," not when one goes to death, but where he was going after death. And so, not understanding, they answered these words.

4. omit. *nec,* following BA.
5. Cf. Jn 13.33.

4. And what does the Lord say to those who savored the earth? "And he said to them, 'You are from beneath.'" You savor the earth precisely because like serpents you eat the earth. What does it mean, you eat the earth? You are fed with earthly things, you delight in earthly things, with open mouth you covet earthly things, you have not lifted up your hearts. "You are from beneath, I am from above. You are of this world, I am not of this world." For how was he through whom the world was made of the world? All who are of the world are after the world, because the world is first; and so man is of the world. But first there was Christ, then the world, because Christ was before the world, before Christ was nothing; for "in the beginning was the Word" and "all things were made through him."[6]

(2) So therefore, he was from above. From what above? From the air? Perish the thought! Even birds fly there. From the sky which we see? Perish this thought, too! The stars also and the sun and the moon go about there. From the angels? That is not what it means, either. The angels, too, were made through him "through whom all things were made." So, from what above does Christ come? From the Father himself. There is nothing farther above than that God who begot the Word equal to himself, coeternal with himself, only-begotten, without time, through whom he would create times. Therefore, so understand Christ from above that in your thought you go out beyond all that was made, out totally beyond the whole of creation, out beyond every body, every created spirit, every thing in any way changeable; go out beyond everything, as John went out that he might reach to this: "In the beginning was the Word, and the Word was with God, and the Word was God."[7]

5. Therefore, he said, "I am from above. You are of this world, I am not of this world. Therefore I said to you that you will die in your sins." He explained to us, brothers, how he wanted "You are of this world" to be understood. In fact he

6. Jn 1.1, 3.
7. Jn 1.1.

said, "You are of this world," precisely because they were
sinners, because they were wicked, because they were unbelieving, because they savored earthly things. For what do you
think about the holy Apostles? how much difference was there
between the Jews and the Apostles? As much as between darkness and light, as between belief and unbelief, as between
piety and impiety, as between hope and despair, as between
love and lust—that much difference was there. Well now, because there was such a great difference, were the Apostles not
of the world? If you should consider how they were born and
where they came from, since all had come from Adam, they
were of this world. But what did the Lord himself say to them?
"I have chosen you out of this world."[8] They who were of the
world were made to be not of the world and began to belong
to him through whom the world was made. But these men
continued to be of the world, to whom it was said "You will die
in your sins."

6. Therefore, let no one say, brothers, I am not of this
world. Whoever of you is a human being is of this world; but
he who made the world has come to you and has freed you of
this world. If the world delights you, you forever wish to be
unclean; but if this world no longer delights you, you are now
clean.[9] But if nevertheless through some weakness the world
still delights you, let him who cleanses dwell in you and you
will be clean. But if you are clean, you will not remain in the
world nor will you hear what the Jews heard: "You will die in
you sins." For we have all been born with sin; in living we all
have added to that with which we had been born and we have
become more of the world than when we were born of our
parents.

(2) And where would we be, if he who had no sin at all had
not come to loose all sin? And the Jews, because they did not
believe in him, justly heard, "You will die in your sins," because in no way could you not have had sin, you who were

8. Jn 15.19.
9. The Latin contains an untranslatable play on the noun for world,
mundus, and homonymous adjective, *mundus*, clean, its privative, *immundus*,
and its derivative verb, *mundare*.

born with sin; but yet if you believe in me, he said, you indeed were born with sin, but you will not die in your sin. Therefore, the whole misfortune of the Jews was exactly this, not to have sin, but to die in sin. This is what every Christian ought to flee. For this reason one runs to baptism. For this reason they who are in danger from sickness or any other thing desire to be helped. For this reason even a suckling child is brought by his mother to the Church with devout hands that he may not pass away without baptism and may not die in the sin with which he was born. Oh, most unhappy state, oh, wretched lot of these who heard from a truth-speaking mouth, "In your sins you will die."

7. All the same, he explains why this happens to them. "For if you do not believe that I am, you will die in your sins." I believe, brothers, that in that multitude which heard the Lord there were also those who would believe. But as if that most severe sentence had come forth against all of them, "In your sin you will die," and through this even from those who would believe, hope had been taken away, some were furious, some were afraid, nay rather, not afraid, but already in despair. He recalled them to hope; for he added, "If you do not believe that I am, you will die in your sins." Therefore, if you do believe that I am, you will not die in your sins. Hope has been granted to the despairing, awakening has come to the sleeping, they have wakened in their hearts. Because of this, very many believed, as what follows in the Gospel itself attests.[10]

(2) For there were there members of Christ who had not yet adhered to the body of Christ; and among that people by whom he was crucified, by whom he was hung on wood, by whom he was mocked while he hung, by whom he was wounded with a spear, by whom he was given gall and vinegar to drink, there were members of Christ for whom he said, "Father, forgive them, for they know not what they do."[11] Now what is a convert not forgiven if the spilled blood of Christ is forgiven? What murderer should despair if he by whom even Christ was murdered has been returned to hope? Because of

10. Cf. Jn 8.30–32.
11. Lk 23.34.

this many believed; the blood of Christ was granted to them that they might drink it more to be freed than to be held guilty of the spilling of it. Who should despair? And if on the cross a robber was saved, who not long before was a murderer and shortly thereafter was accused, convicted, condemned, hung, and freed, do not be amazed. Where he was convicted, there he was condemned; but where he was changed, there he was freed. Therefore, among this people to whom Christ was speaking, there were those who would die in their sin; there were also those who would believe in him who was speaking and be freed from all sin.

8. Yet observe this which the Lord Christ said, "If you do not believe that I am, you will die in your sins." What does this mean: "if you do not believe that I am"? "I am" what? He added nothing; and because he added nothing, what he brought to our notice is much. For there was expectation that he would say what he was; and yet he did not. What was he expected to say? Perhaps, If you do not believe that I am the Christ. If you do not believe that I am the Son of God. If you do not believe that I am the Word of the Father. If you do not believe that I am the maker of the world. If you do not believe that I am the fashioner and refashioner of man, the creator and recreator, the maker and the remaker. "If you do not believe that I am" this, "you will die in your sins." This very thing which he said here, "I am", is much; for God also had so spoken to Moses, "I am who am".[12]

(2) Who may worthily proclaim what "I am" means? Through his angel God was sending his servant Moses to set his people free from Egypt (you have read what you have heard, and you know; still, I remind you); he sent Moses trembling, making excuses, but obeying. When he was making excuses, he said to God, whom he understood to be speaking in the angel, "If the people say to me, 'And who is the God who sent you?' what shall I say to them?" And the Lord said to him, "I am who am." And he repeated it, "You will say to the children of Israel, he who is has sent me to you."[13] There too

12. Ex 3.14.
13. Ex 3.13–14.

he did not say, I am God, or, I am the builder of the world, or, I am the creator of all things, or, I am the propagator of the freeing of this people. But he said only this, "I am who am" and "You will say to the children of Israel, he who is." He did not add, He who is your God, he who is the God of your fathers, but he said only this, "He who is has sent me to you."

(3) Perhaps it was much even for Moses himself, as it is much also for us, and much more for us, to understand what was said, "I am who am" and "He who is has sent me to you." And if perchance Moses understood, when would they to whom he was being sent understand? Therefore, the Lord put aside what man could not grasp and added what he could grasp. For he added and said, "I am the God of Abraham, and the God of Isaac, and the God of Jacob."[14] This you can grasp. But what mind can grasp, "I am who am"?

9. What then about us? Shall we dare to say something about this which was said: "I am who am"? Or rather about this which you heard the Lord say: "If you do not believe that I am, you will die in your sins"? So, since these powers of mine are so slight and practically nonexistent, shall I dare to discuss the meaning of what the Lord Christ said: "If you do not believe that I am"? Shall I dare to ask the Lord himself? Listen to me, asking rather than discussing, seeking rather than assuming, learning rather than teaching; and you also, ask at least in me or through me. The Lord himself, who is everywhere, is also present here. Let him hear the feeling underlying the question and let him offer the result of understanding. For with what words can I, even if I perhaps grasp something, introduce what I grasp to your hearts? What sound suffices? What eloquence is sufficient? What strength of understanding? What ability to explain?

10. I shall speak, therefore, to our Lord Jesus Christ; I shall speak, and may he hear me. I believe he is present; I do not at all doubt it. For he himself said, "Behold, I am with you, even unto the consummation of the world."[15] O Lord, our God, what is the meaning of what you said, "If you do not believe

14. Ex 3.15.
15. Mt 28.20.

that I am"? For what *is* not part of the things that you have
made? Can it be that the sky *is* not? That the earth *is* not? That
the things which are in the sky and on the earth *are* not? That
man himself, to whom you are speaking, *is* not? That the
angel whom you send *is* not? If all these things which were
made through you *are,* what is it which you have kept for
yourself to be, as something special to you which you have not
given to other things, so that you alone might be? How do I
hear, "I am who am," as if other things were not? And how do
I hear, "If you do not believe that I am"? Were they who heard
you not? And if they were sinners, they were men. Then what
do I do? Let him say to the heart what it is that he is, let him
say within, let him speak within. Let the inner man hear. Let
the mind grasp true being; for it is *to be always in the same way.*

(2) For some thing, any thing at all (I have, as it were, begun
to discuss and have stopped seeking; perhaps I want to speak
what I have heard. May he give joy to my hearing[16] and to
yours when I speak), for any thing at all, absolutely of whatever excellence, if it is changeable, does not have true being;
for true being is not there where non-being also is. For whatever can be changed, when it has been changed, is not what it
was; if what was is not, a kind of death has occurred there.[17]
Something there which was has been completely taken away,
and is not. The color black has died on the head of a man
whose hair is turning white; beauty has died in the body of a
weary and bowed old man; strength has died in the body of a
sick man; standing has died in the body of a man walking;
walking has died in the body of a man standing still; walking
and standing have died in the body of a man lying down;
talking has died in the tongue of a man keeping silence.
Whatever is changed and is what it was not, there I see a kind
of life in that which is and a death in that which was.

(3) Moreover, when it is said about someone who is dead,
"Where is that man?", the answer is, "He was." O Truth, you
who truly are! For in all our actions and movements, and in
absolutely every activity of a created being I find two times,

16. Cf. Ps 50 (51).10.
17. Cf. *Tractate* 2.2.

the past and the future. I look for a present; nothing stands still. What I have said no longer is; what I am going to say is not yet. What I have done no longer is; what I am going to do is not yet. What I have lived no longer is; what I am going to live is not yet. I find past and future in every motion of things. In the truth which abides I do not find past and future, but only the present and what is without corruption—something which does not exist in a created being. Analyze changes in things; you will find, it was and it will be. Think about God; you will find, *he is,* where *he was* and *he will be* cannot be.

(4) Therefore, that you too may *be,* transcend time. But who will transcend by his own strength? Let him lift you up there who said to the Father, "I will that where I am, they also may be with me."[18] And so, promising this, that we will not die in our sins, the Lord Jesus Christ seems to me to have said in these words, "If you do not believe that I am," nothing else; indeed he seems to me to have said nothing else in these words than this, If you do not believe that I am God, "you will die in your sins." It is a good thing, thanks be to God, that he said, "If you do not believe." He did not say, If you do not comprehend. For who can comprehend this? Or, because I have dared to speak and you seemed to understand, have you truly comprehended something of such great ineffableness? Therefore, if you do not comprehend, faith sets you free. And so the Lord did not say, If you do not comprehend that I am; but he said what they could do, "If you do not believe that I am, you will die in your sins."

11. And those men, always savoring earthly things and always hearing and answering according to the flesh, what did they say to him? "Who are you?" For when you said, "If you do not believe that I am," you did not add what you were. Who are you that we may believe? And he said, "The beginning."[19]

18. Jn 17.24.
19. The text of John 8.25 is quite unclear and remains a serious problem both for textual critics and exegetes. The weight of contemporary scholarship inclines toward making τὴν ἀρχήν (*principium* in the Latin text) adverbial and not substantive as Augustine does; but there is less agreement on how to translate and interpret the resultant text. Cf. NAB, John 8.25, note; B. Vawter, JBC 2.442; R. E. Brown, *The Anchor Bible* 29.347–48; R. W. Funk, "Pa-

See what being is. The beginning cannot be changed; the beginning abides in itself and renews all things. He is the beginning to whom it was said, "But you are the selfsame, and your years will not fail."[20] He said, "The beginning, because I also speak to you." Believe that I am the beginning that you may not die in your sins. For as if in that which they said, "Who are you?", they said nothing other than, What are we to believe you are?, he answered, "The beginning", that is, Believe that I am the beginning.

(2) For a distinction is made in the Greek language which cannot be made in Latin. For in Greek 'beginning' is feminine;[21] among us 'law' is feminine, whereas among them it is masculine; as 'wisdom' is feminine both among them and among us.[22] Linguistic usage in different languages, therefore, varies the genders of words because you do not find sex in the things themselves. For wisdom is not really female, since Christ is the Wisdom of God,[23] and 'Christ' is put in the masculine gender and 'wisdom' in the feminine. Therefore, when the Jews said, "Who are you?", he who knew that there were some there who would believe and who had said, "Who are you?" precisely that they might know what they ought to believe him [to be]; he answered, "The beginning," not as if he were to say, "I am the beginning," but as if he were to say, "Believe that I am the beginning." And this is quite clear, as I said, in the Greek language where the word for beginning is of the feminine gender.[24] Just as if he wanted to say that he

---

pyrus Bodmer II (P66) and John 8, 25," *Harvard Theological Review* 51 (1958) 95–100. Augustine prefers to accept the sense generally ascribed from the Latin translation rather than to analyze fully the Greek text; cf. Comeau, *Saint Augustin,* 62–64. One might note that Ambrose, *Expositio Evangelii Secundam Lucam* 10.112 (CCL 14.377) interprets this text as Augustine does, whereas Chrysostom, *Homiliae in Ioannem* 53.1 (PG 59.293), takes τὴν ἀρχήν as an adverb.

20. Ps 101 (102).28.

21. But in Latin "beginning," *principium,* is neuter.

22. The Latin *principium* and Greek ἀρχή, *lex* and νόμος, *sapientia* and σοφία.

23. Cf. 1 Cor. 1.24.

24. St. Augustine means that the feminine ἀρχή distinguishes in form between the nominative and accusative cases, ἀρχή and ἀρχήν, but the Latin

was the truth and to those saying, "Who are you?", he would answer truth, [*veritatem*], although it would seem that he ought to have answered that which was said, "Who are you?", truth, [*veritas*], that is, I am the truth [*veritas sum*]. But he answered more profoundly, when he saw that they had said, "Who are you?", so as if they were to say, Because we have heard from you, "If you do not believe that I am," what are we to believe that you are?, he answered to them, "The beginning," as though he were to say, "Believe that I am the beginning."

(3) And he added, "because I also speak to you," that is, because, having become lowly for your sake, I have descended to these words. For if the Beginning, as he is, had so remained with the Father that he did not take the form of the servant[25] and speak as a man to men, how would they believe him, since weak hearts could not hear the intelligible Word without the perceptible voice? Therefore, he says, believe that I am the beginning, because, that you may believe, I not only am, but I also speak to you. But there is still much to say to you on this subject. And so may it please you, my beloved people, that, with his help, we save what remains and discharge our obligation tomorrow.

---

neuter *principium* can in form be either the nominative or the accusative. If "the beginning" represented "I am the beginning," ἀρχή would occur; but if it means, "Believe that I am the beginning," ἀρχήν would occur as in fact it does in the Greek text, assisted further by the Greek article τήν. Latin has only *principium* for both possibilities. By concentrating on the Latin text and not carefully analyzing the Greek text, as suggested above, Augustine overlooked the possibility that τὴν ἀρχήν is an adverbial accusative; see note 18.

25. Cf. Phil 2.7.

TRACTATE 39

On John 8.25–27

HE WORDS of our Lord Jesus Christ which he exchanged with the Jews, so controlling his language that the blind might not see and the believers might open their eyes, which were read aloud from the holy Gospel today are these: "Therefore the Jews said, 'Who are You?'" For the Lord had said before, "If you do not believe that I am, you will die in your sins."[1] To this, then, they [answered], "Who are You?", as if seeking to know in whom they ought to believe, that they might not die in their sin. He answered those who were asking, "Who are you?", and he said, "The beginning, because I also speak to you."[2]

(2) If the Lord said that he was the beginning, it can be asked whether the Father is also the beginning. For if the Son who has the Father is the beginning, how much more easily ought God the Father to be understood to be the beginning, who does indeed have the Son to whom he is the Father but has no one of whom he is? For the Son is the Son of the Father, and the Father is, of course, the Father of the Son; but the Son is called God of God, the Son is called Light of Light. The Father is called Light, but not of Light; the Father is called God, but not of God. If, therefore, God of God, Light of Light is the beginning, how much more easily is the Light of which he is Light and the God of whom he is God to be understood as the beginning? And so it seems ridiculous, my dearest people, that we should call the Son the beginning but should not call the Father the beginning.

1. Jn 8.24.
2. Cf. *Tractate* 38.11, notes 18 and 23.

2. But what shall we do? Will there be two beginnings? One must beware of saying this. Well, then, if the Father is the beginning and the Son is the beginning, how are there not two beginnings?[3] As we say the Father is God and the Son is God and yet we do not say there are two Gods. It is sacrilege to say there are two Gods; it is sacrilege to say there are three Gods. And yet he who is the Father is not the Son, and he who is the Son is not the Father; moreover, the Holy Spirit is the Spirit of the Father and the Son, but is neither Father nor Son.[4] Therefore, as Catholic ears have been instructed upon the breast of Mother Church, although he who is the Father is not the Son, nor is he who is the Son the Father, nor is the Holy Spirit of the Father and the Son either the Father or the Son, nevertheless we do not say that there are three Gods; although if someone asks about them individually, we must admit about whichever one we are questioned that he is God.

3. And these things seem absurd to men who ascribe the usual to the unusual, the visible to the invisible, who compare the creature to the Creator. For sometimes the unbelievers ask us and say, He whom you say is the Father, do you say he is God? We answer, He is God. He whom you say is the Son, do you say he is God? We answer, He is God. He whom you say is the Holy Spirit, do you say he is God? We answer, He is God. Therefore, they say, Are the Father and the Son and the Holy Spirit three Gods? We answer, No. They are troubled because they are not enlightened; they have a closed heart because they do not have the key of faith.

(2) Therefore, brothers, with [our] faith which heals the eye

3. Browne, LFC 26.534, states that Eastern theologians, in reaction to the Gnostics and the Manichaeans, restricted the term *beginning* to the Father alone, emphasizing that there was *one* beginning. The Western theologians, however, in reaction to the Arians, to assert the co-equality of the Son, saw the Father and the Son together as the *one* beginning, so that consequently the Holy Spirit proceeds from the Father and the Son. Cf. Augustine, *De Trinitate* 5.13–14 (CCL 50.220–23 or FOTC 45.191–194); G. Prestige, *God in Patristic Thought*, 140–46, 242–62, for the Greek Fathers only; J. Kelly, *Early Christian Doctrines*, 262–63, 271–76; B. de Margerie, *The Christian Trinity in History*, trans. E. Fortman (Still River, Mass., 1982) 161–65.

4. Cf. *Tractate* 9.7.

of our heart preceding [us], let us grasp without obscurity what we understand; let us believe without doubting what we do not understand. Let us not depart from the foundation of faith that we may come to the rooftop of perfection. The Father is God, the Son is God, the Holy Spirit is God; and yet the Father is not he who is the Son, nor is the Son he who is the Father, nor is the Holy Spirit, the Spirit of the Father and the Son, either the Father or the Son. The Trinity is one God; a Trinity, one eternity, one power, one majesty. Three, but not three Gods. Let not the slanderer reply to me, What then are the three? For if there are three, he says, you ought to say what the three are. I answer, The Father and the Son and the Holy Spirit. Look, he says, you mentioned three, but explain what the three are. Nay, rather you do the counting; for I complete three when I say, the Father and the Son and the Holy Spirit. For that which the Father is to himself is God; what he is to the Son is Father. What the Son is to himself is God; what he is to the Father is Son.

4. You can come to know these things which I am saying from everyday example. For instance, a man and another man, if the one should be a father, the other a son. That he is a man is in respect to himself; that he is a father is in respect to the son. And that the son is a man is in respect to himself; but that he is a son is in respect to the father. For the name *father* has been said in respect to something, and *son* in respect to something; but these are two men. But in truth, God the Father is Father in respect to something, that is, to the Son; and God the Son is Son in respect to something, that is, to the Father. But as those men are two men, not so are these two Gods. Why is it not thus in that case? Because this is different from that because that is divinity. There is something ineffable there which cannot be explicated in words, that there be number and not be number. See if number does not seemingly appear, Father and Son and Holy Spirit, the Trinity. If there are three, what are the three? Number fails. Thus God neither departs from number, nor is he comprehended by number. Because they are three, it is as if there is a number; if you ask what are the three, there is not number. Whence it has

been said, "Great is our Lord and mighty is his power, and of his wisdom there is not number."[5]

(2) Where you begin to reflect, you begin to number; where you number, you cannot answer what you have numbered. The Father is the Father, the Son is the Son, the Holy Spirit is the Holy Spirit. What are these three, the Father and the Son and the Holy Spirit? Are there not three Gods? No. Are there not three omnipotent Beings? No. Are there not three Creators of the world? No. Then is the Father omnipotent? Yes, he is omnipotent. Is not the Son, then, omnipotent? Yes, the Son too is omnipotent. And is the Holy Spirit, then, not omnipotent? He too is omnipotent. Therefore, are there three omnipotent Beings? No, but one omnipotent Being. They convey the idea of number in this alone, what they are in respect to each other, not what they are in respect to themselves. For, because God the Father in respect to himself is God together with the Son and the Holy Spirit, there are not three Gods; because he is in respect to himself omnipotent together with the Son and the Holy Spirit, there are not three omipotent Beings. But because he is Father, not in respect to himself, but in respect to the Son, and the Son is not Son in respect to himself but in respect to the Father, and the Spirit, in that he is called the Spirit of the Father and the Son, is not in respect to himself, there is nothing that I can call the three, except Father and Son and Holy Spirit, one God, one omnipotent Being. Therefore, one Beginning.

5. Learn something from the holy Scriptures by which in one way or another you may grasp this which is said. After our Lord Jesus Christ arose and ascended when he wished into Heaven, after ten days were there fulfilled, he sent the Holy Spirit from there. And they who were in one room were filled with him and began to speak in the languages of all nations.[6] The murderers of the Lord were quite frightened by the miracle and, feeling remorse, they were sorry; being sorry, they were changed; being changed, they believed. There were ad-

5. Ps 146 (147).5.
6. Cf. Acts 2.2–6.

ded to the body of Christ, that is to the number of believers, three thousand men. Likewise, when a certain other miracle happened,[7] another five thousand were added. And this not insignificant number of people became one in which all, after the Holy Spirit was received, by whom spiritual love was enkindled, were brought into one group by the very love and fervor of the Spirit and began in the very unity of fellowship to sell all that they had and to place the money at the Apostles' feet that it might be distributed to each one as anyone had need. And the Scripture says this about them, "They had one soul and one heart" in God.[8]

(2) Observe, therefore, brothers, and recognize from this the mystery of the Trinity, how we say: There is both the Father, and there is the Son, and there is the Holy Spirit, and yet there is one God. Look, those were so many thousands, and there was one heart. Look, there were so many thousands, and there was one soul. But where? In God. How much more is God himself? Do I err in word when I say that two men are two souls, or three men three souls, or many men many souls? Of course I say it rightly. Let them come to God, there is one soul of all. If, coming to God, many souls through love are one soul, and many hearts are one heart, what does the very Fountain of love do in the Father and the Son?[9] Is not the Trinity there even more one God? For love comes to us from there, from the Holy Spirit himself, as the Apostle says, "The love of God has been poured forth in our hearts by the Holy Spirit who has been given to us."[10] If, therefore, "the love of God has been poured forth in our hearts by the Holy Spirit who has been given to us" makes many souls one soul and many hearts one heart, how much more does it make the Father and the Son and the Holy Spirit one God, one Light, and one Beginning?

6. Let us hear, then, the Beginning which is speaking to us. He says, "Many things I have to speak concerning you and to judge." You remember what he said, "I do not judge any

---

7. The healing of a man lame from his mother's womb; see Acts 3.1–11.
8. Acts 4.32.   9. Cf. *Tractate* 14.9.
10. Rom 5.5.

one."[11] Look, now he says, "Concerning you I have many things to say and to judge." But "I do not judge" he said for the present; for he had come to save the world, not to judge the world.[12] But his words, "Many things I have to say concerning you and to judge" indicate a future judgment. For he ascended for the reason that he may come to judge the living and the dead. No one will judge more justly than he who was judged unjustly.

(2) He said, "Many things I have to say concerning you and to judge; but he who sent me is true." See how the equal Son gives glory to the Father. For he affords us an example, and as if in our hearts he speaks: O man of faith, if you hear my gospel, the Lord your God says to you, where I, in the beginning the Word, God with God, equal to the Father, coeternal to the Begetter, give glory to him whose Son I am, how are you proud against him whose servant you are?

7. He said, "Concerning you I have many things to say and to judge; but he who sent me is true," as if he were to say, I judge truly precisely because I am the truth, the Son of the one who is true.

(2) The Father is true, the Son is truth; which do we adjudge is greater? Let us think, if we can, which is greater, true or truth? Let us examine certain examples. Is a pious man or piety more? But piety itself is more; for the pious stems from piety, not piety from the pious. For piety can exist even if he who was pius becomes impious. He himself has lost his piety; but he takes nothing away from piety. Likewise what about beautiful and beauty? Is beauty more than beautiful? For beauty makes one beautiful, beautiful does not make beauty. Chaste and chastity? Chastity is certainly more than chaste. For if there were no chastity, one would not have the means to be chaste; but if one does not wish to be chaste, chastity remains unimpaired. Therefore, if piety is more than pious, beauty more than beautiful, chastity more than chaste, shall we say that truth is more than true?

(3) If we say this, we shall begin to say that the Son is greater

11. Jn 8.15.
12. Cf. Jn 12.47 and *Tractate* 36.4.

than the Father. For the Lord most clearly said, "I am the way and the truth and the life."[13] Therefore, if the Son is the truth, what is the Father except what Truth itself said, "He who sent me is true"? The Son is truth, the Father is true. I seek which is more, but I find equality. For the true Father is not true from that truth, a part of which he took, but which he wholly begot.

8. I see that this must be expressed more clearly. And indeed, for fear that I may detain you too long, let the discussion come to this point today; when I finish what I want to say, with God's help, let the discourse be closed. I have said this precisely to make you attentive.

(2) Because every soul is changeable, and however great a creature, nevertheless, it is a creature, however better than the body, nevertheless, it is made; therefore, because every soul is changeable, that is, now it believes, now it does not believe, now it wishes, now it does not wish, now it is adulterous, now it is chaste, now good, now evil—it is changeable. But God is this which is; therefore he has kept for himself as his proper name: "I am who am."[14] The Son is this, in saying, "If you do not believe that I am",[15] to this also belongs, "Who are you? The Beginning." Therefore, God is immutable; the soul is mutable.

(3) When the soul takes from God that by which it is good, by participation it becomes good, as your eye sees by participation. For if the light is taken away, it does not see; but being made a participant in it, it sees. Therefore, because the soul becomes good by participation, if it has been changed and has begun to be evil, the goodness of which it was a good participator, abides. For it became a participant in a certain goodness when it was good; but when the soul was changed for the worse, goodness remains unimpaired. If the soul should withdraw and become evil, goodness is not lessened. If the soul should turn back and become good, goodness does not increase. Your eye has become a participant in this light and you see. Has it been closed? You have not lessened this light.

13. Jn 14.6.
15. Jn 8.24.

14. Ex 3.14; cf. *Tractate* 38.10.

Has it been opened? You have not increased this light. By the presentation of this simile, brothers, understand that if the soul is devout, there is piety with God in which the soul becomes a participant. If the soul is chaste, there is chastity with God in which the soul is a participant. If the soul is good, there is goodness with God in which the soul is a participant. If the soul is true, there is truth with God in which the soul is a participant. And if the soul is not a participant in this, every man is a liar;[16] if every man is a liar, no man is true of his own.

(4) But the Father is true; he is true of his own, because he begot the Truth. This man is true because he has perceived the truth, is one thing; God is true because he begot the Truth, is something else. Look at how God is true, not by participating in but by generating the Truth.

(5) I see that you have understood and I am glad. Let this suffice for you today. When it pleases the Lord, as he grants, we shall explain the rest.

16. Cf. Ps 115 (116).11 and Rom 3.4.

TRACTATE 40

On John 8.28–32

ROM THE holy Gospel according to John, which you see us carrying in our hands, you have already heard, my beloved people, many things which we have discussed, God granting, as best we could, especially showing you that this Evangelist had chosen to speak about the Lord's divinity by which he is equal to the Father and is the only Son of God; and for this reason the Evangelist has been compared to an eagle; for, of course, no bird is said to fly higher.[1] Accordingly, to those things which follow in order, as the Lord grants us to treat of them, listen most attentively.

2. We have spoken to you about the preceding reading, making known how the Father is understood as true, the Son as truth. But when the Lord Jesus had said, "He who sent me is true,"[2] the Jews did not understand what he said to them about his Father. And he said to them what you have just heard when it was read, "When you shall have lifted up the Son of Man, then you shall know that I am, and that of myself I do nothing: But as the Father has taught me, these things I speak." What does this mean? He seems to have said nothing else than that they would recognize who he was after his passion.

(2) Beyond doubt, therefore, he saw there that some, whom he himself knew, whom he himself in his foreknowledge had chosen with the rest of his saints before the foundation of the world,[3] would believe after his passion. These are they whom we continually commend and whom we set before

1. See introduction, FOTC 78, *Tractates* 15.1 and 36.1.
2. Jn 8.26.
3. Cf. Eph 1.4–5; see also 1 Pt 1.20.

you with great exhortation for imitation. For, after the Holy Spirit was sent from above after the Lord's passion and resurrection and ascension, when miracles were done in the name of him whom the persecuting Jews had despised as dead, they felt remorse in their hearts, and they who killed him in their rage were changed and believed.[4] The blood which they poured out in rage they drank in belief: those three thousand and those five thousand Jews whom he saw there when he said, "When you shall have lifted up the Son of Man, then you shall know that I am." As if he were saying, I delay your knowing that I may accomplish my passion; in the proper order for you, you shall know who I am. Not that all of those who heard would believe then, that is, after the Lord's passion; for a little later the Gospel says, "When he was speaking these things, many believed in him," and the Son of Man had not yet been lifted up.

(3) He speaks, of course, of the lifting up of his passion, not of his glorification, of the cross, not of heaven; for he was lifted up there, too, when he was hung on the cross. But that exaltation was humiliation. For then he "became obedient even to the death of the cross."[5] It was necessary for this to be fulfilled through the hands of those who would afterwards believe, to whom he says, "When you shall have lifted up the Son of Man, then you shall know that I am." Why did he say this, except that no one might despair, [however] bad his conscience, over any sin, when he saw that they who had killed Christ were pardoned for their homicide?

3. Therefore, the Lord, recognizing these men in that crowd, said, "When you shall have lifted up the Son of Man, then you shall know that I am." You already know what "I am" is. And it ought not be continually repeated, lest a thing so great produce aversion. Recall the words "I am who am" and "He who is sent me"[6] and you will recognize what has been said, "then you shall know that I am," but also, the Father is and the Holy Spirit is. The whole Trinity pertains to the same Being.

4. Cf. Acts 2.37, 41; 4.4.   5. Phil 2.8.
6. Ex 3.14.

(2) But because the Lord was speaking as the Son, so that, in that which he said, "Then you shall know that I am," the error of the Sabellians, that is, the Patripassianists,[7] might not perhaps steal in, and I have instructed you that this error must not be held but must be guarded against, the error, namely, of those who said, the same one is the Father, the same one is the Son, there are two names, but one thing—therefore in order to guard against this error, when the Lord had said, "Then you shall know that I am," that he himself might not be understood to be the Father, he immediately added, "and that of myself I do nothing: but as the Father has taught me, these things I speak." The Sabellian had already begun to rejoice since he had found an occasion for his error; as soon as he extolled himself in the dark, as it were, he was confounded by the light of the following sentence. You had thought that he was the Father because he had said, "I am." Hear that he is the Son, "and that of myself I do nothing." What does it mean, "of myself I do nothing"? I am not of myself. For the Son is God of the Father; the Father is God, but not of the Son. The Son is God of God, the Father is God, but not of God. The Son is Light of Light; the Father is Light, but not of Light. The Son is, but there is one of whom he is; the Father is, but there is not one of whom he is.

4. Therefore, as for what he added, "As the Father has taught me, these things I speak," let no carnal thought creep up on any of you, my brothers. For human weakness can only think of what it has been accustomed to do or hear. Do not, therefore, set before your eyes two men, as it were, one a father, the other a son, and the father speaking to the son, as you do, when you say some words to your son, advising him and instructing him how he should speak so that whatever he has heard from you, he commits to memory, that when he has committed it to memory, he may also express with his tongue, may formulate through sounds, and may carry to another's ears what he perceived in his own.[8] Do not think that way, that you may not fashion idols in your heart.

7. Cf. *Tractates* 29.7 and 36.8.
8. Cf. *Tractates* 18.5, 20.9, and 21.2.

(2) The human form, the lines of human limbs, the shape of human flesh, these external senses, the stature and movements of the body, the function of the tongue, the distinctions of sounds, do not think that [any of these] are in that Trinity, except as far as pertains to the form of the servant[9] which the only-begotten Son received when the Word became flesh to dwell among us.[10] There, I do not forbid you, human weakness, to think what you know; rather, I even compel you. If the faith in you is true, think that Christ was such, but think that he was such from the Virgin Mary, not from God the Father. He was a baby, he grew as a man, he walked as a man, he hungered, thirsted as a man, he slept as a man, then at the last he suffered as a man, was hung on the wood, was killed, was buried as a man. In the same form he arose, in the same form he ascended into heaven before the eyes of his Apostles, in the same form he will come in order to judge. For the pronouncement of the angels has been related in the Gospel: "He shall so come as you have seen him go into heaven."[11]

(3) When, therefore, you think about the form of the servant in Christ, think of his human shape, if there is faith in you. But when you think of: "In the beginning was the Word and the Word was with God, and the Word was God,"[12] let every human configuration vanish from your heart; let there be driven from your thought whatever is limited by a bodily boundary, whatever is confined by the extent of a place or is extended with any bulk whatsoever; let such a fictitious image disappear from your heart. Think, if you can, of the beauty of wisdom; let the beauty of justice occur to you. Is it form? Is it size? Is it color? It is none of these, and yet it is. For if it were not, neither would it be loved nor justly praised; nor, loved and praised, would it be held fast in our heart and habits. But now men do become wise. How could they if there were no wisdom? Now, O man, if you cannot see your own wisdom with the eyes of the flesh, nor think of it with such imaginings as bodily things are thought of, do you dare to impose the form of the human body on the wisdom of God?

9. Cf. Phil 2.7.
11. Acts 1.11.
10. Cf. Jn 1.14.
12. Jn 1.1.

5. What, then, do we say, brothers? How did the Father speak to the Son, since the Son says "As the Father has taught me, these things I speak"? Did he speak to him? When the Father taught the Son, did he use words as you do when you teach your son? How does he use words with regard to the Word? What abundance of words might be used with regard to the only-begotten Word? For did the Word of the Father have ears for the Father's mouth? These are bodily things; let them vanish from your hearts.

(2) For I say this: Look, if you understood what I said, I assuredly spoke and my words sounded, they struck your ears with sounds, and through your sense of hearing they brought my sentence to your heart, if you understood. Suppose that someone who knew the Latin language heard, but only heard, and did not understand what I said. As far as pertains to the noise which was emitted from my mouth, he who did not understand became a participant in it just as you did; he heard the sound, the same syllables struck his ears, but they begot nothing in his heart. Why? Because he did not understand. But if you understood, how did you understand? I made sound for the ear; did I enkindle a light in the heart?

(3) Without doubt, if what I said is true and you not only heard this true thing but also understood it, two things happened there; distinguish them, hearing and understanding. Hearing occurred through me; through whom did understanding occur? I spoke to the ear that you might hear; who spoke to your heart that you might understand? Without a doubt, someone also said something to your heart so that not only did that sound of words strike your ear, but something of truth descended into your heart. Someone spoke also to your heart; but you did not see him. If you understood, brothers, your heart has also been spoken to. Understanding is a gift of God. If you understood, who spoke this in your heart? He to whom the psalm says, "Give me understanding that I may learn your commands."[13]

(4) For example, the bishop spoke. What did he say? some-

13. Ps 118 (119).73; also, cf. *De Magistro* 11.38, 12.40, 13.46 (CCL 29.195–96, 197–99, 202–3; ACW 9.177, 179–81, 185–86).

one asks. You answer what he said, and you add, He said a true thing. Then another who did not understand says, What did he say, or what is it that you praise? Both heard me; I spoke to both. But God spoke to [only] one of them. If one is allowed to compare small things to great—for what are we to him? Yet God effects something or other in us incorporeally and spiritually; for it is neither sound which strikes the ear, nor color which is discerned by the eyes, nor odor which is caught by the nostrils, nor flavor which is judged by the palate, nor hard or soft which is perceived by touching—yet it is something which is easy to perceive, impossible to explain.

(5) Therefore, if, as I had begun to say, God speaks in our hearts without sound, how does he speak to his Son? In this way, then, brothers, in this way think, as best you can, as I said. If one may somehow compare small things to great, think in this way. The Father spoke incorporeally, because he begot him incorporeally. Nor did he teach him in such a way as if he had begot him untaught; but to have taught him is the same as to have begotten him knowing; and "the father has taught me" is the same as the Father begot me knowing. For if— something which few understand—the nature of Truth is simple, for the Son, *to be* is the same as *to know*. Therefore, from whom he has that he is, he has from him that he knows, not that he is from him first and then knows from him, but just as he gave him *to be* by begetting him, so he gave him *to know* by begetting him. For, as was said, to the simple nature of Truth, *to be* and *to know* are not two different things, but this same thing.

6. Therefore, he said these things to the Jews, and added, "And he who sent me is with me." He had already said this before:[14] but he continually recalls an important matter: "He sent me" and "He is with me." Therefore, if he is with you, O Lord, one was not sent by the other, but you both have come. And yet although they are both together, one was sent, the other did send, because the sending is the incarnation, and the incarnation itself is only of the Son, not also of the Father.

14. Cf. Jn 8.16.

And so the Father sent the Son, but did not withdraw from the Son. It is not the case that the Father was not there where he sent the Son. For where is he not who made all things? Where is he not who said, "I fill heaven and earth"?[15] But is the Father perhaps everywhere and the Son not everywhere? Hear the Evangelist: "He was in the world, and the world was made through him."[16] Therefore, he said, "He who sent me", by whose paternal authority, so to speak, I have been made incarnate, "is with me; he has not left me." Why has he not left me? He said, "He has not left me alone because I do always the things that are pleasing to him." The equality itself is "always," not from some beginning and from then on, but without beginning, without end. For God's begetting does not have a beginning of time, since times were made through the one begotten.

7. "When he was speaking these things, many believed in him." Would that, when I speak, many who hold a contrary view might also understand and believe in him. For perhaps some in this crowd are Arians.[17] I do not venture to suspect that there are Sabellians[18] who say that the Father himself is he who is the Son; for that heresy is rather ancient and has gradually been dissipated. But the Arians still seem to have some twitchings as of a rotting corpse, or surely, at best, as of a man gasping for breath. It is necessary that the rest be freed of it as many have been freed of it. And indeed this town did not have them; but after many foreigners came, some of them came too.[19] Look, when the Lord said these things, many Jews be-

15. Jer 23.24.
16. Jn 1.10.
17. Cf. *Tractate* 1.11, note 27.
18. Cf. *Tractate* 29.7, note 17; 36.8, note 22.
19. During his bishopric Augustine had only occasional contact with isolated Arians, but either by letter or in Cathage or elsewhere, as, e.g., with Elpidius and Pascentius. At Hippo some Arians were among the refugees from the barbarian invasions of Italy after A.D. 410, and in particular a number of Arian Goths came in A.D. 417 in connection with Roman military defence forces. See B. Warmington, *The North African Provinces from Diocletian to the Vandal Conquest* (Cambridge 1954) 13; A.-M. La Bonnardière, *Recherches de chronologie augustinienne* (Paris 1965) 91–101; and J. Randers-Pehrson, *Barbarians and Romans* (Norman, Okla., 1983) 147.

lieved in him; look, when I speak, may the Arians also believe, not in me, but with me.

8. "The Lord therefore said to those Jews who had believed in him, 'If you abide in my word.'" "You abide" precisely because you have been initiated, because you have begun to be there. "If you abide," that is, in the faith which has begun to be in you who believe, where will you arrive? See what sort of beginning [there is], where it leads. You have loved the foundation; observe the rooftop, and from this lowliness seek after the other loftiness.

(2) For faith has lowliness; knowledge and immortality and eternity do not have lowliness but loftiness, eminence, no deficiency, eternal stability, no attack by an enemy, no fear of failing. It is a great thing which begins from faith, but it is despised. Even as in a building it is usual for the foundation to be despised by the ignorant. A big ditch is made; stones are tossed indiscriminately in any which way. There is no polishing here, no beauty appears; just as even in the root of a tree, no beauty appears, yet whatever delights you in the tree, all of it rises up from the root. You see the root and you are not delighted; you see the tree and you are amazed. Stupid man, that at which you are amazed arose from that with which you are not delighted. The faith of those who believe seems something small; you have no balance with which to weigh it. Therefore, hear where it arrives, and see how great it is, as the Lord himself also says in another place, "If you have faith like a mustard seed."[20] What is lowlier, what is more vigorous? What is tinier, what is hotter? Therefore, he also said, "If you abide in my word," in which you have believed, where will you be led? "You shall be my disciples indeed." And what does this profit us? "And you shall know the truth."

9. What does he promise to those who believe, brothers? "And you shall know the truth." Well, now, did they not know it when the Lord was speaking? If they did not know it, how did they believe? They did not believe because they knew, but they believed that they might know. For we believe that we

20. Mt 17.19 (NAB 17.20).

may know; we do not know that we may believe.[21] For what we shall know "neither eye has seen, nor ear has heard, nor has it ascended into the heart of man."[22] For what is faith except to believe what you do not see? Faith, therefore, is to believe what you do not see; truth is to see what you have believed, as he himself says in a certain place.[23] And so the Lord first walked on earth in order to bring about faith. He was a man; he had become humble. He was seen by all, and yet not recognized by all. He was reproached by many, he was slain by a crowd, he was mourned by few. But still, even by those by whom he was mourned, he was not yet recognized as he was. All of this is, as it were, the beginning of the outlines of the faith and the structure that was going to be. And the Lord himself, observing this, said in a certain place, "He who loves me keeps my commandments; and he who loves me will be loved by my Father, and I will love him and reveal myself to him."[24] They who heard him, of course, were already seeing him; yet he was promising them, if they loved, to see himself. So also here, "You will know the truth." Well now, is not what you have said the truth? It is the truth, but it is still believed, it is not yet seen. If one abides in that which is believed, he comes to that which is to be seen. Concerning this the holy Evangelist John himself in his epistle says, "Beloved, we are the sons of God, but it has not yet appeared what we shall be."[25] We are now something and we shall be something. What more shall we be than we are? Listen. "It has not yet appeared what we shall be. We know that, when he shall appear, we shall be like to him." How? "For we shall see him as he is." A great promise, but it is the recompense of faith. You seek recompense; let work precede. If you believe, demand the recompense of faith; but if you do not believe, with what effrontery do you seek the recompense of faith?

(2) Therefore, "if you abide in my word, you shall be my disciples indeed," that you may gaze upon the Truth itself as it is, not through resounding words, but through gleaming

---

21. Another repetition of this common theme; see *Tractate* 36.7, note 21.
22. 1 Cor 2.9, quoting Is 64.4 (NAB 64.3).
23 Cf. Jn 20.29.   24. Jn 14.21.
25. 1 Jn 3.2.

light, when he has satisfied[26] us, as we read in the psalm, "The light of your countenance has been sealed upon us, O Lord."[27] We are God's money; a coin, we have wandered away from the treasury. What had been stamped upon us was worn off by our wandering. He comes who may reform us because he had formed us; he himself seeks his own coin, as Caesar sought his coin. Thus he says, "Render to Caesar the things that are Caesar's, and to God the things that are God's,"[28] to Caesar his coins, to God you yourselves. Then, therefore, truth will be expressed in us.

10. What am I to say to you, my beloved people? Oh, would that the heart were sighing, in anyway whatever, in that ineffable glory! Oh, if only we would perceive our exile in moaning and not love the world, and with pious mind knock constantly upon the door of him who has called us! Longing is the heart's bosom; we shall receive if we would stretch out our longing as far as we can. Divine Scripture, the congregation of peoples, the celebration of mysteries, holy baptism, the songs of God's praise, this exposition of ours all aim at this with us: that this longing may not only be sown and germinate, but also that it may be increased to a measure of such great capacity that it may be able to take what "eye has not seen nor ear heard nor has it ascended into the heart of man."[29]

(2) But love with me. He who loves God does not love money much. And I have treated his weakness gently; for I did not venture to say, he does not love money, but, he does not love money *much*, as if money ought to be loved, but not much. Oh, if only we should love God worthily, we shall not love money at all! Money will be for you fare for a voyage, not an incitement to greed, a thing which you employ for a need, not which you enjoy for delight.[30] Love God, if what you hear

26. Or, with a variant reading, "when he has impressed his seal upon us."
27. Ps 4.7 (LXX).
28. Mt 22.21; Cf. Mk 12.17; Lk 20.25.
29. 1 Cor 2.9, quoting Is 64.4 (NAB 64.3).
30. Sections 10 and 11 constitute the peroration of this semon, and it is a very rhetorical peroration. This sentence in particular contains sound effects difficult to translate: . . . *instru*mentum *peregrinationis, non irrita*mentum *cupidi*tatis, *quo ut*aris *ad necessi*tatem, *non quo fru*aris *ad delectationem.* The translation strives to give a feeling of this type of sound effect.

and praise has had any effect on you. Use the world; let not the world seize hold of you. You are making a journey which you have entered upon; you have come to go away, not to stay. You are making a journey; this life is an inn. Use money as, in an inn, a traveler uses the table, the cup, the pitcher, the bed: as one who is going to leave, not going to stay.

(3) If you are such, lift up your heart, you who can, and hear me; if you are such, you will come to his promises. It is not much for you, because the hand of him who has called you is strong. He has called; let him be called upon. Let it be said to him: You called us, we call upon you. Look, we heard you calling. Hear us calling upon you: lead us where you promised, finish what you have begun, do not desert your gifts, do not desert your field, let your sprouts come into the granary. Temptations abound in the world, but greater is he who made the world; temptations abound, but he does not fail who places hope in him in whom there is no failing.

11. I have urged these things, brothers, for this reason, because the freedom about which our Lord Jesus Christ speaks is not of this time. See what he added: "You shall be my disciples indeed, and you shall know the truth, and the truth shall free you." What does "shall free you" mean? He will make you free. Now the Jews, carnal men and judging carnally, not those who had believed, but those who were in that crowd who did not believe, thought that he had done them a wrong, because he said to them, "The truth shall free you." They were indignant that they had been marked as slaves. They were truly slaves. And he explains to them what slavery is and what the freedom which he promises will be. But it would take too long for us to discuss this freedom and that slavery today.

TRACTATE 41

On John 8.31–36

HE END of the previous reading which has been read aloud to us from the holy Gospel, I put off speaking about on that occasion because I had already said many things; and one ought not to discuss cursorily nor carelessly the freedom into which the grace of the Savior calls us. With the Lord's help, we intend to speak to you about this today.

(2) Now those to whom the Lord Jesus Christ was speaking were Jews, a great part of them indeed his enemies, but also a certain part of them had already become, and were soon to be, his friends; for he saw there certain ones, as we have already said,[1] who were going to believe after his passion. Looking upon these, he had said, "When you have lifted up the Son of Man, then you will know that I am."[2] There were also there those who, when he spoke these words, believed immediately; to them he spoke what we have heard today: "Jesus therefore said to the Jews who had believed in him, 'If you abide in my word, you will indeed be my disciples.'" By abiding you will be; for because you are believers now, by abiding you will be beholders. And so he continues: "And you will know the truth."

(3) Truth is unchangeable. Truth is bread, it restores the mind and does not run short. It changes the one who eats it; it is not itself changed into the one who eats it. Truth itself is the Word of God, God with God, the only-begotten Son. This Truth was clothed in flesh for our sakes, that he might be born of the Virgin Mary and the prophecy fulfilled: "Truth sprang

1. See *Tractate* 40.2–3.
2. Jn 8.28.

out of the earth."[3] And so this Truth, when he spoke to the
Jews, was hiding in flesh; he was hiding, however, not that he
be denied but that there be a delay,[4] a delay that he might
suffer in the flesh, but suffer in the flesh so that flesh might be
redeemed from sin.

(4) And so, our Lord Jesus Christ standing there, visible in
conformity with the weakness of flesh, yet hidden in accordance with the majesty of divinity, said to those who had believed in him when he was speaking these words, "If you abide
in my word, you will indeed be my disciples." "For he who has
persevered all the way to the end will be saved."[5] "And you will
know the truth," which now is concealed from you and yet
speaks to you. "And the truth shall set you free." The Lord
has taken this verb from *freedom:* "will set you free." For *sets
free* is, in a strict sense, nothing other than *makes free.* Just as
saves is nothing other than *makes safe,* as *heals* is nothing other
than *makes healthy,* as *enriches* is nothing other than *makes rich,*
that is, wealthy, so *sets free* is nothing other than *makes free.*
This is clearer in the Greek.[6] For in Latin usage we very often
say that a man is freed, pertaining not to freedom but only to
health, as someone is said to be freed from an infirmity. This
is said in common usage, nevertheless not in the strict sense.
But the Lord so applied this verb, that he might say, "And the
truth will set you free," so that in the Greek language no one
would doubt that he spoke about freedom from bondage.

2. In fact, the Jews also understood this. "And they answered him," not those who had already believed, but those in
the crowd who were not yet believers. "They answered him,
'We are the seed of Abraham, and never have we been slaves
to anyone. What do you mean by saying, You will be free?'"
But the Lord had not said, You will be free, but "The truth
will set you free." Yet in this verb those men only understood

3. Ps 84 (85).12; cf. *Tractate* 27.4.
4. I.e., a delay in the revelation of his divinity.
5. Mt 10.22.
6. The Greek text reads: ἐλευθερώσει ὑμᾶς. Augustine means that the
Latin verb *liberare* should be understood in the Greek verb's narrower meaning, "to make a person ἐλεύθερος," that is, to set one free from enslavement,
and that one should not be misled by other connotations.

political freedom because, as I said, this is unambiguous in the Greek; and they prided themselves because they were the seed of Abraham, and they said, "We are the seed of Abraham, and never have we been slaves to anyone. What do you mean by saying, 'You will be free'?" Oh, windbag! This is not grandeur, but pomposity!

(2) And, as regards the freedom of this period in time, how did you even say this truly: "Never have we been slaves to anyone"? Was not Joseph sold?[7] Were not the holy prophets led into captivity?[8] And then, is this not the very people who were making bricks in Egypt and were enslaved to hard kings, not even in gold and silver but in mud?[9] If you were never slaves to anyone, O you ungrateful people, why is it that God constantly ascribes to you his setting you free from the house of slavery?[10]

(3) Or is it perhaps that your fathers were slaves, but you who are speaking never were slaves to anyone? How then were you paying tribute taxes to the Romans at that very time? And from this very fact you even proposed for Truth himself a snare, a quibbling sophism, to wit, so that you said, "Is it lawful to give tax to Caesar?"[11] In order that, if he had said, It is lawful, you might gain control over him on the grounds that he had opted ill for the freedom of Abraham's seed; but if he had said, It is not lawful, you might malign him before the kings of the earth since he prohibited the payment of taxes to the kings. Justly, after a coin was presented, were you defeated and you yourselves were compelled to respond to your quibbling sophism.[12] For there it was said to you, "Give to Caesar the things that are Caesar's, and to God the things that are God's,"[13] when you yourselves had answered that the coin had Caesar's image. For as Caesar seeks his own image on the coin, so God seeks his own in a human being. This answer,

7. Cf. Gn 37.28.   8. Cf. 4 Kgs (2Kgs) 24.10–16.
9. Cf. Ex 1.11–14.   10. E.g., Ex 13.3, 20.2; Dt 5.6.
11. Mt 22.17.

12. Or this could mean: "to correspond to your trap," that is, to be caught in your own trap. Innes LNPF 7.230, translates "to concur in your own capture."

13. Mt 22.21.

then, he gave to the Jews. For the vain pride of men distresses me, my brothers, men who lied even about their own freedom which they understood carnally, saying, "Never have we been slaves to anyone."

3. But what the Lord answered, this let us hear better and more attentively so that we ourselves may not also be found slaves. "Jesus answered them, 'Amen, amen, I say to you, everyone who commits sin is the slave of sin.'" He is a slave—I wish it were of a man and not of sin. Who would not quake at these words? Let the Lord our God grant to us, that is, to you and to me, that I speak knowledgeably about seeking this freedom and avoiding that slavery. "Amen, amen, I say to you," Truth says. And what is the nature of this expression of the Lord our God's: "Amen, amen, I say to you"? He very much affirms what he proclaims in this way; in a certain sense, if it is right for it to be said, it is his oath: "Amen, amen, I say to you." In fact, "Amen" is translated as "truly" and yet it has not been translated although it could be expressed: "Truly, I say to you." Neither the Greek nor the Latin translator has dared to do this; for the word "Amen" is neither Greek nor Latin but Hebrew. So it has remained, has not been translated so that it might be honored by a veil of mystery, not that it be disavowed but that it be not cheapened by being laid bare. And yet it was said by the Lord not once but twice: "Amen, amen, I say to you." Now learn from the repetition how great an affirmation has been made.

4. What, then, has been affirmed? Truly, truly, I say to you: Truth speaks. And certainly, even if he were not saying, "I say truly," not at all could he lie. Still he affirms, he inculcates. In a sense, he rouses the sleeping, he makes them attentive, he does not want to be scorned. Saying what? "Amen, amen, I say to you, everyone who commits sin is the slave of sin."

(2) Oh, pitiable slavery! Very often when men are afflicted with wicked masters, they request to have themselves put up for sale, not seeking to not have a master, but simply to change [masters]. But the slave of sin, what can he do? To whom can he appeal? Before whom can he appeal? Before whom can he request to have himself put up for sale? Then too, the slave of

a man sometimes, when exhausted by his master's harsh orders, finds rest in flight. Where does the slave of sin flee? He drags himself with himself wherever he flees. An evil conscience does not flee itself; there is nowhere for it to go, it pursues itself. Nay, it withdraws not from itself, for the sin which one commits is within. He committed a sin to obtain some bodily pleasure; the pleasure passes, the sin remains. What delighted has gone past; what may sting has remained. Evil slavery! Sometimes men flee to the Church; and very often we endure them as undisciplined men, wishing to be without master but who do not want to be without sins. Moreover, sometimes, too, men who are subjected to an unlawful and unrighteous yoke flee to the Church because, although freeborn, they are held in slavery, and the bishop is appealed to; and if he should not care to undertake an effort to undo the oppressing of free-birth, he is considered unmerciful.[14]

(3) Let us all flee to Christ. Against sin let us appeal to God, the giver of freedom.[15] Let us request to have ourselves put up for sale that we may be redeemed by his blood. For the Lord says, "You were sold for nothing, and without money you shall be redeemed."[16] Without payment, without your payment, because by mine. The Lord says this; for he gave the payment himself, not silver, but his own blood. For we had remained both slaves and in need.

5. The Lord alone, then, sets [us] free from this slavery; he, who did not have it, himself sets [us] free from it. Indeed, he alone came in this flesh without sin. For little children whom you see being carried in their mothers' hands do not yet walk and they have already been shackled; for they have contracted from Adam what is to be broken by Christ. This grace which the Lord promises also pertains to them when they are bap-

---

14. A subtle word-play runs through this sentence but is not translatable. There are several important words beginning with the prefix *in-* with both of the prefix's meanings and with alliterative assimilation: *illicito . . . improbo . . . ingenui . . . impendere . . . ingenuitas . . . immisericors.*

15. I.e., *Liberator.*

16. Is 52.3.

tized;[17] for he alone can set free from sin, who came without sin and became a sacrifice for sin.

(2) For you have heard, when the Apostle was read, "For Christ," he says, "we are ambassadors, God, as it were, exhorting by us. We beseech you for Christ,"[18] that is, as though Christ were beseeching you. What? "To be reconciled to God." If the Apostle exhorts and beseechs us to be reconciled to God, we were enemies to God. For no one is reconciled except from enmities. Not nature, however, but sins made us enemies. We are the slaves of sin from the same source from which we are his enemies. God does not have free men as his enemies; they must be slaves and they will remain slaves unless they are set free by him to whom they wished to be enemies by their sinning. "We beseech" therefore, he says, "for Christ, to be reconciled to God."

(3) But how are we reconciled unless what separates us and him is broken? For he says through the prophet: "He has not made heavy the ear that it not hear, but your sins separate between you and God."[19] Therefore, because we are not reconciled unless what is in the middle has been removed and what should be in the middle has been put there—for there is a separating middle, but over against it is a reconciling mediator; the separating middle is sin; the reconciling Mediator is the Lord Jesus Christ: "For there is one God and one mediator of God and man, the man Christ Jesus."[20] And so, in order that the separating wall which is sin may be taken away, that

17. In advocating infant baptism Augustine not only emphasizes the washing away of original sin and the attaining of eternal life but also declares that the child experiences a kind of seminal participation in the life of the Church, some sort of spiritual life through the inner workings of the Word and the Spirit, that is, the sacrament has efficacy even before moral development occurs. See especially *Epistula* 98 (PL 33.359–64 or FOTC 18.129–38), *De Baptismo* 4.23.30–24.31 (PL 43.174–76), and *De Peccatorum Meritis et Remissione* 1.16.21–26.39 (PL 44.120–31); also E. Fairweather, "Saint Augustin's Interpretation of Infant Baptism," *Augustinus Magister* II (Paris 1954) 897–903; P. Brown, *Augustine of Hippo*, 280, 344, and 385; TeSelle, *Augustine the Theologian*, 259, 262, 265–66, 279–80, and 323–24; and Van der Meer, *Augustine the Bishop*, 308–11 and 350–51.

18. 2 Cor 5.20. 19. Is 59.1–2.
20. 1 Tm 2.5.

Mediator has come, and the Priest himself has become the sacrifice.

(4) And because he became the sacrifice for sin, offering himself as a holocaust on the cross of his passion, the Apostle, when he had said, "We beseech you for Christ to be reconciled to God,"—as if we were to say, How will we be able to be reconciled?—continues and says, "Him," that is, Christ himself, "who knew not sin, he made to be sin," he says, "for our sakes, so that we might be the justice of God in him."[21] "Him" himself, he says, Christ, God, "who knew not sin." For he came in the flesh, that is, "in the likeness of sinful flesh,"[22] yet not in sinful flesh, not having any sin at all; and thus he became a true sacrifice for sin because he himself had no sin.

6. But perhaps it is according to my own understanding of the meaning that I have said that "sin" is a sacrifice for sin. Let those who have read it acknowledge it. Let those who have not read it not be lazy; let them not, I say, be lazy in reading, so that they may be truthful in judging. For when God was giving instruction about offering sacrifices for sin,[23] and in these sacrifices there was not expiation of sins, but a shadow of the future, the very same sacrifices, the very same sacrificial animals, the very same victims, the very same beasts which were presented to be immolated for sins, and in whose blood that blood was prefigured, these the Law calls *sins*,[24] to such an extent that in certain passages[25] it has been written thus, that priests, about to immolate, place their hands over the head of *sin*, that is, over the head of the victim to be immolated for sin.

21. 2 Cor 5.21.
22. Rom 8.3.
23. Cf. Lv 4.1–7.10.
24. One meaning of the Greek word for sin, ἁμαρτία, in the Septuagint is "sacrifice for sin." Augustine interprets this to be the meaning of the Latin word *peccatum* in Paul. Here, for Augustine, that Christ was made sin means that he assumed the likeness of human flesh and then by the death of that likeness of human flesh on the cross there occurred symbolically the sacrifice of the old man in his sinful flesh and the birth of the new man. For a full discussion of this topic see S. Lyonnet and L. Sabourin, *Sin Redemption and Sacrifice: A Biblical and Patristic Study* (Rome 1970) 187–289, esp. 211–15 on Augustine.
25. Cf. Lv 4.4, 15, 24, 29, and 33.

Therefore such a "sin," that is, a sacrifice for sin, did our Lord Jesus Christ become, "who knew not sin."

7. Rightly does he set free from this slavery of sin, he who says in the psalms, "I have become as a man without help, free among the dead."[26] He alone was free, because he did not have sin. For he himself says in the Gospel, "Lo, the prince of this world is coming," signifying that the devil would come in the persons of his Jewish persecutors. "Lo," he says, "he is coming and he will find nothing in me."[27] Not as he finds sins of some sort or other among those whom he kills, even though just, in me he will find nothing. And as if it were said to him, If he will find nothing in you, why will he kill you?, he added and said, "But that all may know that I do the will of my Father, arise, let us go from here."[28] I do not, he says, pay the penalty of death by the necessity of my sin, but in that I die, I do the will of my Father; and there I am doing rather than suffering, because if I were unwilling, I would not even have suffered. You have him saying in another place, "I have the power to lay down my life, and I have the power to take it up again."[29] Look, truly a free man among the dead.

8. Therefore, since everyone who commits sin is a slave of sin, hear what hope of freedom there is for us. "But the slave," he says, "does not remain in the house forever." The house is the Church, the slave is the sinner. Many sinners enter the Church. He did not therefore say, "The slave" is not in the house, but "does not remain in the house forever." If, then, there will be no slave there, who will be there? For when "a just king sits on the throne," as Scripture says, "who will boast that he has a pure heart? Or who will boast that he is cleansed of sin?"[30]

(2) He has greatly frightened us, brothers, by saying, "The slave does not remain in the house forever." But he adds and says, "But the son remains forever." And so will Christ alone be in his house? Will no people be united with him? For of

26. Ps 87 (88).5 (LXX).
27. Jn 14.30.
28. Jn 14.31, perhaps under the influence of Jn 4.34, 5.30, and 6.38.
29. Jn 10.18.
30. Prv. 20.8–9 (LXX).

whom will he be the head if there will be no body? Or is the Son perhaps this whole, head and body? Not without cause has he both frightened and given hope: he frightened that we might not love sin; he gave hope that we might not despair of the removal of sin. "Everyone," he says, "who commits sin is the slave of sin. But the slave does not remain in the house forever." What hope, then, is there for us who are not without sin? Hear your hope: "The son remains forever. If therefore the Son shall set you free, then you will really be free." This is our hope, brothers, that we be set free by the one who is free; and by setting us free, he makes us slaves. For we were slaves of lust; freed, we are made slaves of love.

(3) The Apostle also says this: "But you, brothers, have been called into freedom; only do not make freedom an opportunity to the flesh, but serve one another by love."[31] Therefore, let the Christian not say, I am free, I was called into freedom; I was a slave, but I have been redeemed, and by that redemption I have been made free, I shall do what I will.[32] Let no one restrain me from my will, if I am free. But if you commit sin by that sort of willing, you are a slave of sin. Do not, therefore, abuse freedom to sin freely, but use it not to sin. For your will will be free if it will be pious. You will be free if you will be a slave: free of sin, a slave to justice, as the Apostle says: "When you were the slaves of sin, you were free from justice; now, however, freed from sin and become slaves to God, you have your fruit for sanctification, and the end, life everlasting."[33] Let us try this, let us aim at it.

31. Gal. 5.13.
32. This seems to conflict with a well-known expression of Augustine, *Dilige et quod vis fac* (Love and do what you will) from *Tr in Io Ep* 7.8, a sermon delivered to this same congregation some time before this one. The same idea was expressed in identical or very similar words in *Expositio Epistulae ad Galatas* 57 (PL 35.2144), *Sermo* 56.13.17 (PL 38.385), and *Sermo Frangipane* 5.3, G. Morin, *Miscellanea Agostiniana*, 214–15. There is no contradiction. If one has a truly Christian love that is motivating and formative, then from a properly formed conscience one wills only what is good and so one may do what one will. The freedom of the will is not the justification for this, but the freely accepted assistance of God's grace and the free formation and motivation of the will by genuine love. See J. Gallay, "*Dilige et quod vis fac,*" RSR 43 (1955) 545–55, and P. Brown, *Augustine of Hippo*, 209.
33. Rom 6.20 and 22.

9. The first freedom is to be without crimes. Pay attention, my brothers, pay attention, in case perhaps I can convey to your understanding both what sort of thing this freedom is now and what it will be.

(2) You may examine any man whatsoever, exceedingly just in this life; however worthy he may now be of the term just, still he is not without sin. Hear holy John himself, whose Gospel this also is, speaking in his epistle: "If we say," he says, "that we do not have sin, we deceive ourselves and the truth is not in us."[34] Only the one free among the dead could say this; about him alone who knew not sin could it be said. About him alone could it be said; for he experienced all things according to his likeness, without sin.[35] He alone could say, "Lo, the prince of the world will come, and he will find nothing in me."[36] Although you will examine any other just man whatever, he is not altogether without sin. Neither was Job such a one, to whom the Lord bore such testimony that the devil was envious and requested that he should be tempted,[37] and tempting him, was overcome so that that man might be proven. And thus that man was proven, not because he was unknown to God as worthy to gain a crown, but that he might be made known to humanity as worthy to be imitated. What does even Job himself say? "For who is clean? Not even a baby whose life on earth lasts one day."[38]

(3) But clearly many have been called just without complaint, because [the term] is understood as without crime; for no complaint is just in human affairs about these who have no crime. But crime is serious sin, most deserving of accusation and condemnation. Consequently, God does not condemn certain sins, but justify and praise certain others; he praises

34. 1 Jn 1.8.   35. Cf. Heb 4.15.
36. Jn 14.30.
37. Cf. Jb 1.6–12.
38. Cf. Jb 14.4–5 (LXX). Augustine's quotation is a variant reading of LXX and differs from the text as it is given in A. Rahlfs, *Septuaginta* (Wurttemberg 1935) 2.294. Augustine does not cite this verse in his commentary on chapter 14 of Job in his *Annotationum in Job Liber Unus* (PL 34.840–41); he has a similar but different version in *En in Ps* 50.10 and 103.4.6. The verse is a troubled one even in the Hebrew texts; see R. MacKenzie, JBC 1.50, and M. Pope, *Job*, in *The Anchor Bible* 15 (New York 1965) 101.

none, he hates all. Just as a doctor hates the sickness of the sick man and in healing directs his effort so that the sickness be driven away and the sick man be relieved, so God by his grace directs his effort in us, so that the sin be destroyed and the person set free. But when is it destroyed? you will ask. If it is lessened, why is it not destroyed? That which is destroyed in the life of the perfect is lessened in the life of those who are progressing.

10. The first freedom, then, is to be without crimes. And so when the Apostle Paul chose either priests or deacons to be ordained, and when anyone is to be ordained to take charge of a church, he does not say, If anyone is without sin. For if he were to say this, every person would be rejected, no one would be ordained. But he says, "If anyone is without crime,"[39] such as homicide, adultery, and uncleanness of fornication, theft, fraud, sacrilege, and other things of this sort. When a person begins not to have these—and no Christian ought to have these—he begins to lift his head to freedom; but his freedom has only been begun, it has not been brought to perfection.

(2) Why, someone asks, has freedom not been brought to perfection? Because "I see another law in my members, warring against the law of my mind; for I do not perform what I wish," he says, "but I do that which I hate."[40] "Flesh," he says, "lusts against the spirit, and the spirit against the flesh, so that you do not do those things that you will."[41] In part freedom, in part slavery: it is not yet whole, not yet pure, not yet full freedom, because it is not yet eternity. For in part we have weakness, in part we have received freedom.

(3) Whatever sin has been done by us earlier has been erased in baptism. Because the whole wickedness has been erased, can it be that no weakness remained? If it had not remained, we would be living here without sin. But who would dare to say this except the proud, except one unworthy of the mercy of the giver of freedom, except one who wishes to deceive himself and in whom truth is not? Therefore, from

39. Ti 1.6; cf. 1 Tm 3.10.   40. Rom 7.23; cf. 7.15.
41. Gal 5.17.

the fact that some weakness remained, I dare to say: insofar as we are slaves to God, we are free; insofar as we are enslaved to the law of sin, we are still slaves. Hence the Apostle says what we began to say, "I am delighted with the law of God according to the inner man."[42] See wherein we are free, wherein we are delighted with the law of God. Freedom delights. For as long as you do what is just out of fear, God does not delight you. As long as you do it, still as a slave, he does not delight you; let him delight you and you are free. Do not fear punishment, but love justice. Are you not yet able to love justice? Fear punishment, at least, that you might attain the love of justice.

11. Therefore, that man thought that he was already free in the higher part, from which he said, "I am delighted with the law of God according to the inner man."[43] The law delights me, what the law orders delights me, justice itself delights me. "But I see another law in my members," this is the weakness which remained, "warring against the law of my mind, and imprisoning me in the law of sin that is in my members."[44] In this part, he perceives imprisonment where justice has not been fulfilled; for when he is delighted with the law of God, he is not a prisoner but a friend of the law, and thus free, because he is a friend.

(2) What, then, in regard to what remains? What, unless we should look to him who said, "if the Son shall set you free, then you will really be free"? Indeed he who was speaking also himself looked to him: "Unhappy man that I am! Who will set me free from the body of this death? The grace of God by Jesus Christ our Lord."[45] Therefore, "if the Son shall set you free, then you will really be free." Finally he concluded thus: "Therefore I myself with the mind serve the law of God but with the flesh, the law of sin."[46] "I myself," he says; for we are not two, contrary to each other, coming from diverse beginnings; but "I myself with the mind serve the law of God but

---

42. Rom 7.22.
44. Rom 7.23.
46. Rom 7.25.

43. Rom 7.22.
45. Rom 7.24–25.

with the flesh the law of sin," as long as weakness struggles with health.[47]

12. But if you serve with the flesh the law of sin, do what the Apostle himself says: "Therefore, let sin not rule in your mortal body and make you obey its lusts, and do not offer your members to sin as weapons of iniquity."[48] He does not say, Let it not be, but "let it not rule." As long as it is necessary for sin to be in your members, at least let rule be taken away from it, let what it orders not be done. Does anger arise? Give not the tongue to anger for uttering abuse; give not the hand or foot to anger for striking. This irrational anger would not arise unless sin were in your members; but take its rule away, let it not have weapons with which it may fight against you. It will learn, too, not to arise when it begins not to find weapons.

(2) "Do not offer your members to sin as weapons of iniquity." Otherwise, you will be completely captive and it will not be possible to say, "with the mind I serve the law of God."[49] For if the mind were to hold the weapons, the members would not be moved to the support of the raging sin. Let the inner emperor hold the citadel because it stands under a greater Emperor and will receive help: let it rein in anger, let it restrain lust. Yet there is present something which should be reined in, there is present something which should be restrained, there is present something which should be held back.

(3) But for what did that just man, serving the law of God with the mind, wish, except that what should be reined in not be at all? And everyone who strives for perfection ought to attempt this, that even lust itself, which the members are not given way to obey, may daily be lessened in the one making progress. "To will," he says, "is there for me, but to accomplish the good is not."[50] Did he say, to do good is not there for me? If he had said this, there would be no hope. He did not say, to do is not there for me, but "to accomplish is not there for me."

47. The Latin word is *salus;* it carries the double connotation of health and salvation, carrying out the metaphor used throughout this section of the sermon. See *Tractate* 7.19, 17.12, 30.4, and 34.3.

48. Rom 6.12–13.   49. Rom 7.25.

50. Rom 7.18.

(4) What is the accomplishing of good except the cessation and end of evil? But what is the cessation of evil except what the Law says, "You shall not lust"?[51] To lust not at all is the accomplishing of good because it is the cessation of evil. He said this: "To accomplish good is not there for me," because he was unable to bring it about that he did not lust; he only brought it about that he reined in lust, that he not consent to lust and that he not offer his members to lust for its service. "To accomplish good" therefore, he says, "is not there for me." I am not able to fulfill what was said: "You shall not lust." What then is needed? That you fulfill: "Go not after your lusts."[52] Do this in the meantime, as long as illicit lusts are present in your flesh: "Go not after your lusts." Remain in the slavery of God, in the freedom of Christ; with the mind serve the law of your God. Do not give yourself to your lusts. By following them, you add strength to them. By giving strength to them, how do you prevail when you nourish your enemies against yourself with your own strength?

13. What, then, is the full and perfect freedom in the Lord Jesus who said, "If the Son shall set you free, then you will really be free"? When will there be full and perfect freedom? When there are no enmities, when "death, the last enemy shall be destroyed. For this corruptible must put on incorruption and this mortal must put on immortality; but when this mortal has put on immortality, then shall come to pass the saying which is written, 'Death is swallowed up in victory, Where, O death, is your strife?'"[53] What is "Where, O death, is your strife?" "Flesh" lusted "against the spirit, and the spirit against the flesh,"[54] but when the flesh of sin was vigorous. "Where, O death, is your strife?" Now we shall live, now we shall not die, in him who died for us and rose up "so that those who live," he says, "might now live no longer for themselves but for him who for their sakes died and rose up."[55]

(2) Let us, the wounded, entreat the Physician, let us be

51. Rom 7.7, quoting Ex 20.17; the usual translation, covet, is here adapted to the context.

52. Ecclus (Sir) 18.30.   53. 1 Cor 15.26, 53–55.
54. Gal 5.17.   55. 2 Cor 5.15.

carried to the inn to be healed.[56] For it is he who promises health, who pitied the man left half-dead on the road by the robbers. He poured oil and wine, he healed the wounds, he lifted him onto his beast, he brought him to an inn, he entrusted him to the innkeeper. To what innkeeper? Perhaps to him who said, "We are ambassadors for Christ."[57] He also gave two coins to pay for healing the wounded man; perhaps these are the two precepts on which the whole law and the prophets are based.[58] Therefore, brothers, in this time the Church, too, in which the wounded man is healed, is the inn of the traveler; but for the Church itself the possessor's inheritance is on high.

56. With the help of the Good Samaritan; see Lk 10.30–35.
57. 2 Cor 5.20.
58. See Mt 22.34–40.

TRACTATE 42

On John 8.37–47

UR LORD, promised freedom to those believing in him in the form of a servant certainly, but not a servant. Yet certainly the Lord was in the form of a servant,[1] that form of the flesh was servile, but although there was a likeness of sinful flesh,[2] there was not the sinful flesh. But the Jews, as if taking pride in their own freedom, disdained to become free, although they were the slaves of sin. But the reason why they said that they were free was that they were the seed of Abraham.[3] We heard, then, when today's reading was read, what the Lord answered to them in regard to this.

(2) "I know," he said, "that you are the children of Abraham; but you seek to kill me because my word takes no hold in you." I recognize you, he says, "you are the children of Abraham; but you seek to kill me." I recognize the origin of the flesh, but not the faith of the heart. "You are the children of Abraham," but in the flesh. And so, he says, "you seek to kill me," for "my word takes no hold in you." If my word were taken hold of, it would take hold; if you were taken hold of, you would be enclosed with the nets of faith like fish. What does "takes no hold in you" mean? It does not take hold of your heart because it is not received by your heart. For so is the word of God, and so it ought to be for the faithful, like a hook for a fish; when it is taken hold of, then it takes hold. Harm does not come to those who are taken; for of course, they are taken for their salvation, not for their destruction. For this reason the Lord says to his Apostles, "Come after me, and I will make you fishers of men."[4] These men, then, were

1. Cf. Phil 2.7.
2. Cf. Rom 8.3.
3. Cf. Jn 8.33.
4. Mt 4.19.

not such, and yet they were children of Abraham; they were the children of a man of God, they were wicked men. For they drew [from him] the generation of their flesh, but had become degenerate by not imitating the faith of that one whose children they were.

2. Surely you heard the Lord saying, "I know that you are the children of Abraham." Hear what he says afterwards: "I speak that which I have seen with my Father; and you do the things which you have seen with your father." He had already said, "I know that you are the children of Abraham." But what do they do? What he said to them: "You seek to kill me." This they never saw with Abraham. The Lord, however, wants God the Father to be understood when he says, "I speak that which I have seen with my Father." I have seen truth, I speak truth because I am Truth. For if the Lord speaks the truth which he has seen with the Father, he has seen himself. He speaks himself because he is himself the Truth of the Father which he saw with the Father; for he is himself the Word, the Word which was with God.[5] The evil, then, which these men are doing, which the Lord rebukes and reproaches, where did they see it? With their father.

(2) When in what follows[6] we hear it said more clearly who their father is, we shall understand what kinds of things they saw with such a father; for he still does not name their father. A little before he mentioned Abraham, but as to the origin of their flesh, not from a likeness to their lives; he is going to speak of their other father who neither begot them nor created them to be human beings. But still they were his children in as much as they were evil, not as they were human beings, in what they imitated, not because they were created.

3. "They answered and said to him, 'Our father is Abraham.'" As if, what will you say against Abraham? Or, if you can do anything, dare to find fault with Abraham. Not because the Lord would not dare to find fault with Abraham, but Abraham was such a one who would not be faulted by the Lord, but rather praised. Nevertheless, these men seemed to

5. Cf. Jn 1.1.
6. I.e., verse 44.

be challenging him to say something evil about Abraham, and
there would be an opportunity to do what they were planning.
"Our father is Abraham."

4. Let us hear how the Lord answered them, joining a condemnation of them with praise for Abraham. "Jesus says to
them: 'If you are Abraham's children, do the works of Abraham. Now, however, you seek to kill me, a man who has spoken the truth to you, which I have heard from God. Abraham
did not do this.'" Look, that one was praised; they were condemned. Abraham was not a murderer. I do not say, he says, I
am the Lord of Abraham; but if I were to say [this], I would
say the truth. For he said in another place, "Before Abraham,
I am."[7] Then they wanted to stone him; he did not say this.
Meanwhile, as to what you see, what you are looking at, what
you think that I am only, I am a man. Why do you wish to slay
a man saying to you what he has heard from God, except that
you are not the children of Abraham? And yet he said earlier,
"I know that you are the children of Abraham." He does not
deny their origin, but he does condemn their deeds; their
flesh was from that man, but their life was not.

5. But we, my beloved people, have we come from the stock
of Abraham, or was Abraham in any way our father in the
flesh? The flesh of the Jews takes its origin from his flesh,
but not the flesh of the Christians; we have come from other
races, and yet, by imitating, we have become the children
of Abraham. Hear the Apostle: "To Abraham and his seed
promises were spoken. He does not say," he says, "and to his
seeds, as of many, but as of one, and to your seed, who
is Christ. But, if you are Christ's then you are the seed of
Abraham, heirs according to the promise."[8] We then have
become the seed of Abraham by the grace of God. Not from
the flesh of Abraham did God make coheirs for him. He disin-
herited the former, he adopted these; and from that tree of
the olive whose root is in the patriarchs, he pruned away the
haughty natural branches and engrafted the lowly wild olive.[9]

(2) And thus when the Jews came to John to be baptized, he

7. Jn 8.58.   8. Gal 3.16 and 29.
9. Cf. Rom 11.16–21.

burst out against them and said to them, "Brood of vipers!"
For they were boasting particularly about the highness of
their origin; but he called them a brood of vipers, not of men,
to be sure, but of vipers. He saw the shape of human beings,
but he recognized the poison. Yet they had come to be
changed[10] because of course they had come to be baptized.
And he said to them, "Brood of vipers, who has shown you to
flee from the wrath to come? Bring forth, then, fruits worthy
of repentance. And do not say within yourselves, 'We have
Abraham as our father.' For God can raise up children to
Abraham from these very stones."[11] If you do not bring forth
fruits worthy of repentance, do not flatter yourselves about
that lineage; God can both condemn you and not cheat
Abraham of his children. For he has a means by which he can
raise up children to Abraham. They will become his children
who have imitated his faith: "God can raise up children to
Abraham from these very stones." We are they! In our parents we were stones when we were worshipping stones instead
of God; from such stones God made a family for Abraham.[12]

6. Why, then, does that empty and useless boasting extol
itself? Let the children of Abraham stop boasting now; they
have heard what they ought to have heard: "If you are the
children of Abraham," prove it by deeds, not by words. "You
seek to kill me, a man." For now I do not say the son of God, I
do not say God, I do not say the Word, because the Word does
not die; I say this which you see because you can kill what you
see and you can offend him whom you do not see. Therefore,
"Abraham did not do this. You are doing the works of your
father." And still he does not say who this father of theirs is.

7. Now what did they answer? For, to some extent, they
began to realize that the Lord was not speaking about the
begetting of the flesh but about their way of life. And because
it is the practice of the Scriptures which they read to use the
word fornication in a spiritual sense, when the soul—
prostituted, so to speak—is made subject to many false gods,

10. Some editions read: "to be cleansed."
11. Mt 3.7–9.
12. Cf. *Tractate* 9.16.

154   ST. AUGUSTINE

they answered this: "Therefore they said to him, 'We have not been born of fornication. We have one Father, God.'" Already Abraham had lost his value. For they were confuted as they ought to have been confuted by the mouth speaking truth; for Abraham, whose deeds they did not imitate, was such a one, and they were boasting about their descent from him. And they changed their answer, saying among themselves, I believe: As often as we name Abraham, he will say to us, Why do you not imitate him about whose kinship you boast? We cannot imitate so great a man, holy, just, guiltless. Let us say that God is our father; let us see what he will say to us.

8. Immediately falsehood found something to say, and would Truth not find an answer to give? Let us hear what they say. Let us hear what they hear. "We have one Father, God," they say. "Jesus therefore said to them, 'If God were your Father, you would indeed love me; for I proceeded from God and have come. For I have not come of myself, but he sent me.'" You say that God is your father; recognize me at least as your brother. Nevertheless, for those who understand he has stirred up their hearts and has touched upon what he frequently says: "I have come not of myself; he sent me; I proceeded from God and have come." Remember what we frequently say: he came from him, and he came with him from whom he came. The sending of Christ, then, is the incarnation.[13]

(2) Indeed, that the Word proceeded from God is an eternal procession; he does not have a time, through whom time was made. Let no one ask in his heart: before the Word was, in what way did God exist? You should never say, Before the Word of God was. God never was without the Word because the Word is abiding, not transient; God, not a sound; he through whom heaven and earth were made, not that which passes away together with the things which were made on the earth.

(3) Therefore, he proceeded from him as God, as equal, as the only Son, as the Word of the Father; and he came

13. See *Tractate* 36.8 amd 40.6.

to us because the Word was made flesh that he might dwell among us.[14] His coming is his humanness; his abiding is his divinity. His divinity is that to which we are going; his humanity is the way by which we are going. Unless there were a way for us by which we might go, we would never reach him who abides.

9. "Why," he says, "do you not know my speech? Because you cannot hear my word." And so they could not know because they could not hear. But why could they not hear except that they were unwilling to be corrected through believing? And why is this? "You are of your father, the devil." How long will you keep mentioning your father? How long will you keep changing fathers, now Abraham, now God? Hear from the Son of God whose children you are: "You are of your father, the devil."

10. Now at this point one must watch out for the heresy of the Manichees. It maintains that there is a certain nature of evil and a certain race of dark spirits with their own leaders which dared to do battle against God. But that God, [they say], in order that this hostile race might not vanquish his kingdom, had sent against it his own entrails, so to speak, leaders from his own light; and that race had been vanquished from which the devil takes his origin.[15]

(2) They say that our flesh takes its origin from this source and they think it was in accord with this that it was said by the Lord, "You are from your father, the devil," because those men[16] were, so to speak, the nature of evil, taking their origin from the opposed race of the dark spirits. In this they err, in this they are blinded, in this they make themselves the race of dark spirits, by believing what is false against him by whom they were created.

14. Cf. Jn 1.14.
15. For a good short account of Mani's particular form of dualism, his conception of evil and "The Prince of Darkness and his Archons," and his whole cosmology, see G. Widengren, *Mani and Manichaeism*, 43–58. Connecting this with the concept of free will as developed by Augustine against Manichaean fatalism, see L. Koenen, "Augustine and Manichaeism in the Light of the Cologne Mani Codex," *Illinois Classical Studies* 3 (1978) 154–61.
16. I.e., the Jews.

(3) For every nature is good;[17] but man's nature has been spoiled through ill-will. What God made cannot be evil if man himself were not evil to himself. But clearly the Creator is the Creator, the creature is the creature; the creature cannot be equal to the Creator. Distinguish him who made from what he made. The bench cannot be equal to the carpenter, the column cannot be equal to the mason. And yet if the carpenter made the bench, he did not himself create the wood. But the Lord, our God, because he is omnipotent, also made what he made by the Word; he did not have anything from which he might make all things which he made, and yet he made them. For they were made because he willed, they were made because he spoke; but the things made cannot be compared to the Maker. You seek something to compare. Acknowledge the only Son.

(4) In what way, then, were the Jews children of the devil? By imitation, not by birth. Hear the common usage of holy Scripture. The prophet says to the Jews themselves, "Your father was an Amorite and your mother was a Cethaean."[18] The race of Amorite was a certain one from which the Jews derived no origin; the Cethaeans themselves also had their own nation altogether foreign to the race of the Jews. But because the Amorites and Cethaeans were impious and the Jews imitated their impieties, they found parents for themselves; and the Jews were not born from them, but by following their customs they were equally condemned.

17. For Augustine's views on the goodness of creation against the Manichaeans, see *DCD* 11.20–23; *De Genesi contra Manichaeos* 6.2.4 and 21.32 (PL 34.175 and 188–89); and *De Natura Boni,* esp 1–17 (PL 42.551–60 or A. Moon, *The De Nature Boni of Augustine,* esp. 67–77).

18. Ez 16.3. The Old Testament identifies the Amorites as an Hamitic race related to the Canaanites and located at various places in Palestine, especially southern Palestine; yet, while the name appears frequently, the usage is somewhat loose and sometimes more geographic than ethnic. The ancient Greek and Latin translations of the Bible introduce a variety of forms for the name of the ancient Hittites: Hethites, Hethaeans, Cethites, Cethaeans. Hence the Cethaean was a Hittite, one of the peoples who were living in Canaan before the Israelites settled there. On the Amorites and Hittites, see J. McKenzie, NCE 1.451–52; F. Hartman, NCE 6.1090–91; J. Hunt, JBC 1.221; and J. Steinmueller and K. Sullivan, *Catholic Biblical Encyclopedia* (New York 1956) 61–62, 219, 468–69.

(5) But do you perhaps ask where the devil himself is from? From that place, of course, where the rest of the angels are also from. But the rest of the angels persisted in their obedience; that angel, by disobedience and pride, fell and became the devil.

11. But now hear what the Lord says. "You are," he says, "of your father, the devil, and you will do the desires of your father." Behold from what source you are his children, because you desire such things, not because you were born from him. What are his desires? "He was a murderer from the beginning." Behold what "the desires of your father you will do" means: "You seek to kill me, a man who speaks to you the truth." And that one envied man and killed man. For when the devil envied man, clothed in a serpent,[19] he spoke to the woman, and from the woman he poisoned also the man. They died by listening to the devil,[20] whom they would not have listened to if they had willingly listened to the Lord; for mankind, placed between him who created and him who fell, ought to have obeyed the Creator, not the deceiver. Therefore "he was a murderer from the beginning."

(2) See the kind of murder, brothers. The devil is called a murderer, not armed with a sword, not girded with a weapon; he came to man, he planted an evil word, and he killed him. Do not, then, think that you are not a murderer when you persuade your brother to do evils; if you persuade your brother to do evils, you kill him. And, that you may know that you kill him, hear the psalm: "The sons of men, their teeth are weapons and arrows, their tongue a sharp sword."[21]

(3) You, then, "the desires of your father you will do." Therefore, you rage against the flesh because you cannot against the mind. "He was a murderer from the beginning," against the first man, of course. From that time from which it was possible to commit murder, he was a murderer; from that time from which man was made, it was possible to commit

19. I.e., assuming the form of a serpent. See Gn 3.1; cf. Wis 2.24 and Apoc (Rv) 12.9 and 20.2 where the serpent is identified with the devil.
20. Cf. Gn 3.3–4 and 19.
21. Ps 56 (57).5 (LXX).

murder. For man could not be killed unless man were first made. Thus "he was a murderer from the beginning." And in what way was he a murderer? "And he stood not in the truth." Therefore, he was in the truth and fell by not standing. And why "did he not stand in the truth"? "Because truth is not in him." Not as it is in Christ; the truth is in him in this way—that Christ himself is the Truth. If, then, he had stood in the truth, he would have stood in Christ, but "he stood not in the truth, because the truth is not in him."

12. "When he speaks a lie, he speaks of his own because he is a liar and the father thereof."[22] What is this? You heard the words of the Gospel; paying attention, you received them. Look, I repeat them, that you may realize what you should ask about. The Lord was saying about the devil the things which ought to have been said about the devil by the Lord. "He was a murderer from the beginning." That is true: for he killed the first man. "And he stood not in the truth," because he fell from the truth. "When he," of course, the devil himself, "speaks a lie, he speaks of his own because he is a liar and the father thereof."

(2) From these words some have thought that the devil has a father, and they have asked who is the devil's father. And here, in fact, the loathsome error of the Manichees has found yet another way whereby to deceive the uninformed. For they are accustomed to say: Suppose the devil was an angel and fell; sin began from him, as you say. Who was his father? We on the other hand say: Why, who of us ever said the devil had a father? And they say in reply, The Lord speaks it, the Gospel says it. Speaking about the devil, he asserts, "He was a murderer from the beginning, and stood not in the truth because the truth is not in him. When he speaks a lie, he speaks of his own because he is a liar *and his father is a liar.*"

13. Hear. Understand. I do not send you far away. Under-

---

22. This translation reproduces an ambiguity in the Latin which reads: *quia mendax est et pater eius,* because he is a liar and the father of it, i.e. of lying. This could be taken to say: because he is a liar and his father is a liar. Hence the exegetical problem discussed by Augustine. English translation does not tolerate the ambiguity; hence both NAB and CCD have "father of lies."

stand from the words themselves. The Lord said the devil is the father of lying. What is this? Hear what it is; just go back again over the words themselves and understand. For not everyone who lies is the father of his lying. For if you received the lie from another and told it, you indeed lied by making known the lie; but you are not the father of the lie itself because you received the lie from another. But the devil is a liar on his own; he himself begot his own lying, he heard it from no one. As God the Father begot his Son, Truth, so the devil after his fall begot a son, so to speak, lying.

(2) Now that you have heard this, go back again and cultivate again the words of the Lord. O Catholic mind, observe what you have heard; pay attention to what he says. "He"— who? the devil—"was a murderer from the beginning." We understand; he killed Adam. "And he stood not in truth." We understand, because he fell from the truth. "Because the truth is not in him." It is true; by withdrawing from the truth, he does not have the truth. "When he speaks a lie, he speaks of his own"; he does not receive from anywhere else what he would speak, "when he speaks a lie, he speaks of his own, because he is a liar *and the father thereof.*" He is a liar and the father of lying. Now perhaps you are a liar because you tell a lie; but you are not its father. For if you received what you say from the devil and you believed the devil, you are a liar, you are not the father of the lie. But that one, because he did not receive the lie from elsewhere, the lie with which the serpent might kill mankind as if with poison, he is the father of the lie, as God is the Father of the Truth. Depart from the father of lying, run to the Father of Truth. Embrace Truth that you may receive freedom.

14. It was, then, with their father that those Jews saw what they were saying. What, except a lie? And it was with his Father that the Lord saw what he was to say. What, if not himself? What, except the Word of the Father? What, if not the Truth of the Father, eternal and coeternal to the Father? Thus, "he was a murderer from the beginning, and he stood not in the truth because the truth is not in him. When he speaks a lie, he speaks of his own because he is a liar." And not

only is he a liar, but "also the *father thereof*"—that is, he is the father of the lie itself which he speaks because he himself begot his own lie. "But because I speak the truth, you do not believe me. Who of you convicts me of sin?" As I convict both you and your father. "If I am telling the truth, why do you not believe me?" Except that you are children of the devil.

15. "He who is of God hears the words of God. The reason you do not hear is that you are not of God." Again concentrate not on their nature but on their impairment.[23] Thus, these men are of God and they are not of God; by nature they are of God, by impairment they are not of God. I beg you, pay attention. In the Gospel you have the means by which you may be made sound against the poisonous and sacrilegious errors of the heretics. For the Manichees are also accustomed to say about these words: See that there are two natures, one good and the other evil; the Lord says it. What does the Lord say? "The reason you do not hear is that you are not of God." The Lord says these words. What, then, he asks, do you say to this? Hear what I say! They both are of God and they are not of God; by nature they are of God, by impairment they are not of God. For the good nature, which is of God, sinned through will, by believing what the devil persuaded, and it was impaired; therefore, it seeks the Physician because it is not healthy. See what I am saying.

(2) But it seems impossible to you that they be of God and yet not be of God; hear that it is not impossible. They are of God and they are not of God, just as they are the children of Abraham and are not the children of Abraham. Here you have it; it is not such as you say. Hear the Lord himself. He said to them, "I know that you are the children of Abraham." Would the Lord lie? Perish the thought! Is it true, then, what the Lord said? It is true. Is it true, then, that those men were the children of Abraham? It is true. Hear him denying it himself. For he who said, "You are the children of Abraham," himself denied that they were the children of Abraham: "If you are Abraham's children, do the deed of Abraham. But

23. The Latin word is *vitium*. Perhaps one might also translate it "a defect of their character" or simply "fault."

now you seek to kill me, a man who says to you the truth which I have heard from God. Abraham did not do this. You do your father's works." That is, the works of the devil. How, therefore, were they both the children of Abraham and not the children of Abraham? He showed both in them; they were the children of Abraham on account of the origin of the flesh, and they were not the children of Abraham on account of the impairment of the devil's persuasion.

(3) So, too, pay attention to our Lord and God; they were both of him and not of him. How were they of him? Because he himself created the man from whom they were born. How were they of him? Because he himself is the builder of nature, he himself is the creator of flesh and soul. How then were they not of him? Because by their own efforts they had become impaired. They were not of him because, by imitating the devil, they had become children of the devil.

16. Therefore, the Lord God came to man the sinner. You have heard two names, both man and sinner. In that he is a man, he is of God; in that he is a sinner, he is not of God. Let the impairment be distinguished from the nature. Let the nature be recognized from which the Creator is to be praised; let the impairment be recognized on account of which the Physician is to be summoned.

(2) What the Lord said, then, "He who is of God hears the words of God. The reason you do not hear is that you are not of God," [here] he did not distinguish the worth of natures or find, beside his own[24] soul and flesh, any nature in men which had not been impaired by sin; but because he had foreknown who would believe, these he said were of God because they would be reborn of God by the adoption of regeneration. To these pertains "he who is of God hears the words of God."

(3) But the following words, "The reason you do not hear is that you are not of God," were said to those who not only were impaired because of sin (for this evil was common to all), but who also were foreknown that they would not believe with that

24. or "their" since *suus* in Christian Latin sometimes is used for *eorum;* see A. Blaise, *Manuel des latin chrétien* (Strasbourg 1955) 114. I take this to mean that only Christ's "soul and flesh" were unimpaired by sin.

faith by which alone they could have been freed from the bond[25] of sin. Accordingly, he foreknew that those to whom he was saying such things would persist in that which they were of the devil, that is, that they would die in their own sins and impiety, in which they were like him, and that they would not come to the regeneration in which they would be children of God, that is, born of God by whom they had been created as men. The Lord spoke in accord with this predestination,[26] not because he found some person who either already was of God as regards regeneration or as regards nature was no longer of God.

25. Cf. Acts 8.23.

26. Augustine's complex, difficult, and somewhat pessimistic views on predestination are not easy to summarize, especially since he seems to have been still thinking about the problem in the last years of his life when his seemingly set teaching was challenged by the monks of Hadrumetum. While all men have the capacity for salvation through faith and love, God freely chooses or elects only some men to give them aid in exercising this capacity; he gives some a prevenient grace to overcome original sin and accept the faith, and this is one type of predestination. For those who have the faith, he gives efficacious graces to assist them in persevering through love to salvation, and this is a second type of predestination. God both pre-elects these individuals and prepares graces for them; he foreknows whom he will choose and what graces they need to attain salvation. But human beings still have complete freedom of will and must choose to cooperate with God's grace. Original and particular sin condemn the sinner and he deserves punishment; therefore the condemned are justly punished and the saved are the beneficiaries of God's mercy. God wills that all be saved, but why he does not give the necessary graces to all is a deep and inscrutable secret which he does not reveal. See E. Teselle, *Augustine the Theologian*, 176–82, 319–38; E. Gilson, *The Christian Philosophy of Saint Augustine*, 154–57; P. Brown, *Augustine of Hippo*, 398–407. M. Pontet discusses predestination as presented in Augustine's sermons in *L'Exégèse de s. Augustin Prédicateur* (Paris, 1946?) 480–514. See also the brief remarks in the introduction (28)–(30), FOTC 78.

TRACTATE 43

On John 8.48–59

N THE passage of the holy Gospel which was read today, we learn patience from power. For what are we, servants to the Lord, sinners to the Just, a creature to the Creator? Nevertheless, just as if we are something evil, we are of ourselves, so whatever good we are, we are from him and through him.

(2) And nothing does a man so seek as power. He has the Lord Christ, a great power; but first let him imitate his patience that he may come to power. Who of us would listen patiently if it were said to someone, "You have a devil"? And this was said to him who not only saved men, but also gave orders to devils.

2. For when the Jews had said, "Do not we say well that you are a Samaritan and have a devil?" he denied one of these two accusations against him; he did not deny the other. For he answered and said, "I do not have a devil." He did not say, "I am not a Samaritan." And there were definitely two accusations. Although he did not return abuse for abuse, although he did not refute insult with insult, nevertheless it suited him to deny one thing, not to deny the other.

(2) Not without reason, brothers. For Samaritan is interpreted as guard.[1] He knew that he was our guard. For "he neither slumbers nor sleeps, who guards Israel"[2] and "Unless

---

1. Augustine's definition of Samaritan as guard is one of the two meanings given the name by the Fathers; the other is observer or keeper of the Law. Jerome defines it both ways; see *Liber Interpretationis Hebraicorum Nominum* s.v., 4 Kgs, Is, Lk, and Acts (CCL 72.117, 122, 142, 148) and *Epistula* 75.5 (PL 22.688). These two meanings conform to modern etymologies; see J. Montgomery, *The Samaritans* (New York 1907 and 1968) 317–19.

2. Ps 120 (121).4

the Lord guard the city, in vain do they who guard watch."[3]
He who is our Creator is our guard. For did it suit him that we
be redeemed but not that we be saved?

(3) Accordingly, that you may know more fully the mystery
of why he ought not to have denied that he was a Samaritan,
consider that well known parable when a certain man was
going down from Jerusalem to Jericho and fell upon robbers
who wounded him seriously and left him half-dead on the
road. A priest came along and ignored him; a Levite came
along and he, too, passed him by. A certain Samaritan came
by; he is our guard. He approached the wounded man and he
exercised mercy, and he showed himself a neighbor to him
whom he did not consider a foreigner.[4] To their objections,
then, he only answered that he did not have a devil, but not
that he was not a Samaritan.

3. Then, after such an insult, he said only this about his
own glory: "But I honor," he said, "my Father, and you have
dishonored me." That is, I do not honor myself, that I may
not seem arrogant to you. I have one whom I may honor. But
if you would recognize me, as I honor the Father, so also you
would honor me. I do what I ought; you do not do what you
ought.

4. "But I," he said, "seek not my own glory; there is one
who seeks and judges." Whom does he intend to be understood except the Father?

(2) Just as in another place he says, "The Father does not
judge anyone, but has given all judgment to the Son,"[5] here
also he says, "I seek not my own glory; there is one who seeks
and judges." If, therefore, the Father judges, how does he not
judge anyone and has given all judgment to the Son?

5. That we may resolve this question, pay attention; it can
be resolved by a similar expression. You have it written: "God
tempts no one."[6] Again you have it written: "For the Lord
your God tempts you to learn whether you love him."[7] Surely

3. Ps 126 (127).1.
4. See Lk 10.30–37.
5. Jn 5.22; cf. *Tractates* 19.5, 21.11–15, and 23.13.
6. Jas 1.13.
7. Dt 13.3 (NAB 13.4).

this is the question, you see. For how does "God tempt no one" and how does "the Lord your God tempt you to learn whether you love him"? Likewise it has been written: "Fear is not in love, but perfect love casts out fear."[8] And in another place it has been written: "The fear of the Lord is pure, enduring forever."[9] And there is the same question. For how does "perfect love cast out fear" if "fear of the Lord is pure" endures "forever?"

6. We understand, therefore, that there are two temptings, one which seduces, the other which proves: as to the one which seduces, "The Lord tempts no one," as to the one which proves, "The Lord, your God, tempts you to learn whether you love him."

(2) But again also here another question arises, how "He tempts to learn" from whom nothing can be concealed before he tempts? God is not unknowing; but it is said, "to learn," that is, that he may make you learn. Such expressions are in our ordinary conversations and are also found in eloquent authors. I shall mention something from our ordinary conversation. A ditch is called blind, not because it has itself lost its eyes but because, by being concealed, it causes people to not see it. I shall mention something also from those authors. A certain one [of them][10] says that lupines are sad, that is, bitter, not because they are themselves sad but because, when tasted, they sadden, that is, they make people sad. Now there are also expressions of this kind in the Scriptures. They who exert effort in posing such questions do not exert effort in resolving such questions. Thus "the Lord your God tempts you to learn." What is "to learn"? That he may make you learn "whether you love him." Job was unknown to himself but he was not unknown to God; he permitted a tempter and made him a knower of himself.

7. And what about the two fears? There is a servile fear and a pure fear; there is a fear that you may suffer punishment and another fear that you may lose justice.[11] That fear, that

8. 1 Jn 4.18.
9. Ps 18 (19).10.
10. Vergil, *Georgics* 1.75.
11. The two fears mentioned in section 5 from 1 Jn 4.18 and Ps 18 (19).10.

you may suffer punishment, is the servile one. What great thing is it to fear punishment? Both the most wicked slave does this and the cruelest robber does this. It is not a great thing to fear punishment, but it is a great thing to love justice. Then, does he who loves justice fear nothing? Surely he fears, not that he may fall into punishment, but that he may lose justice. My brothers, believe this and judge from that which you love. One of you loves money. Will I find someone, do you think, who does not love it? Nevertheless, from that very thing which he loves let him understand what I am saying. He fears loss. Why does he fear loss? Because he is fond of money. He fears that he may lose his money with as much intensity as he loves his money. Therefore, someone is found to be a lover of justice; and he may have more fear of loss in his heart, he may have more fear that he will be despoiled of justice than you have that you will be despoiled of your money. This is a pure fear, this endures forever. Love does not take it away nor cast it out, but rather embraces it and holds it as a companion as long as it possesses it. For we come to the Lord that we may see him face to face; there a pure fear protects us, for that fear does not disturb, but strengthens. An adulterous woman fears that her husband may come and a pure one fears that her husband may leave.

8. Therefore, as regards one temptation, "God tempts no one," but as regards the other, "The Lord, your God tempts you." And as regards one fear, "Fear is not in love, but perfect love casts out fear," but as regards the other fear, "Pure fear of the Lord" endures "forever." So also in this passage, as regards one judgment, "The Father does not judge anyone, but has given all judgment to the Son," but as regards the other judgment, "I," he says, "seek not my own glory; there is one who seeks and judges."

9. And let this question be resolved from the word itself. In the Gospel you have a punitive judgment mentioned: "He who does not believe has already been judged."[12] And in another place: "The hour will come when those who are in the

12. Jn 3.18; cf. *Tractate* 12.12.

graves will hear his voice and those who have done good shall come forth unto the resurrection of life, those who have done evil unto the resurrection of judgment."[13] See how he put judgment for damnation and punishment.

(2) And yet if judgment were always taken for damnation, would we hear in the psalm, "Judge me, God?"[14] There judgment has been put as regards affliction, here as regards distinction. How, as regards distinction? As he himself who said, "Judge me, God," explains. For read and see what follows. What does "Judge me, God" mean? "And distinguish my cause," he says, "from the nation that is not holy." Therefore, as regards that which was said, "Judge me, God, and distinguish my cause from the nation that is not holy," the Lord Christ now says, "I seek not my own glory; there is one who seeks and who judges."

(3) How "is there one who seeks and who judges?" There is the Father to distinguish and separate my glory from your glory. For you glory in regard to this world; I do not glory in regard to this world, I who say to the Father, "Father, glorify me with that glory I had with you before the world was."[15] What does "with that glory" mean? Distinguished from human pretentiousness. As regards this, the Father judges. What is "judges?" He distinguishes. What does he distinguish? The glory of his Son from the glory of human beings; for thus was it said, "God, your God, has anointed you with the oil of gladness above yours fellows."[16] For, because he became man, he ought not immediately be compared to us. We are men with sin; he is without sin. We are men acquiring both death and transgression from Adam; he has acquired mortal flesh from the virgin but no iniquity. Furthermore, we were neither born because we wanted to be, nor do we live as long as we want to, nor do we die as we want. He chose from whom he could be born before he was born; after he was born, he brought it about that he be adored by the Magi. As an infant he grew and showed that he was God by his miracles, and presented him-

---

13. Jn 5.28–29; cf. *Tractate* 19.17–18.
14. Ps 42 (43).1.   15. Jn 17.5.
16. Ps 44 (45).8.

self as a human by his weakness. Finally he chose also the kind of death, that is, that he hang on a cross and that he fix the cross itself on the foreheads of the faithful, so that the Christian may say, "God forbid that I should glory except in the cross of our Lord Jesus Christ."[17] On the cross itself, when he wanted, he abandoned his body and departed; he lay in the tomb itself as long as he wanted and, when he wanted, he rose up as from a bed.

(4) Therefore, brothers, as regards the very form of the servant (for who worthily says this: "In the beginning was the Word, and the Word was with God, and the Word was God"?[18]), as regards the very form, I say, of the servant there is much difference between the glory of Christ and the glory of the rest of mankind.[19] About this glory he was speaking when he heard that he had a devil: "I seek not my own glory; there is one who seeks and who judges."

10. But you, O Lord, what do you say about yourself? "Amen, amen, I say to you, if anyone keeps my word, he will not see death forever." You say, he says, "You have a devil." I call you to life; keep my word and you will not die. They heard: "He who keeps my word will not see death forever." And they were angered because they had already died by that death which was to be avoided. "The Jews therefore said, 'Now we know that you have a devil. Abraham is dead, and the prophets; and you say, If anyone keeps my word, he will not taste death forever.'"

(2) See the Scriptures' mode of expression: "He will not see death," that is, "will taste." "He will see death, he will taste death." Who sees? Who tastes? What eyes does a person have that he may see when he dies? When at its coming death closes the eyes themselves that they might not see anything, how is it said: "He will not see death"? Likewise with what palate, with what jaws is death tasted that what he is tasting may be discerned? When it takes away all sensation, what will remain on the palate? But "will see" and "will taste" were said in place of "will experience."

17. Gal 6.14.   18. Jn 1.1.
19. Cf. Phil 2.3–11.

11. The Lord, about to die, was saying these things (it is insufficient for me to say) to those about to die; for "the Lord's also are the passageways of death,"[20] as the psalm says. Since, then, he was speaking to those who were also going to die, and he was speaking as one who was about to die, what do his words mean: "He who keeps my word will not see death forever," except that the Lord sees another death from which he came to free us, a second death, an everlasting death, the death of Gehenna, the death of damnation with the devil and his angels? That one is the true death, for this one is a passage. What is this death? The leaving behind of the body, the putting off of heavy baggage; but only if other baggage should not be carried by which a person would be hurled into Gehenna. Therefore, about this death the Lord said, "He who keeps my word will not see death forever."

12. Let us not dread this death, but let us fear that one. What is more serious, however, many, perversely, by fearing this death, have fallen into that one. It was said to some: Adore idols; and if you do not do it, you will be killed. Or just as that well-known Nabuchodonosor said, "If you do not do it, you will be sent into the furnace of burning fire."[21] Many were afraid and adored; not wishing to die, they died. By fearing the death from which there is no escape, they fell into the death from which they could happily escape if they were not unhappily afraid of that one from which there is no escape.

(2) You were born a human being; you are going to die. Where will you go so as not to die? What will you do so as not to die? That he might comfort you who are going to die of necessity, your Lord deemed it good to die of his own will. When you see that Christ died, do you disdain to die?[22] Thus you *will* die; you have no means to escape from this. Let it be today, let it be tomorrow; it *will* be, the debt must be paid. What then does a person do, fearing, fleeing, hiding himself that he may not be found by the enemy? Does he do something so that he will not die? Only that he may die a little later.

20. Ps 67 (68).21.
21. Dn 3.15; cf. 3.6.
22. Cf. *Tractate* 3.13.

He does not receive a release from the debt, but asks for a delay. However long it is delayed, what is delayed will come.

(3) Let us fear that death which the three men feared when they said to the king, "Our God can free us even from this flame; but even if he will not . . ."[23] There was the fear of that death which the Lord is now threatening, when they said, But even if he is unwilling to free us openly, he can crown us secretly. Accordingly, the Lord himself also, about to make martyrs and about to be the head of martyrs, said, "Do not be afraid of those who kill the body and after have not what they can do."[24] How "have not what they can do"? What if, when they killed, they threw the body out to be torn by beasts and ripped apart by birds? Cruelty still seems to have something that it can do. But to whom does it do it? To him who has departed. The body is present, but there is no sensation. The dwelling place lies there, the dweller has departed. Therefore, afterwards "they have not what they can do," for they can do nothing to that which is without sensation. "But fear him who has the power to kill both the body and the soul in the Gehenna of fire."[25] See the death about which he was speaking when he said, "He who keeps my word will not see death forever." Let us, then, brothers, keep his word in faith; we are going to reach the vision when we shall have received the fullest freedom.

13. But these dead men, indignant and predestined to eternal death, answered insolently and said, "Now we know that you have a devil. Abraham is dead, and the prophets." But neither Abraham nor the prophets died with this death which the Lord intends to be understood. For they are dead, yet they live; these men were living, and yet they were dead. For in a certain place, answering to the Sadducees who were proposing a question about the resurrection, the Lord himself said this: "But have you not read about the resurrection of the dead" as the Lord said to Moses from the bush, "I am the God of Abraham, the God of Isaac, the God of Jacob? He is not the God of the dead, but of the living."[26] Therefore, if they live, let

23. Dn 3.17–18.   24. Lk 12.4; cf. Mt 10.28.
25. Mt 10.28; cf. Lk 12.5.   26. Mt 22.31–32, quoting Ex 3.6.

us work to live thusly so that we can live with them when we have died. "Whom do you make yourself?" they say, that you may say, "He who keeps my word will not see death forever" when you know that both Abraham is dead and the prophets.

14. "Jesus answered, 'If I glorify myself, my glory is nothing. He who glorifies me is my Father.'" He says this because of that which they said, "Whom do you make yourself?" For he refers his glory to the Father, from whom it is that he is God.

(2) Sometimes the Arians misrepresent our faith from this sentence; and they say, See, the Father is greater because, of course, he glorifies the Son. Heretic, have you not read the Son himself also saying that he glorifies his Father?[27] If he glorifies the Son and the Son glorifies the Father, put aside your obstinacy; acknowledge their equality, correct your perversity.

15. "He who gives me glory," therefore, he says, "is my Father of whom you say that he is our God, and you have not known him." See, my brothers, how he shows that the Father of Christ is God himself who was announced also to the Jews. I say this precisely because, again, certain heretics say that the God announced in the Old Testament is not the Father of Christ, but some leader or other of the evil angels. The Manichees[28] are ones who say this; the Marcionites[29] are ones who say this. There are also other heretics, perhaps either those whom I need not mention, or all of whom cannot be recalled by me at the present; there were not lacking, nonetheless, those who would say this. Therefore, pay attention that you may have something to say against them also.

27. Cf. Jn 17.4.

28. E.g., see Augustine, *De Haeresibus* 46.15 (CCL 46.318).

29. The Marcionites were a Christian Gnostic sect founded by Marcion, fl. c. A.D. 140–160. He held that the Creator God of the Old Testament was the Demiurge, an intermediate being between man and the perfect God; the Demiurge had created this world and was its tyrannical ruler as described in the Old Testament. He was a God of Law, wholly unlike the God of Love whom Jesus came to reveal; Jesus was in fact the visible embodiment of this perfect God, not of the Demiurge. See A. Stephenson, "Marcion," NCE 9.193–94, and ODCC² 870–71. For a modification of this standard view see E. Blackman, *Marcion and His Influence* (London 1948).

(2) The Lord Christ says that he is his Father whom they said was their God and they knew him not; for if they had known him, they would have accepted his Son. "But I," he says, "know him." To those judging in regard to the flesh he could have seemed arrogant also from this, that he said, "I know him." But see what follows: "If I shall say that I do not know him, I shall be like you—a liar!" Therefore, let arrogance not be so guarded against that truth is abandoned. "But I do know him and I do keep his word." He, as the Son, was speaking the word of the Father, and he was himself the Father's Word, who was speaking to men.

16. "Abraham your father rejoiced that he might see my day; he saw it and was glad." He, the seed of Abraham, the creator of Abraham, gives great testimony to Abraham. "Abraham rejoiced," he says, "that he might see my day." Not, He feared, but "he rejoiced that he might see." For there was in him the love which casts out fear.[30] He did not say, He rejoiced because he saw, but "he rejoiced that he might see." Believing, of course, he rejoiced by hoping that he might see by understanding. "He saw." And what more could the Lord Jesus Christ have said or what more ought he have said? "He saw," he said, "and was glad." Who will describe this joy, my brothers? If those for whom the Lord opened the eyes of the flesh rejoiced, what sort of joy was there for him who saw with the eyes of the heart the ineffable Light, the enduring Word, the Brightness shining upon godly minds, the unfailing Wisdom, God remaining with the Father and one day to come in flesh and yet not withdraw from the breast of the Father? Abraham saw all this.

(2) For, as regards what he said, "my day," it can be uncertain of what he was speaking, whether the temporal day of the Lord on which he was to come in the flesh or the day of the Lord which knows not a rising, knows not a setting. But I have no doubt that father Abraham knew the whole. And where shall I find it? Can it be that the testimony of our Lord Jesus Christ ought to suffice for us? Let us think that we cannot find

30. Cf. 1 Jn 4.18 and sections 5–8, above.

because it is perhaps difficult how it is clear that Abraham "rejoiced that he might see the day" of Christ, "and he saw and was glad." And if we do not find it, could Truth have lied? Let us believe in the Truth, and let us not at all doubt about the good deserts of Abraham.

(3) Nevertheless, hear one place which occurs to me at the moment. When father Abraham sent his slave to seek a wife for his son Isaac, he bound him by this oath,[31] that he should faithfully fulfill what he was ordered and that he also himself might know what he was doing.[32] For an important thing was being done when a spouse was being sought for the seed of Abraham. But that the servant might learn this which Abraham knew, that he did not desire grandchildren carnally and that he did not have any carnal conception about his progeny, he said to his slave whom he was sending, "Put your hand under my thigh and swear by the God of heaven."[33] What does the God of heaven want to signify in respect to the thigh of Abraham? Already you understand the hidden meaning:[34] by the thigh, his progeny. Therefore, what was that swearing but a signifying that the God of heaven would come in the flesh from the progeny of Abraham? The stupid reproach Abraham because he said, "Put your hand under my thigh." They who reproach the flesh of Christ reproach the action of Abraham. Let us, however, my brothers, if we acknowledge that the flesh of Christ is to be honored, not despise that thigh, but let us receive what was said in prophecy. For Abraham was a prophet. The prophet of whom? Of his seed and of the Lord. He signified his seed by saying, "Put your hand under my thigh." He signified the Lord by adding, "and swear by the God of heaven."

17. The Jews were angered and replied, "You are not yet fifty years old and you have seen Abraham!" And the Lord, "Amen, amen, I say to you, before Abraham came to be, I am!" Weigh the words and learn the mystery! "Before

31. *sacramentum* in its classical connotation.
32. Cf. Gn 24.2–4.
33. Gn 24.2–3.
34. *sacramentum* in its more unusual Christian connotation.

Abraham came to be." Understand: "came to be" refers to the making of the human [substance]; but "I am" refers to the divine substance. "Came to be" because Abraham is a creature. He did not say, Before Abraham was, I was, but, "Before Abraham *came to be*"—who would not come to be except through me—"I am." Neither did he say this: Before Abraham came to be, I came to be. For "in the beginning God made heaven and earth",[35] for "in the beginning was the Word."[36] "Before Abraham came to be, I am." Acknowledge the Creator, distinguish the creature. He who was speaking came to be the seed of Abraham; and that Abraham might come to be, he himself was before Abraham.

18. Now at this, as if at a quite obvious insult of Abraham, they were more bitterly disturbed. The Lord Christ seemed to them to have blasphemed because he said, "Before Abraham came to be, I am." "Therefore they took up stones to throw at him." Where would such great hardness run except to its like? "But Jesus," as a man, as in the form of a servant, as lowly, as about to suffer, as about to die, as about to redeem us by his blood, not as he who is, not as "in the beginning was the Word and the Word was with God." For when they took up stones to throw at him, what great thing was it were the earth, straightway gaping open, to swallow them up and they would find hell instead of stones? It was not a great time for God; but patience was more to be recommended than power displayed. Therefore, "He hid himself" from them so that he not be stoned. As a man, he fled from stones, but woe to those from whose stony hearts God has fled!

35. Gn 1.1.
36. Jn 1.1.

TRACTATE 44

On John 9

HE DAY will not be long enough if we should try to explicate the whole of the lengthy reading just heard concerning the man born blind, whom the Lord Jesus enlightened, in accordance with its own worth, considering each detail as best we are able. And so I ask each of you and I advise you, my beloved people, that you not require of us a discourse on those matters which are clear; for it will be too tedious to tarry on every point. Therefore, I present briefly the mystery of the enlightenment of this blind man. Of course, those things, both the words and deeds, that our Lord Jesus Christ did should produce astonishment and wonder: the deeds because they were things done, the words because they were signs.[1]

(2) If, then, we should think about what that which was done signifies, this blind man is the human race, for this blindness happened through sin in the first man from whom we all have taken the origin not only of death, but also of wickedness. For if the blindness is lack of faith and the enlightenment faith, whom does Christ find faithful when he comes?[2] In as much as the Apostle, who was born in a nation of prophets, says, "All of us, too, were once by nature children of wrath, even as the rest."[3] If "children of wrath," then children of vengeance, children of punishment, children of Gehenna. How "by nature," except that when the first man sinned, a

---

1. Cf. *Tractate* 24.2 and 25.2, 5.
2. A word play is obscured in the English: Whom does Christ *come upon* as a faithful one when he *comes?*
3. Cf. Eph 2.3.

175

flaw[4] grew in the place of nature?[5] If the flaw has grown in the place of nature, every man is born blind as regards his mind. For if he sees, he has no need of a leader; if he has need of a leader and an enlightener, then he is blind from birth.

2. The Lord came. What did he do? He set forth a great mystery. "He spat on the ground." From his saliva he made mud because the Word was made flesh.[6] And he besmeared the eyes of the blind man. He was besmeared and yet did not see. He sent him to the pool which is called Siloe. And the Evangelist was concerned to explain to us the name of this pool, and he said, "which is interpreted 'Who has been sent.'" You already know who has been sent; for unless he had been sent, no one of us would be sent away from wickedness. Therefore, he washed his eyes in that pool which is interpreted "Who has been sent"; he was baptized in Christ. If then, when in some way he baptized him in himself, he then enlightened him; perhaps when he besmeared him, he made him a catechumen. Indeed the profundity of a symbol so great and mysterious can be explained and expounded in various ways.[7] But let this be enough for you, my beloved people; you have heard a great mystery.

(2) Ask a man: Are you a Christian? If he is a pagan or a Jew, he has answered you: I am not. But if he said, "I am," you still ask him: Are you a catechumen or one of the faithful? If he answered, A catechumen, he was besmeared, not yet washed. But besmeared with what? Ask and he answers; ask him in whom he believes. For the very reason that he is a catechumen, he says: In Christ. Look now, I am speaking both to the faithful and to the catechumens. What did I say about the spittle and the mud? That the Word was made flesh. The catechumens also hear this; but for the purpose for which they have been besmeared this does not suffice for them.

---

4. In Latin, *vitium*.

5. Surely with Rom 5.12–19 in mind; cf. *Tractate* 30.5 and 49.12.

6. Cf. Jn 1.14.

7. Some codices read this sentence as follows: Indeed the nature of so great a symbol can be explained and its profundity can be expounded in various ways.

Let them hurry to the baptismal font if they seek light.[8]

3. Now then, on account of certain questions in this reading itself, rather than give a complete exegesis, let us run rapidly through the words of the Lord and of the whole reading itself. "As he passed by, he saw a man blind," not blind in any way whatever, but "from birth. And his disciples asked him, 'Rabbi.'" You know that Rabbi means teacher. They called him teacher because they very much wanted to learn; so, of course, they proposed a question to the Lord as to a teacher. "'Who sinned, this man or his parents, that he should be born blind?' Jesus replied, 'Neither has this man sinned, nor his parents,'" that he should be born blind.

(2) What is this that he has said? If no man is without sin, were the parents of this blind man without sin? Was he himself born blind even without original sin? Or had he while living added nothing? Can it be that because he had closed eyes, his lusts were not at all awake? How great are the evils the blind commit! From what evil does the evil mind abstain, even with closed eyes? He could not see, but he knew how to think, and perhaps to lust for something which as a blind man he could not accomplish; but in his heart he could be judged by the Searcher of the heart.

(3) If then both his parents had sin and this man had sin, why did the Lord say, "Neither has this man sinned, nor his parents," except with regard to what he had been asked about: "that he should be born blind"? For his parents had sin; but it did not happen that he was born blind because of sin itself. If then it did not happen because of his parents' sin that he was born blind, why was he born blind? Hear the Master teaching; he seeks one who believes that he may make him one who understands. He himself tells the reason why that man was born blind. "Neither has this man sinned," he says, "nor his parents, but it was to let God's works show forth in him."

4. What follows then? "I must work the works of him who sent me." Look, he is "Who has been sent,"[9] in whom the blind

---

8. Cf. *Tractate* 11.3–4.
9. See section 2 on Jn 9.7: Siloe, which means "Who has been sent."

man washed his face. And see what he said, "I must work the works of him who sent me while it is day." Remind yourself how he gives total glory to that one from whom he is because that one has a Son who is from him but he does not himself have one from whom he is.[10] But why, O Lord, did you say, "while it is day"? Hear why. "The night comes when no one can work." Not even you, Lord? Will that night have such great power that not even you, whose work the night is, can work in it? For I think, Lord Jesus, rather, I do not think, but I believe and I assert, that you were there when God said, "'Let there be light,' and light was made."[11] For if he made it by the Word, he made it through you. And therefore, it has been said, "Through him all things were made, and apart from him nothing was made."[12] "God divided between the light and the darkness; he called the light 'day' and the darkness he called 'night.'"[13]

5. What is that night on which, when it comes, no one will be able to work? Hear what the day is and then you will understand what the night is. From whom will we hear what this day is? Let him speak himself: "As long as I am in this world, I am the light of the world." Look, he is himself the day. The blind man will wash his eyes in the day that he may see the day. "As long as I," he says, "am in the world, I am the light of the world." Therefore, there will be a night of some sort—when Christ is not there; and for this reason no one will be able to work.

(2) It remains to inquire, my brothers, bear with me patiently as I inquire. Together with you I seek; together with you I shall find him by whom I seek. It is certain, it is clearly and definitively set down that the Lord mentioned himself as the day in this passage, that is, as the light of the world. "As long as I," he says, "am in this world, I am the light of the world." Therefore, he himself works. But how long is he in this world? Do we think, brothers, that he was here then and is not here now? If we think this, then, now, after the ascension

10. See, e.g., *Tractates* 19.13, 29.5, and 43.14.
11. Gn 1.3.   12. Jn 1.3.
13. Gn 1.4–5.

of the Lord, this night has come to be fearful when no one can work. If this night has come to be after the ascension of the Lord, from what source did the Apostles do such great works? Was this night when the Holy Spirit, coming and filling all who were in the one place, gave to them to speak in the tongues of all nations?[14] Was it night when that lame man was made whole at the word of Peter,[15] or rather at the word of the Lord dwelling in Peter? Was it night when the sick were put down with their beds, when the Apostles were passing by, so that they might be touched even by their shadow as they passed by?[16] But when the Lord was here, he made no one whole by his shadow as he passed by; but he himself had said to his disciples, "You will do greater [works] than these."[17] The Lord has indeed said, "You will do greater [works] than these." But let flesh and blood not exalt itself; let it hear him saying, "Without me you can do nothing."[18]

6. Well then, what shall we say about this night? When will it be, when no one can work? This will be the night of the ungodly, this will be the night of those to whom it is said at the end, "Go into everlasting fire which has been prepared for the devil and his angels."[19] But night was named, not flame, not fire. Hear that it is also night. About a certain slave he says, "Bind him hands and feet and cast him into the exterior darkness."[20]

(2) Therefore, let a person work while he is alive that he may not be prevented by that night when no one can work. Now is the time for faith to work through love; and if we work now, this is day, this is Christ. Hear what he promises and do not think him absent. He himself said, "Behold, I am with you." How long? Let there not be anxiety in us who live. If it were possible, we would also make our posterity, who are yet to be, most secure about this word. "Behold," he says, "I am with you even to the consummation of the world."[21] This day which is completed by the circuit of this sun has a few hours;

14. See Acts 2.1–12.   15. See Acts 3.1–10.
16. See Acts 5.15.   17. Jn 14.12.
18. Jn 15.5.   19. Mt 25.41.
20. Mt 22.13.   21. Mt 28.20.

the day of the presence of Christ is prolonged even to the consummation of the world.

(3) Indeed, after the resurrection of the living and the dead, when he has said to those on his right, "Come, blessed of my Father, take possession of the kingdom,"[22] and when he has said to those on the left, "Go into everlasting fire which has been prepared for the devil and his angels," there will be the night when no one can work but can receive the results of his work. There is one time for working, another for receiving; for the Lord will render to each one according to his works.[23] While you live, act, if you are going to act; there will then be a mighty night which is to envelop the ungodly.

(4) But even now every faithless person, when he dies, is caught up in that night; it is not possible to do any work therein. In that night the rich man was burning and he sought a drop of water from the finger of the poor man.[24] He suffered pain, was tortured, and confessed; yet no help was given to him and he tried to do some good. He said to Abraham, "Father Abraham, send Lazarus" to my brothers, that he may tell them what occurs here "so they may not also come to this place of torments."[25] O unhappy man! When you were living, then was the time of working; now you are already in the night in which no one can work.

7. "When he had said these things, he spat on the ground and made mud with his saliva; and he smeared the mud on his eyes and said to him, 'Go, and wash in the pool of Siloe' (which is interpreted 'Who has been sent'). So he went off, and washed, and came seeing." Since this is clear, let us pass over it.

8. "The neighbors, therefore, and they who had seen him before as a beggar, said, 'Is not this he who used to sit and beg? Some said, 'This is he.' But others, 'Not at all, but one like him.'" His opened eyes had changed his facial appearance. "He said, 'I am he.'" A grateful voice, in order that an ungrateful one not be condemned. "They said therefore to him,

22. Mt 25.34.
24. See Lk 16.19–31.
23. Cf. Mt 16.27.
25. Cf. Lk 16.24, 27–28.

'How were your eyes opened?' He answered, 'That man who is called Jesus made mud and anointed my eyes, and said to me, "Go to the pool of Siloe and wash," and I went and washed, and I saw.'" Look, he became a proclaimer of grace; look, he preaches the Gospel. Seeing, he confesses. That blind man confessed, and the heart of the ungodly was broken because they had not in their heart what that man now had in his face. "They said to him, 'Where is he who opened your eyes?' He said, 'I do not know.'" In these words his mind was like one now anointed but not yet seeing. Let us put it in this way, brothers, as though he had that anointing in his mind. He preaches and knows not whom he preaches.

9. "They took the man who had been blind to the Pharisees. (Now it was the Sabbath when Jesus made the mud and opened his eyes.) Again the Pharisees asked him how he had recovered his sight. But he said to them, 'He put mud on my eyes, and I washed, and I see.' Therefore, some of the Pharisees said." Not all, but *some;* for some were already being anointed. What then were they saying, neither seeing nor anointed? "This man, who does not keep the Sabbath, is not from God." Rather, he himself who was without sin was keeping it. For the spiritual Sabbath is this:[26] not to have sin. In fact, brothers, God apprises [us] of this when he consigns the Sabbath: "You will not do any servile work whatever."[27] These are the words of God consigning the Sabbath: "You will not do any servile work whatever." Now inquire of the previous readings what servile work is, and hear the Lord: "Everyone who commits sin is a slave of sin."[28] But they, neither seeing, as I said, nor anointed, were observing the Sabbath carnally, but violating it spiritually. "Others said, 'How can a man who is a sinner perform these signs?'" Look, they are anointed. "And there was a division among them." That day had divided between the light and the darkness.

(2) "Therefore they say to the blind man again, 'What do you say about him who opened your eyes?'" What do you

26. Some codices read: For spiritually the Sabbath is this . . .
27. Lv 23.8.
28. Jn 8.34; cf. *Tractates* 3.19 and 20.2.

perceive about that one? What do you think? What do you judge? They were seeking a way to accuse the man falsely that he might be driven from the synagogue, but be found by Christ. But he unswervingly expressed what he perceived. He said, "He is a prophet." At this point, anointed in his heart indeed, he does not yet confess the Son of God, and yet he does not lie. For the Lord himself said about himself, "A prophet is not without honor except in his own country."[29]

10. "The Jews therefore did not believe concerning him that he had been blind and had recovered his sight until they called the parents of him who had recovered his sight," that is, who had been blind and now saw. "And they asked them saying, 'Is this your son who you say was born blind? How then does he now see?' His parents answered them and said, 'We know that this is our son and that he was born blind. But we do not know how he now sees, or who opened his eyes we do not know.' And they said, 'Ask him. He is old enough; let him speak for himself.'" He is indeed our son, but we might justly be compelled to speak for an infant because he could not speak for himself. For a long time now he has spoken, and now he sees. We know that he was blind from birth. We know that he has spoken for a long time now. We now see him seeing. Ask him himself that you may be informed. Why reproach us? "His parents said these things because they feared the Jews. For the Jews had already agreed that if anyone should confess him [to be] the Christ, he would be put out of the synagogue." It was no longer an evil thing to be put out of the synagogue; they were expelling, but Christ was receiving. "That was why his parents said, 'He is old enough, ask him.'"

11. "Therefore, they again called the man who had been blind and said to him, 'Give glory to God.'" What is, "Give glory to God"? Deny what you have received. Clearly this is not to give glory to God but rather to blaspheme God. "'Give,'" they say, "'glory to God. We know that this man is a sinner.' He said, 'If he is a sinner, I do not know; one thing I know, that although I was blind, I now see.' Therefore, they

29. Mt 13.57; cf. *Tractates* 15.23–24 and 24.7.

said to him, 'What did he do to you? How did he open your eyes?'" And he, now getting angry at the hardness of the Jews, and from being blind, [now] seeing, but not enduring the blind, "answered them, 'I have told you already and you have heard. Why do you want to hear it again? Do you also want to become his disciples?'" What is, "Do you also," except that I already am? "Do you also want." Now I see but I do not be-grudge sight.[30]

12. "They cursed him and said to him, 'You be his disci-ple.'" Let such a curse be upon us and upon our children! For it is a curse if you should search their heart, not if you should carefully consider their words. "But we are the disciples of Moses. We know that God spoke to Moses, but we do not know where this man is from." Would that you knew "that God spoke to Moses." Would that you knew that God was pro-claimed through Moses. For you have the Lord saying, "If you did believe Moses, you would also believe me; for he wrote about me."[31] Do you thus follow the servant and turn your back on the Lord? But you do not even follow the servant; for through him you would be led to the Lord.

13. "That man answered and said to them, 'Herein is a wonderful thing, that you do not know where he is from and he has opened my eyes. Now we know that God does not hear sinners, but if anyone is a worshipper of God and does his will, he listens to him.'" He speaks, as yet only anointed. For God also listens to sinners. For if God would not listen to sinners, in vain would that publican, casting his eyes to the ground and striking his breast, say, "O Lord, be merciful to me, a sinner."[32] And that confession won justification as this blind man won enlightenment. "From the beginning of the world it has not been heard of that anyone ever opened the eyes of one born blind. If this man were not from God, he could not do any-thing." Freely, firmly, truthfully. For these things which have been done by the Lord, by whom would they be done except

30. A difficult to translate play on words: *Iam video, sed non invideo.* Liter-ally, "I now see, but I do not envy."
31. Jn 5.46.
32. Lk 18.13.

by God? Or when would such things be done by the disciples unless the Lord dwelt in them?

14. "They answered and said to him, 'You were wholly born in sins.'" What is "wholly"? With closed eyes. But he who opened the eyes also heals the person wholly; he who has given enlightenment to the face will himself give resurrection at his right hand.[33] "'You were wholly born in sins, and do you teach us?' And they cast him out." They themselves made him a teacher, they themselves asked over and over that they might learn; and without gratitude they threw him out when he taught them.

15. But as I said a while ago,[34] brothers, they drive out, the Lord receives; for because he was expelled, the more did he become a Christian. "Jesus heard that they had cast him out; and when he had found him, he said to him, "Do you believe in the Son of God?"[35] Now he washes the face of his heart. "He answered and said," as yet only anointed, "'Who is he, Lord, that I may believe in him?' And Jesus said to him, 'You have seen him, and it is he who is speaking with you.'" He is the one who has been sent, the one washing his face in Siloe, which is interpreted "Who has been sent." Finally now, with the face of his heart washed and his conscience cleansed, recognizing not only that he is the Son of Man—which he had believed before—but now that he is the Son of God who has taken flesh, "he said, 'I do believe, Lord.'" It is not enough, "I believe." Do you wish to see in what sort of being he believes? "And falling down, he worshiped him."[36]

16. "And Jesus said to him." Now it is that day which distinguishes between the light and the darkness. "I came into this world for judgment, that they who see not may see and they

33. This is a reference to the last judgment; see Mt 25.31–34.
34. In sections 9 and 10.
35. NAB follows the Greek text which has "the Son of man." The Vulgate reads as Augustine does. See R. E. Brown, *The Anchor Bible* 29.375. Some late Greek and the Latin manuscripts have "the Son of God" which Brown sees as coming from the use of this passage in the baptismal liturgy and exegesis where the more customary and complete formula of the Christian faith is substituted. See also B. Vawter, JBC 2.444.
36. Jn 9.38 is omitted in many of the best early manuscripts; it exhibits certain non-Johanine peculiarities. See R. E. Brown, *The Anchor Bible* 29.375–76. B. Vawter, JBC 2.444, suggests that the omission is probably accidental.

who see may become blind." What is this, Lord? You have imposed a great problem on weary men, but restore our strength that we may be able to understand what you said: "that they who see not may see." Rightly, because you are light. Rightly, because you are day. Rightly, because you set free from darkness. Every soul accepts this, every soul understands it. What is that which follows: "and that they who see may become blind"? Is it for this reason that you came—that they who were seeing will become blind? Hear what follows, and perchance you will understand.

17. Therefore, "some of the Pharisees" were stirred up by these words "and they said to him, 'Are we also blind?'" Hear now what it is which provoked them; "and that they who see may become blind." "Jesus said to them, 'If you were blind, you would not have sin.'" Although the blindness itself is a sin. "If you were blind," that is, if you realized you were blind, if you admitted you were blind and raced to the Physician. Therefore "if you were blind" in this way, "you would not have sin," because I have come to take sin away. "But now you say, 'We see.' Your sin remains." Why? Because by saying "We see," you do not seek the Physician, you remain in your blindness. This, then, is what we had not understood a little before about the words, "I came that they who do not see may see." What is "that they who do not see may see"? That they who confess that they do not see and who seek the Physician may see. "And that they who see may become blind." What is "that they who see may become blind"? That they who think that they see and who do not seek the Physician may remain in their blindness.

(2) Therefore, he calls that distinction judgment when he says, "I came into this world for judgment," by which he distinguishes the cause of those who believe and confess from the proud who think that they see and are thereby more seriously blinded, as if the sinner who confesses and seeks the Physician said to him, "Judge me, O God, and distinguish my cause from an unholy nation,"[37] of those, of course, who say, "we see," and their sin remains. However, he has not imposed on

37. Ps 42 (43).1 (LXX).

the world that judgment by which he will judge about the living and the dead at the end of [this] age. For as regards this he had said, "I do not judge anyone,"[38] because he came before "not to judge the world, but that the world may be saved through him."[39]

38. Jn 8.15.
39. Jn 3.17.

TRACTATE 45

On John 10.1–10

HE LORD'S discourse to the Jews began from the enlightenment of that man who was born blind. You ought, therefore, to know and be reminded, my beloved people, that today's reading is closely connected with that one. For when the Lord had said, "I came into the world for judgment that they who do not see may see, and they who see may become blind,"—and we explained this at that time when it was read, insofar as we could—some of the Pharisees said, "Are we also blind?" And he answered them, "If you were blind, you would not have sin. But now you say, 'We see,' and your sin remains."[1] To these words he added those which we heard today when they were read out.

2. "Amen, amen, I say to you, he who does not enter the sheepfold through the gate but climbs in some other way is a thief and a robber." For they said that they were not blind; but then they would be able to see if they were Christ's sheep. How did they who were raging against the day appropriate the light to themselves?[2] Because of their vain, proud and incurable arrogance, the Lord Jesus conjoined these words, in which he, looking after our well-being, if we should pay heed to them, advised us.

(2) For there are many who, according to a certain common usage of this life, are called good persons, good men, good women, innocent and, as it were, keeping those precepts which were given in the Law, bearing honor to their parents,

---

1. Jn 9.39–41.
2. There is a subtle word play in this sentence: The thief (*fur*) and his fellows who rage (*furebant*) against the day (i.e., Christ) appropriate (*usurpabant*), i.e., take possession of by illegal means, the light (*lumen*).

187

not engaging in adultery, not committing murder, not stealing, not bearing false witness against anyone, and, in effect,
keeping the other things which have been enjoined by the
Law, and they are not Christians. Often, like these men, they
brag about themselves, "Are we also blind?" Now, because
they do all these things which they do in vain and they do not
know to what end they pertain, the Lord, concerning his own
flock and the gate by which it enters the sheepfold, presented
an analogy in today's reading. Let the pagans say, We live well.
If they do not enter through the gate, what profit is there to
them from the things of which they boast? For to live well
ought to profit each one for this purpose: that it be given him
to live always. For to him to whom it is not given to live always,
what profit is there in living well? For those who either by
their blindness do not know the purpose of living well or who
by their haughtiness despise it must not even be said to live
well. But no one has the true and certain hope of living always
unless he should acknowledge the Life, that is to say, Christ,
and enter the sheepfold through the gate.

3. Often, therefore, such men seek also to persuade men to
live well and yet not to be Christians. They wish to climb over
through another part, to seize and to kill, not, like the shepherd, to defend and save. Thus, there have been certain philosophers, discussing many fine points about virtues and vices,
making distinctions, defining, deducing very sharply-pointed
inferences, filling books, airing their wisdom from their
loudly prattling mouths. And they would even dare to say to
me, "Follow us, hold to our sect if you wish to live happily."
But they had not entered through the gate; they wanted to
destroy, to slaughter and kill.[3]

3. The sentiment expressed here so strongly is somewhat surprising, given
Augustine's earlier devotion to philosophical pursuits, from the inspiration of
Cicero's *Hortensius* to his thorough grounding in Neoplatonism. But this is
more an attack on philosophers, not on philosophy, not on the use of reason
to gain understanding and truth. The relationship between faith and reason
is a constant and frequent theme in his writings; Is 7.9 (LXX) is a favorite
quotation. Augustine sees two sources for religious knowledge, faith (which
he equates with authority) and reason; both have as their goal understanding
and both interact. Reason establishes the necessity for faith and guarantees

4. What shall I say about these? Look, the Pharisees themselves were reading, and in what they were reading they were making the sound, "Christ." They were hoping that he would come, and they did not recognize him when he was before them. They themselves were also bragging that they were among those who see, that is, among those who are wise; and they were denying Christ and were not entering through the gate. Therefore, they themselves, too, if perhaps they would seduce some, would seduce them in order to slaughter and kill them, not to set them free. Let us dismiss these; let us look at those—whether perhaps they themselves enter through the gate—who boast in the name of Christ himself.

5. For countless are they who not only brag of themselves as ones who see but want to be seen as enlightened by Christ; but they are heretics. Perhaps they themselves will have entered through the gate? Perish the thought!

(2) Sabellius[4] says: He himself who is the Son is the Father.

---

the authority of the witness to be believed. Faith assents to the acceptance and truth of the concept. Reason then leads the human mind, as far as it can go, to an understanding of the concept of faith; this in turn increases the faith of the believer as well as his understanding. See e.g., besides the many references to this topic in these tractates, *Epistulae* 120.1–10 (PL 33.452–57 or FOTC 18.300–309) and 147.2–11 (PL 33.597–601 or FOTC 20.171–79); *Sermo* 43 (PL 38.254–58); *En in Ps* 118.18.3 and 29.1. (CCL 40.1724–25 and 1763–64); *De Vera Religione* 24.45–25.46 and 29.52–30.54 (CCL 32.215–16 and 221–23); and *De Utilitate Credendi* 11.25 (PL 42.82–84 or FOTC 4.423–26). A good note on this topic is found in J. O'Meara, *Saint Augustine Against the Academics*, ACW 12.197–98, note 66. See also E. Portalie, *A Guide to the Thought of Saint Augustine*, 114–24, and B. Reardon, "The Relation of Philosophy to Faith in the Teaching of St. Augustine," *Studia Patristica* 2 (1957) 288–94. Augustine's attack on philosophers is more than the traditional Christian distrust of reason, which was strong in North Africa; he is especially distressed at the pride underlying their unending and captious word-splitting which has as its goal their own glory more than the truth, and in their failure to match their active lives with their comtemplative conclusions. See e.g., *Tractate* 2.4; *En in Ps* 140.19; *Sermo* 141 (PL 38.776–78); *De Vera Religione* 4.6–5.8 (CCL 32.192–93); *De Moribus Ecclesiae Catholicae et de Moribus Manichaeorum* 1.21.38 (PL 32.1327–28 or FOTC 56.32–33), *Confessiones* 5.3.3–6 (PL 32.707.–8 or FOTC 21.103–7), and *De Spiritu et Littera* 2.12.19–13.22 (PL 44.211–15).

4. See *Tractate* 29.7, note 17.

But if he is the Son, he is not the Father. He who says that the Son is the Father does not enter through the gate.

(3) Arius[5] says: The Father is one thing, the Son is another thing. He would say it rightly if he were to say "another person," not "another thing." For when he says "another thing," he contradicts him from whom he hears, "The Father and I, we are one thing."[6] Therefore, he does not himself enter through the gate; for he proclaims a Christ such as he draws up for himself, not such as Truth declares. You have the name, you do not have the reality. Christ is the name of a certain thing; hold this reality if you wish the name to profit you.

(4) Another fellow from somewhere or other, like Photinus,[7] says, Christ is a human being; he is not God. Neither does he himself enter through the gate, because Christ is both a human being and God.

(5) And what need is there to run through many [examples] and enumerate the many vanities of heresies? Hold to this: the sheepfold of Christ is the Catholic Church. Let whoever wishes to enter the sheepfold enter through the gate. Let him proclaim the true Christ. Let him not only proclaim the true Christ, but let him seek Christ's glory, not his own. For many, by seeking their own glory, have scattered Christ's sheep rather than gathered them together. For he is a lowly door, Christ the Lord. The man who enters through this door must lower himself that he may enter with an unharmed head. But he who does not lower himself, but exalts himself, wishes to climb over the wall; but he who climbs over the wall is raised up for this very reason, that he may fall.[8]

6. Nevertheless, the Lord Jesus is still speaking covertly; he is not yet understood. He names the gate, he names the sheepfold, he names the sheep; he makes all these things known, but he does not yet explain them. Let us read therefore, because he is about to go on to those words in which he may deign to explain to us some things which he has said; and

---

5. See *Tractate* 1.11, note 27.　　6. Jn 10.30.
7. See *Tractate* 26.5, note 18.　　8. Cf. Mt 23.12, Lk 18.14.

from the explanation of these he will perhaps give us an understanding also of those things which he has not explained. For he feeds us with those things which are evident; he exercises us with those things which are obscure.

(2) "He who does not enter the sheepfold through the gate but climbs in some other way." Woe to the wretch, because he is going to fall! Let him be humble, let him enter through the gate. Let him come on the level ground[9] and he will not stumble. "That one," he says, "is a thief and a robber." He wishes to call someone else's sheep his own sheep; *his own*, that is, taken away in theft, for this purpose, not that he may save them but that he may kill them. He is a thief, therefore, because he calls his own what is another's; and he is a robber because he also kills what he has stolen.

(3) "But he who enters through the gate is the shepherd of the sheep; the keeper opens [the gate] for him." Let us inquire about this keeper, then, when we shall have heard from the Lord himself what the gate is and who the shepherd is. "And the sheep hear his voice and he calls his own sheep by name." For he has their names written in the book of life.[10] "He calls his own sheep by name." Because of this the Apostle says, "The Lord knows who are his."[11] "And he leads them out. And when he has let out his own sheep, he goes before them, and the sheep follow him because they know his voice. But they do not follow a stranger, but flee from him, because they do not know the voice of strangers." These are covert things, full of questions, pregnant with mysteries. Let us continue, therefore, and hear the Teacher opening something from these

9. The Latin is *plano pede*. This phrase means "level with the ground" both as an architectural term in classical usage and in general usage in the postclassical periods. See OLD 1388; H. Rönsch, *Itala und Vulgata* and H. Nettleship, *Contributions to Latin Lexicography* (Oxford, 1889) 552.

10. See Phil 4.3 and Apoc (Rv) 3.5, 13.8, and 17.8; also Ex 32.32–33, Ps 68 (69).29, and Dn 12.1 In *DCD* 20.14–15 Augustine first interprets the book of life to be an action of God at the judgment whereby each person is illuminated so as to "read" the record of his own deeds, and then he takes it as a figure of the predestination of those who are to receive eternal life. In *En in Ps* 68.2.13 he explains Ps 68 (69).29 in terms of predestination.

11. 2 Tm 2.19.

obscure things and causing us, perhaps, to enter through that which he opens.

7. "This proverb Jesus spoke to them, but they did not understand what he was saying to them." And perhaps neither do we. What difference is there between them and us before we too come to know these words? It is because we knock that it is opened to us;[12] but they, by denying Christ, were unwilling to enter to be saved but wished to remain outside to perish. Because, therefore, we hear these words reverently, because before we understand them, we believe them to be true and divine, we differ from these men considerably. For when two men hear the word of the Gospel, the one irreverent, the other reverent, and when there are some things such that, perhaps, both of them do not understand, the one says, It said nothing, but the other says, It said the truth and what it said is good, but we do not understand. This man, because he believes, now knocks and is worthy that it be opened to him, if he should continue to knock. But that man still hears, "Unless you believe, you will not understand."[13] Why do I point these things out? Because, even when I have explained these obscure words, as far as I am able, or, inasmuch as they are exceedingly hidden, either I will not have secured an understanding of them, or I will not have possessed the ability of presenting clearly what I understand, or someone will have been so slow that he does not follow my exposition. Let him not despair of himself. Let him abide in the faith. Let him walk in the way. Let him hear the Apostle saying: "If you understand anything in another way, this also God will reveal to you; still in what we have attained, let us proceed to walk in that."[14]

8. Therefore, let us begin to hear him exposing, the one we have heard proposing. "Therefore, Jesus said to them again, 'Amen, amen, I say to you, I am the sheepgate.'" Look, that gate which he had posited as closed he has opened. He himself

12. Cf. Mt 7.7, Lk 11.9.
13. Is 7.9 (LXX); see *Tractate* 29.6.
14. Phil 3.15–16.

is the gate. We acknowledge it. Let us enter or let us rejoice that we have entered.

(2) "All, as many as have come, are thieves and robbers." What is this, O Lord, "all, as many as have come?" How is this? Have you not come? But understand. I said, "all as many as have come," of course, besides me.[15] Let us, then, recollect. Before his coming the prophets came. Were they thieves and robbers? Perish the thought! They did not come besides him because they came together with him. When he was about to come, he sent heralds, but he had in his keeping the hearts of those whom he had sent. Do you want to know that they came together with him who is always the same?[16] Of course he took his flesh in time. Therefore what is he always? "In the beginning was the Word."[17] Therefore, they who came with the Word of God came together with him. "I am," he said, "the way, and the truth and the life."[18] If he himself is the truth, they who were truthful came together with him. As many, therefore, as were besides him were "thieves and robbers," that is, [they came] to steal and kill.

9. "But the sheep have not heard them." This question is greater, "the sheep have not heard them." Before the coming of our Lord Jesus Christ, whereby he came humbly in flesh, just men went before him, believing in him who was to come just as we now believe in him who has come. The times are varied, not the faith. For the words themselves are also varied in accord with the time,[19] when they are variously inflected. 'He will come' has one sound; 'he came' has another sound. The sound has changed: he will come, and he came. Yet the same faith joins both together, both those who believed that

15. Jn 10.8 presents an interpretation problem because both Augustine's text and the Vulgate have omitted the Greek words πρὸ ἐμοῦ, before me. The use of this phrase by the Manichees and other Gnostic heretics to devalue the Old Testament prophets was perhaps the cause of the omission. See Browne LFC 29.604; Innes LNPF 7.251; R. E. Brown, *The Anchor Bible*, 29.386, and La Grange, *Évangîle selon saint Jean* 277–78.

16. Or, very literally, who is always himself, i.e., who forever exists unchangeably as what he forever is, namely, Being itself, the Word of God.

17. Jn 1.1.   18. Jn 14.6.

19. I.e., the tense.

he would come and those who believed that he had come. We see that both have entered, at different times, indeed, but through the one Gate of faith, that is, through Christ.

(2) We believe that the Lord Jesus Christ was born of a virgin, came in flesh, suffered, arose, ascended into heaven; we now believe that all of this has been fulfilled, as you hear words of past time. With us in the company of this faith are also those fathers who believed that he would be born of a virgin, would suffer, would arise, would ascend into heaven. For the Apostle pointed to them when he said, "But having the same spirit of faith, as has been written, 'I have believed and because of this I have spoken,' we also believe, and because of this we also speak."[20] The prophet said, "I have believed and because of this I have spoken."[21] The Apostle says, "We also believe and because of this we also speak." But, that you may know that the faith is one, hear him saying, "Having the same spirit of faith, we also believe."

(3) So, too, in another passage: "For I would not have you ignorant, brothers, that our fathers were all under the cloud and all passed through the sea; all were baptized into Moses in the cloud and the sea. And all ate the same spiritual food, and all drank the same spiritual drink."[22] The Red Sea signifies baptism. Moses, the leader through the Red Sea, signifies Christ. The people passing through signify the faithful. The death of the Egyptians signifies the abolition of sins.[23] It is the same faith in different signs; in different signs, just as in different words; for words change sounds through the times, and, of course, words are nothing other than signs. For they are words by the fact of signifying; remove signification from the word and there is an empty noise. Therefore, all things have been signified. Were they not believing the same things through whom these signs were provided, through whom the same things which we believe were prophesied and predicted? Of course they believed, but they believed that these things would come; we believe, however, that they have come.

(4) For this reason he also says this: "They drank the same

20. 2 Cor 4.13.
21. Ps 115.10 (116B.1 or 116.10).
22. 1 Cor 10.1–4.
23. Cf. *Tractate* 11.4.

spiritual drink." The same spiritual drink, not the same physical drink. What did they drink? "For they drank from the spiritual rock that was following them, and the rock was Christ."[24] See, therefore, while the faith remains, the signs are changed. There the rock was Christ; for us Christ is what is placed on the altar of God.[25] And they, in accord with a great mystery[26] of the same Christ, drank water flowing out of a rock; the faithful know what we drink. If you look to the visible appearance, they are different; if you look to the intelligible signification, they drank the same spiritual drink.

(5) Therefore, as many as in that time believed either Abraham or Isaac or Jacob or Moses or the other patriarchs and the other prophets predicting Christ, they were sheep and they heard Christ; they heard not another's voice, but his. The judge had been in the crier. For when the judge speaks through the crier, the court clerk does not put, The crier said, but, The judge said.[27] But there are others whom the sheep did not hear, in whom the voice of Christ was not, who were erring, speaking falsity, uttering nonsense, devising vanities, misleading the wretched.

10. Why is it, then, that I said: this question is greater? What does it have that is obscure and difficult to understand? Listen, I beg you. Look, the Lord himself, Jesus Christ, came and preached. Surely it was much more the voice of the shepherd, uttered from the very mouth of the shepherd. For if it was the voice of the shepherd through the prophets, how much more does the very tongue of the shepherd put forth the voice of the shepherd? Not all heard. But what do we think? Were those who heard sheep? Look, Judas heard, and he was a wolf. He was following, but covered with a sheep's skin; he lay in ambush for the shepherd. Indeed some of those who crucified Christ did not hear and yet were sheep; for he saw them in the crowd when he said, "When you have lifted up the Son of Man, then you will realize that I am."[28] Now how is this question resolved? Those who are not sheep hear, and

---

24. 1 Cor 10.4.
26. The Latin word is *sacramentum*.
28. Jn 8.28.

25. Cf. *Tractate* 26.12.
27. Cf. *Tractate* 13.16.

those who are sheep do not hear. Some wolves follow the voice of the shepherd and some sheep gainsay it. Finally, sheep kill the shepherd. The question is resolved; for someone answers and says, But when they were not hearing, they were not yet sheep, then they were wolves. The voice was heard and changed them and from wolves made them sheep. Therefore when they were made sheep, they heard and they found the shepherd and followed the shepherd; they hoped for the promises of the shepherd because they carried out his orders.

11. To some extent this question has been resolved and perchance this is sufficient for some. But it still bothers me, and I share with you what bothers me, in order that, by searching with you in some way or other, through his revelation, I may deserve, with you, to find the answer. Therefore, hear what bothers me.

(2) Through the prophet Ezechiel the Lord rebukes shepherds; and among other things, he says about the sheep, "You did not call back the straying sheep."[29] He says "straying" and also specifies "sheep". If, when it was straying, it was a sheep, whose voice did it hear that it strayed? For without a doubt it would not stray if it heard the voice of the shepherd; but it strayed for the very reason that it heard another's voice; it heard the voice of the thief and robber.

(3) Surely sheep do not hear the voice of robbers. "They who came," he says, and we understand, besides me, that is, "They who came" besides me "were thieves and robbers and the sheep did not hear them." Lord, if the sheep did not hear them, how do the sheep stray? If the sheep hear only you and you are the Truth, whoever hears the Truth surely does not stray. But they were straying and they were designated sheep. For if in the very straying they were not designated sheep, it would not be said through Ezechiel, "You did not call back the straying sheep." How does it both stray and yet remain a sheep? Did it hear another's voice? Certainly "the sheep did not hear them."

(4) Moreover, at the present time many are gathered to the

29. Ez 34.4.

sheepfold of Christ, from heretics they become Catholics; they are taken away from the thieves and returned to the shepherd. And sometimes they murmur; they feel loathing for the one calling them back, and they do not recognize the one cutting their throats. Nevertheless, even when those who are sheep have come, though struggling against it, they recognize the voice of the shepherd and rejoice that they have come and they blush that they have strayed.[30] Therefore, when they were glorying in that straying as if in truth and, of course, were not hearing the voice of the shepherd, and so were following a stranger, were they sheep or were they not? If they were sheep, how do the sheep not hear strangers? If they were not sheep, why are they rebuked to whom it is said, "You did not call back the straying sheep"?

(5) Even among those already become Catholic Christians, among the faithful of good hope, sometimes evil occurs. They are deceived into straying and after their straying are called back. When they have been deceived into straying and have been rebaptized, or when, after association with the Lord's sheepfold, they were again returned to their first straying, were they sheep or were they not? Clearly they were Catholics. If they were faithful Catholics, they were sheep. If they were sheep, how could they hear another's voice, since the Lord says, "the sheep did not hear them?"

12. You have heard, brothers, the profundity of the question. I say, therefore, "The Lord knows who are his."[31] He knows those foreknown, he knows those predestined. For it is said about him, "But those whom he foreknew he predestined to be made conformable to the image of his Son, that he might be the first-born among many brothers. And those he predestined he also called; and those whom he called he also justified; and those whom he justified he also glorified. If God is for us, who is against us?" Add further, "He who did not spare his own Son but handed him over for the sake of us all, how

30. Augustine's attitude toward coercion and compulsion in bringing pagans, schismatics, and heretics into the orthodox Catholic community has been discussed in the introduction (20), FOTC 78.
31. 2 Tm 2.19.

has he not also granted us all things with him?"[32] But to which of us? To the foreknown, the predestined, the justified, the glorified. And about these [the text] continues, "Who shall bring a charge against God's chosen ones?"[33] Therefore "the Lord knows who are his." These are the sheep.

(2) Sometimes they do not know themselves, but the shepherd knows them, as regards this predestination, as regards this foreknowledge of God, as regards the choosing of the sheep before the foundation of the world; for the Apostle also says this: "Even as he chose us in him before the foundation of the world."[34] Therefore, as regards this foreknowledge and predestination of God, how many sheep there are without, how many wolves there are within! And how many sheep there are within and how many wolves without! Why did I say, "How many sheep there are without"? How many now are dissolute but will be chaste! How many blaspheme Christ but will believe in Christ! How many are drunkards but will be sober! How many who will give away their own plunder other people's property! And yet now they hear another's voice, they follow strangers. Likewise, how many are within who praise but will blaspheme, are chaste but will fornicate, are sober but later will bury themselves in wine, are standing but will fall! They are not sheep. (For we are speaking about the predestined; we are speaking about those whom the Lord knows, who are his.) And yet these, as long as they think aright, hear Christ's voice. Look, these hear, those do not hear; and yet, as regards predestination, these are not sheep, and those are sheep.

13. The question still remains; but now, however, it seems to me that it can be resolved as follows. There is a certain voice; there is, I say, a certain voice of the shepherd in which the sheep do not hear strangers, and in which those who are not sheep do not hear Christ. What is this voice? "He who has persevered up to the end, this one will be saved."[35] His own does not neglect this voice; the stranger does not hear it. For

32. Rom 8.29–32.   33. Rom 8.33.
34. Eph 1.4.   35. Mt 10.22.

he also proclaims this to him, that he should persevere with
him up to the end; but, by not persevering with him he does
not hear this voice. He has come to Christ; he has heard some
words and others, these words and those, all true, all health-
ful. And among all these is also that voice: "He who has persevered up to the end, this one will be saved." He who hears this
is a sheep.

(2) But someone or other heard it, and was without understanding; he became indifferent, he heard the stranger's
voice. If he has been predestined, he strayed temporarily, he
was not lost forever; he returns to hear what he neglected, to
do what he heard. For, if he is of those who have been predestined, God foreknew both his straying and his future conversion. If he has gone astray, he returns to hear that voice of the
Shepherd and to follow him saying, "He who has persevered
up to the end, this one will be saved." It is a good voice,
brothers, a true voice, the Shepherd's voice! It is the very voice
of Salvation in the tents of the just.[36] For it is easy to hear
Christ, it is easy to praise the Gospel, easy to applaud the
preacher. To persevere up to the end—this is the characteristic of sheep who hear the Shepherd's voice. A temptation
occurs; persevere up to the end, because the temptation does
not persevere up to the end. Up to what end will you persevere? Until you come to the end of the road.

(3) For, as long as you do not hear Christ, he is your opponent on this road, that is, in this mortal life. But what does he
say? "Agree with your opponent quickly while you are with
him on the road."[37] You heard, you believed, you agreed. If
you were opposed, agree. If it has been offered to you to
agree, do not contend further. For you do not know when the
road may come to its end, but still he knows. If you are a
sheep, and if you persevere up to the end, you will be saved.
And on this account his own do not despise this voice;
strangers do not hear it.

(4) As best I could, as he himself granted, either I have

36. Cf. Ps 117 (118).15.
37. Mt 5.25.

provided you with an answer for this very profound question, or I have investigated it with you. If any have barely understood, let their piety remain and the truth will be revealed. But let those who have understood not exalt themselves, as though the swifter over the slower, so that they do not, by exalting themselves, get off the road and the slower arrive more easily. Rather, let him lead all, him to whom we say, "Lead me, Lord, on your road and I shall walk in your truth."[38]

14. Therefore, through this, which the Lord explained, that he himself is the gate, let us enter to the things which he proposed but did not explain. And indeed who the shepherd is, although he did not say it in this reading which was heard today, nevertheless he says it very openly in that which follows: "I am the Good Shepherd."[39] And, even if he did not say this, whom else besides him ought we to understand in those words where he says, "He who enters through the gate is shepherd of the sheep. The keeper opens the gate for him, and the sheep hear his voice. And he calls his own sheep by name and leads them out. And when he has let out his own sheep, he goes before them; and the sheep follow him because they know his voice"? For who else calls his own sheep by name and leads them from here to eternal life except he who knows the names of the predestined? And for this reason he says to his disciples, "Rejoice that your names have been written in heaven."[40] For he calls them from here by name. And who else lets them out except he who forgives their sins, that, freed from harsh bonds, they may be able to follow him? And who has preceded them where they are to follow him except he who, rising from the dead, dies no more, and death will have no further dominion over him?[41] And when he was visible in the flesh, he said, "Father, I will that where I am, they also whom you have given me may be with me."[42] Similar is the explanation of what he said, "I am the gate. If anyone enters through me, he will be saved. He will go in and he will go out

38. Ps 85 (86).11 (LXX).   39. Jn 10.11.
40. Lk 10.20.   41. Cf. Rom 6.9.
42. Jn 17.24.

and will find pastures." In this, he plainly shows that not only the shepherd but also the sheep enter through the gate.

15. But what does this mean: "He will go in and he will go out and will find pastures"?[43] To be sure, to go into the Church through the gate, Christ, is exceedingly good; but to go out of the Church, as this John the Evangelist himself says in his epistle, "They went out from us, but they were not of us,"[44] is surely not good. Therefore, such a going out could not be praised by the Good Shepherd, so that he should say, "He will go in and he will go out and will find pastures." Therefore, there is not only a good going in, but also a good going out through the good gate which is Christ. But what is this praiseworthy and blessed going out?

(2) I could indeed say that we go in when we think something interiorly, but that we go out when we do something externally; and that, because, as the Apostle says, Christ dwells in our hearts through faith,[45] to go in through Christ is to think according to faith itself, but to go out through Christ is to work according to faith itself even outside, that is, before men. For this reason it is also read in the psalm, "A man will go out to his work."[46] And the Lord himself says, "Let your works shine before men."[47]

(3) But it delights me more that Truth itself, like a good shepherd and thus a good teacher, in some measure advised us how we ought to understand what he said, "He will go in and he will go out and will find pastures," when he continued and added, "The thief comes only to steal and slaughter and destroy. I have come that they might have life and have it more abundantly." For it seems to me that he said that, going in, they might have life, and going out, they might have it more abundantly. But no one can go out through the gate,

---

43. The sentence "He will go in and he will go out" probably does not have two distinct senses as Augustine interprets it, but rather is a Hebraicism meaning "He will come and go freely," as, e.g., in Dt 28.6 or 1 Kgs (1 Sm) 29.6. See Comeau, *Saint Augustin*, 46: La Grange, *Évangile selon saint Jean*, 278; and R. Schnackenburg, *The Gospel According to St. John*, trans. C. Hastings (New York 1980) 292–93.

44. 1 Jn 2.19.   45. Cf. Eph 3.17.
46. Ps 103 (104).23.   47. Mt 5.16.

that is, through Christ, to eternal life, which will be face to face,[48] unless, through the gate itself, that is, through the same Christ, he has entered into his Church, which is his sheepfold, to temporal life, which is in faith. And thus he said, "I have come that they may have life," that is, faith, which works through love;[49] and through this faith they go into the sheepfold that they may live, for "the just man lives by faith."[50] And that they may have it more abundantly," who by persevering up to the end go out through that gate, that is, through the faith of Christ, because they die, true believers: and they will have life more abundantly by coming where that Shepherd preceded, where they are never to die.

(4) Therefore, although even here in the sheepfold itself pastures are not lacking, because we can understand what was said, "and will find pastures," for both, that is, both for going in and for going out, still then they will find true pastures, where they who hunger and thirst after justice are to have their fill.[51] Such pastures did he find to whom it was said, "This day you will be with me in paradise."[52] But how he is himself the gate, himself the shepherd, so that in some measure even he is understood to go in and out, and who is the gatekeeper, it would be too long to search out today and to explain by discussion resulting from his munificence.

48. The Latin is *in specie*. For this meaning see 2 Cor 5.7; Augustine, *Sermo* 216.4 (PL 38.1079) and *De Trinitate* 14.2.4 (CCL 50A.425 or FOTC 45.414–15). Browne translates it "in reality," taking *species* as the Latin technical term for the Platonic ἰδέα, form.

49. See Gal. 5.6.
50. Rom 1.17, quoting Hb 2.4.
51. Cf. Mt 5.6.
52. Lk 23.43.

TRACTATE 46

On John 10.11–13

HE LORD JESUS, speaking to his sheep, both the present ones and the future ones who were then there (for [there] where those already his sheep were, there were those who were going to be his sheep), just so to the present ones and to the future ones, both to those and to us and even to as many as after us will be his sheep, he showed who was sent to them. Therefore, all hear the voice of their Shepherd, saying, "I am the good shepherd." He would not add "good" unless there were evil shepherds. But the evil shepherds, these are the thieves and the robbers,[1] or indeed, at best, the hired hands.

(2) For we ought to search out, to distinguish, to know all the personages which he has posited. For the Lord has already opened up two things which were to some extent closed, once he had proposed them.[2] Now we know that he himself is the gate;[3] we know that he himself is the shepherd. It was made clear in yesterday's reading who the thieves and robbers are; but today we have heard "hired hand," and we have heard "wolf." Yesterday the gatekeeper was named also. Therefore, among the good are the gate, the gatekeeper, the shepherd, and the sheep; among the evil, thieves and robbers, hired hands, the wolf.

2. We learn that the gate is the Lord Christ, the shepherd himself. Who is the gatekeeper? For he himself explained these two things, he left the gatekeeper to us to seek out. And what did he say about the gatekeeper? He said, "The gate-

1. Cf. Jn 10.1, 8.
2. The CCL text erroneously reads *clausus* for *clausas*.
3. Cf. Jn 10.7, 9.

keeper opens for this one."[4] For whom does he open? For the shepherd. What does he open for the shepherd? The gate. And who is the gate itself? The shepherd himself. If the Lord Christ had not explained, had not he himself said, "I am the shepherd" and "I am the gate," would anyone of us dare to say that Christ himself is both the shepherd and the gate? For if he had said, "I am the shepherd," and had not said, "I am the gate," we would be likely to ask what the gate was, and, per-haps, thinking it something else, to remain in front of the gate. By his grace and mercy he explained the shepherd to us; he said it was himself. He explained the gate; he said it was himself. He left the gatekeeper for us to seek out.

(2) Whom are we going to say is the gatekeeper? Whomever we find, we must take care that he not be judged greater than the gate itself because in the houses of people, the gatekeeper is greater than the gate. For the gatekeeper is preferred to the gate, not the gate to the gatekeeper, because the gatekeeper guards the gate, not the gate the gatekeeper. I dare not say that anyone is greater than the gate; for I have already heard what the gate is. It is not concealed from me. I have not been left to my own conjecturing; human guesswork has not been given free rein. God said it, Truth said it; what the Immutable said cannot be changed.

3. Therefore, on this profound question I shall state what seems good to me. Let each one choose what pleases him; nevertheless, let him think devoutly, as it has been written, "Think of the Lord in goodness, and in simplicity of heart seek him."[5]

(2) Perhaps we ought to take the Lord himself as the gate-keeper. For in human affairs the shepherd and the gate are much farther apart from one another than are the gatekeeper and the gate; and yet the Lord said that he was both the shepherd and the gate. Why then should we not understand him also to be the gatekeeper? For if we would examine the proper significations,[6] the Lord Christ is neither a shepherd,

4. Cf. Jn 10.3.
5. Wis 1.1.
6. *proprietates*. For this connotation see OLD, 1495.

as we are accustomed to know and see shepherds, nor is he a gate in that no carpenter made him. But if we would look at it according to a certain likeness, he is both gate and shepherd, I dare to say, and also a sheep. The sheep, of course, is under the shepherd; yet he is both shepherd and sheep. Where is he a shepherd? Look, you have it here. Read the Gospel: "I am the good shepherd." Where is he a sheep? Ask the prophet: "As a sheep he was led to the slaughter."[7] Ask the friend of the bridegroom: "Behold! The Lamb of God. Behold! He who takes away the sin of the world."[8] I am going to say something still more marvelous about these likenesses. For lamb, sheep and shepherd are friendly with one another; but the sheep are usually guarded by the shepherds against lions. And yet about Christ, although he is sheep and shepherd, we read the statement: "The Lion of the tribe of Judah has prevailed."[9] Take all these things, brothers, according to likenesses, not according to their proper significations. We are used to seeing shepherds sitting on a rock and from there guarding the flocks entrusted to them; of course the shepherd is better than the rock on which the shepherd sits. Yet Christ is both shepherd and rock.[10] All of this is according to likeness.

(3) But if you should seek the proper signification from me, "In the beginning was the Word, and the Word was with God, and the Word was God."[11] If you should seek from me the proper signification, he is the only Son begotten from the Father for eternity from eternity, equal to the Begetter, through whom all things were made, with the Father unchangeable, and unchanged in taking the form of a man, a man from the Incarnation, Son of Man and Son of God. All of this which I have said is not likeness but reality.

4. Let us not, then brothers, be reluctant to take him as the gate and as the gatekeeper, according to certain likenesses. For what is a gate? That by which we enter. Who is the gatekeeper? He who opens. Now who opens himself except he who explains himself? Look, the Lord had said a gate; we had

7. Is 53.7.
9. Apoc (Rv) 5.5.
11. Jn 1.1.

8. Jn 1.29.
10. Cf. 1 Cor 10.4.

not understood. When we did not understand, it was closed;
he who opened it is himself the gatekeeper. Therefore, there
is no need to seek something else, no need; but perhaps there
is an inclination.

(2) If there is an inclination, do not deviate, do not desert
the Trinity. If you seek another person for the gatekeeper, let
the Holy Spirit come forward; for the Holy Spirit will not
disdain to be the gatekeeper since the Son deigned to be the
gate itself. See that the gatekeeper is perhaps the Holy Spirit;
the Lord himself said to his disciples about the Holy Spirit,
"He will teach you all truth."[12] What is the gate? Christ. What
is Christ? Truth. Who opens the gate except he who teaches
all truth?

5. But what do we say about the hired hand? This one was
not mentioned among the good.[13] "The good shepherd," he
says, "lays down his life for his sheep. The hired hand (who is
not a shepherd, whose own the sheep are not) sees the wolf
coming, leaves the sheep and flees. And the wolf snatches and
scatters the sheep." Here the hired hand does not display a
good character, and yet he is useful for something; and he
would not be called a hired hand unless he received pay from
his employer. Who, then, is this hired hand, both blamewor-
thy and needed? Here let the Lord himself shine for us,
brothers, that we may understand hired hands, and not be
hired hands.

(2) Who, then, is the hired hand? There are in the Church
certain overseers about whom the Apostle Paul says, "Seeking
their own things, not those of Jesus Christ."[14] What is "seeking
their own things"? Not loving Christ freely, not seeking God
for the sake of God, pursuing temporal advantages, panting
for profits, seeking honors from men. When these things are
loved by the overseer and God is served for the sake of these
things, such a one is a hired hand; let him not count himself
among the sons. For about such men the Lord also said,
"Amen I say to you, they have received their reward."[15]

(3) Hear what the Apostle Paul says about holy Timothy.

12. Jn 16.13.   13. See the end of section 1.
14. Phil 2.21.   15. Mt 6.5.

"Now I hope, in the Lord Jesus, to send Timothy to you soon that I may be of good comfort when I know the things concerning you. For I have no one of the same mind who is genuinely sollicitous of you. For all seek their own things, not those of Jesus Christ."[16] The shepherd groaned among the hired hands; he sought someone who sincerely loved Christ's flock, and among those who had been with him at that time, he did not find one about him. For not that there was no one in the Church of Christ then except Paul and Timothy who was genuinely sollicitous of the flock; but it had happened that at the time when he sent Timothy he did not have around him another of the sons, but there were only hired hands with him, "seeking their own things, not those of Jesus Christ." And yet he himself, though genuinely sollicitous for the flock, preferred to send a son and to remain among the hired hands.

(4) We also find hired hands; only the Lord scrutinizes them. He who sees into the heart scrutinizes them; yet sometimes they are understood by us. For not in vain did the Lord himself also say about wolves, "From their fruits you will know them."[17] Temptations test many and then their thoughts are clear; but many escape their notice.

(5) Let the Lord's sheepfold have overseers, both sons and hired hands. But the overseers who are sons are shepherds. If they are shepherds, how is there one shepherd, unless all those are members of the one shepherd whose own the sheep are? For they themselves are also members of the one sheep himself; for "as a sheep he was led to the slaughter."[18]

6. But hear that hired hands are also needed. To be sure, many in the Church who are pursuing earthly advantages still preach Christ and the voice of Christ is heard through them; and the sheep follow, not the hired hand, but the voice of the shepherd through the hired hand. Hear the hired hands being pointed out by the Lord himself. "The Scribes," he says, "and the Pharisees sit on the chair of Moses; do what they say, but do not do what they do."[19] What else did he say except: through the hired hands hear the voice of the shepherd? For,

---

16. Phil 2.19–21.
18. Is 53.7; see section 3.
17. Mt 7.16.
19. Mt 23.2–3.

by sitting on the chair of Moses they teach God's law; therefore, God teaches through them. But if they should wish to
teach their own teachings, do not listen, do not do. For of
course such men seek their own things, not those of Jesus
Christ;[20] nevertheless, no hired hand has dared to say to the
people of Christ: Seek your own things, not those of Jesus
Christ. For what he does evilly he does not preach from the
chair of Christ; he does harm from the fact that he does evil
things, not from the fact that he says good things.

(2) Pick the cluster, watch out for the thorn. It is good that
you have understood! But for the sake of the slower ones, I
shall say this same thing more plainly. How did I say, Pick the
cluster, watch out for the thorn, although the Lord says, "Did
you ever gather the grape from thorns or the fig from this-
tles?"[21] It is completely true; and yet I also said the truth—pick
the cluster, watch out for the thorn. For the cluster, which has
sprung up from the root of the vine, sometimes hangs on the
fence;[22] the vine-branch grows and is mingled with the thorns
and the thorn carries a fruit not its own. For the vine did not
bear a thorn but the branch lay on thorns. Ask only about the
roots. Seek the root of the thorn; you find it outside, separate
from the vine. Seek the source of the grape; the vine put this
forth from its root.

(3) Therefore, the chair of Moses was the vine; the practices
of the Pharisees were the thorns. True teaching by evil men,
the branch on the fence, the cluster among the thorns. Pick
carefully, so that, while you seek fruit, you do not prick your
hand; and when you hear someone saying good things, do not
imitate him doing evil things. "Do what they say," pick the
grapes; "but do not do what they do," watch out for the thorn.
Hear the voice of the Shepherd even through the hired
hands, but be not hired hands, since you are members of the
Shepherd.

20. Cf. Phil 2.21.
21. Mt 7.16.
22. The Latin is *in sepe*. This is a fence woven together from pliant plants
or branches that have thorns, like a barbed wire fence or a hedge of thorny
plants.

(4) It was Paul himself, the holy Apostle, who said, "I have no one who is genuinely sollicitous for you. For all seek their own things, not those of Jesus Christ."[23] In another place, however, distinguishing between hired hands and sons, see what he said, "Some preach Christ out of envy and contention, but others out of good will. Some out of love, knowing that I have been appointed for the defence of the Gospel. But some proclaim Christ out of contentiousness, not sincerely, thinking to stir up affliction for my bonds."[24] These were hired hands, they envied the Apostle Paul. Why were they envying him except that they were seeking temporal things? But notice what he adds: "But what then? Provided only that in every way, whether by occasion or by truth, Christ is being proclaimed. In this also I rejoice, yes, and I shall rejoice."[25] Truth is Christ. Let truth be proclaimed by hired hands on occasion; let truth be proclaimed by sons in truth. The sons patiently await the eternal inheritance of the Father; the hired hands desire instantly the temporal pay of their employer. For me let human glory, for which I see the hired hands looking jealously, be lessened; and nevertheless through the tongues of both hired hands and sons let Christ's glory be spread abroad when, "whether by occasion or by truth, Christ is being proclaimed."[26]

7. We saw also who the hired hand is. Who is the wolf if not the devil? And what was said about the hired hand? "When he sees the wolf coming, he flees because the sheep are not his own and he has no care for the sheep." Was the Apostle Paul such a one? Far from it! Was Peter such a one? Far from it! Were the other apostles such ones, with the exception of Judas, the son of perdition? Far from it! Were they shepherds then? Clearly they were shepherds. And how is there one shepherd? I have already said that they were shepherds because they were members of the Shepherd. They were rejoic-

23. Phil 2.20–21.   24. Phil 1.15–17.
25. Phil 1.18.
26. A frequent theme in Augustine's writings. See *Tractate* 11.9, *DDC* 4.59; *DCD* 16.2; *En in Ps* 49.23; *Sermo* 101.8.10 (PL 38.610); and *Sermo* 137.5.5. and 9.11 (PL 38.757 and 760), on Jn 10.1–16.

ing in that head, they were united under that head, they were living with one spirit in the structure of one body; and through this, all belonged to the one Shepherd.

(2) Therefore, if they are shepherds, and not hired hands, why did they flee when they suffered persecution? Explain to us, O Lord. In an epistle, I saw Paul fleeing; he was let down in a basket by the wall, that he might escape the hands of the persecutor.[27] Did he have no concern for the sheep which he was abandoning when the wolf came? Clearly he did, but by his prayers he was entrusting them to the Shepherd who was sitting in heaven; moreover, by his flight he saved himself for their benefit, as he said in a certain place: "to remain in the flesh is necessary for your sakes."[28] For all have heard from the Shepherd himself: "If they persecute you in one city, flee into another."[29]

(3) Let the Lord deign to explain this question to us. Lord, you said to those whom you especially wanted to be faithful shepherds, whom you formed to be your members, "If they persecute you, flee." Therefore, you do an injustice to these when you reproach the hired hands who see the wolf coming and flee. We ask that you indicate to us the depth of the question. Let us knock; he will be present who, as gatekeeper of the gate (which he is himself), can open himself.

8. Who is the hired hand? He who sees the wolf coming and flees? He who seeks his own things, not those of Jesus Christ;[30] he does not dare openly to accuse the sinner.[31] Some one or other has sinned; he has sinned grievously. He ought to be reproached; he ought to be excommunicated. But if he is excommunicated, he will be an enemy, he will make plots, he will do harm when he can. Now that one who seeks his own things, not those of Jesus Christ, that he may not lose what he is pursuing, the advantage of a human friendship, and that he may not incur the distress of human enmities—he is quiet, he does not correct. Look, the wolf seizes the sheep's throat; the devil has persuaded a believer [to commit] adultery. You

27. Cf. 2 Cor 11.33; see also Acts 9.23–25.
28. Phil 1.24.   29. Mt 10.23; cf. *Tractate* 28.2.
30. Cf. Phil 2.21.   31. Cf. 1 Tm 5.20.

are silent, you do not scold. O hired hand, you saw the wolf coming and you fled.

(2) Perhaps he answers and says, Look, I am here; I haven't fled. You fled because you kept quiet; you kept quiet because you were afraid. Fear is the flight of the soul. You stood your ground in body; you fled in spirit—the very thing that man did not do who said, "Although I am absent in body, I am with you in spirit."[32] For how was he fleeing in spirit who, although even absent in body, was alleging fornication in a letter? Our feelings are the motions of our minds. Joy is an extension of the mind; sadness, a depression of the mind; desire, a progression of the mind; and fear, a flight of the mind. For you are extended in mind when you are delighted, you are depressed in mind when you are troubled, you advance in mind when you desire, you flee in mind when you fear. Look how that hired hand is said to flee when the wolf has been seen. Why? "Because he has no care for the sheep." Why "has he no care for the sheep? Because he is a hired hand." What is "he is a hired hand"? One seeking temporal reward, and he will not dwell in the house forever.[33]

(3) There are still questions to be asked here and to be discussed with you, but it is not my plan to burden you. For we serve the Lord's food to fellow servants; we feed sheep in the Lord's pastures and are fed at the same time. So just as what is necessary must not be denied, the weak heart must not be weighed down by an excessive amount of food. Therefore, let it not distress you, my beloved people, that I do not discuss today all the things which I think still ought to be discussed here. But the same reading will be recited to us again, please the Lord, on days when a sermon is due, and, with his help, it will be expounded more diligently.

32. Col 2.5, cf. 1 Cor 5.3; the words of the quotation fit Col 2.5 exactly but the context is clearly that of 1 Cor 5.1–3.
33. Cf. Jn 8.35.

TRACTATE 47

On John 10.14–21

YOU WHO listen to our Lord's discourse, not only willingly but also attentively, undoubtedly remember our promise. For the same Gospel reading was also read today which had been read on the last Lord's day because, by spending time on certain unavoidable points, we were unable to discuss all the things which we owed to your understandings. Accordingly, the things which have already been said and expounded we do not bring up today lest, by still repeating the same things, we may not at all be allowed to reach those points which have not yet been stated.

(2) You already know, in the name of the Lord, who the Good Shepherd is and how good shepherds are his members and therefore the Shepherd is one. You know who is the hired hand who must be put up with, who are the wolf, the thieves and the robbers who must be watched out for; who are the sheep, what is the gate by which both sheep and shepherd go in, and how the gatekeeper must be understood. You know also that whoever does not enter through the gate is a thief and a robber and comes only to steal, kill, and destroy. All these things, as I think, were sufficiently discussed and explicated.[1]

(3) Today, insofar as the Lord helps us (because Jesus Christ himself, our Savior, said that he was both shepherd and gate and said that the good shepherd enters by the gate), we ought to say how he enters through himself. For, if no one is a good shepherd except he who enters through the gate, and he himself is especially the good shepherd and yet he is himself the

---

1. In *Tractate* 46, of course.

gate, I cannot understand except that he himself enters through himself to his sheep and gives his voice to them that they may follow him, and that they, going in and going out, find pasture, which is eternal life.

2. Therefore, I say it quickly. I, seeking to go in to you, that is, to your heart, preach Christ; if I preach something else, I shall be trying to climb through another way.[2] And thus Christ is the door for me to you; I go in through Christ, not to your houses but to your hearts. I go in through Christ; you gladly hear Christ in me. Why do you gladly hear Christ in me? Because you are Christ's sheep. You have been bought by Christ's blood. You acknowledge your price which is not given by me but preached through me. For he who pours out his precious blood bought you; precious is the blood of that one without sin.

(2) Yet he himself also made precious the blood of his people for whom he gave the price of his blood; for if he did not make precious the blood of his people, it would not be said, "Precious in the sight of the Lord is the death of his holy ones."[3] and so also in regard to what he says, "The good shepherd lays down his life for his sheep,"[4] he is not the only one who did this; and yet, if those who did [so] are his members, he himself alone likewise did this. For he could do [something] without them, but how could they do [anything] without him since he himself said, "Without me you can do nothing"?[5] From this we show, however, what the others also did: because John the Apostle himself, who preached this Gospel which you have heard, said in his epistle, "As Christ laid down his life for us, so we, too, ought to lay down our lives for our brothers."[6] "We ought to," he said; he who first showed the way made us debtors. Therefore in a certain place it has been written: "If you sit to dine at the table of the ruler, wisely understand what is set before you. And put forth your hand, knowing that you ought to prepare such things."[7] You know what the table of the ruler is; thereupon is the body and blood

2. Cf. Jn 10.1.
4. Jn 10.11.
6. 1 Jn 3.16.

3. Ps 115 (116).15 (115.6 LXX).
5. Jn 15.5.
7. Prv 23.1–2 (LXX).

of Christ. He who approaches such a table, let him prepare such things. What is, let him prepare such things? "As he laid down his life for us, so we, too, ought," for edifying the people and defending the faith, "to lay down our lives for our brothers."

(3) Thus he said to Peter whom he wanted to make a good shepherd, not in Peter himself but in his body; Peter, do you love me? Feed my sheep.[8] This once, this again, this a third time, even making him sad. And when the Lord had asked as much as he judged ought to be asked, so that he who had denied thrice might confess thrice, and when he had for the third time entrusted to him his sheep to be fed, he said to him, "When you were younger, you fastened your belt and walked where you wanted; but when you are old, you will stretch out your hands, and another will fasten your belt and lead you where you do not want."[9] And the Evangelist explained what the Lord said, "Now this," he says, "he said, indicating the sort of death by which he was to glorify God."[10] Therefore, "Feed my sheep" pertains to this, that you lay down your life for my sheep.

3. Now who does not know these words of his, "As the Father knows me and I know the Father"? For he knows the Father through himself; we, through him. That he himself knows through himself, we know. And that we know through him, this we also know, because we know even this through him. For he himself said, "No one has ever seen God, except the only-begotten Son who is in the bosom of the Father, he has declared him."[11] Therefore through him we, too, to whom he has declared him. Likewise elsewhere he said, "No one knows the Son but the Father, and no one knows the Father but the Son—and he to whom the Son shall be pleased to reveal him."[12] As therefore, he himself knows the Father through himself, but we know the Father through him, so he goes in to the sheepfold through himself and we through him. We were saying that we had a gate to you through Christ.

8. Cf. Jn 21.15–17.
9. Jn 21.18.
10. Jn 21.19.
11. Jn 1.18.
12. Mt 11.27.

Why? Because we preach Christ. We preach Christ, and thus we go in through the gate. However, Christ preaches Christ because he preaches himself, and thus the shepherd goes in through himself.

(2) When the light shows other things which are seen in the light, does it need something else for it to be shown? Therefore, the light shows both other things and itself. Whatever we understand, we understand by the understanding. And by what do we understand the understanding except by the understanding? By the eye of the flesh do you thus see both other things and the eye itself? Although men see other things with their eyes, still they do not see their own eyes. The eye of the flesh sees other things; it cannot see itself. But the understanding understands both other things and itself. As the understanding sees itself, so, too, Christ preaches himself. If he preaches himself and by preaching goes in to you, he goes in to you through himself.

(3) And he himself is the gate to the Father; for there is no way by which one may come to the Father except through him. "For there is one God and one mediator of God and men, the man Christ Jesus."[13] Many things are said by a word; these very things which I have said, I have said, of course, by word. If I should wish to speak also the word itself, by what do I speak except by the word? And through this, through the word, also other things are said which are not what the word is. And the word itself cannot be said except through the word. With the Lord's help we have an abundance of examples.

(4) Therefore, hold on to how the Lord Jesus Christ is both the gate and the shepherd, the gate by opening himself, the shepherd by going in through himself. And indeed, brothers, what a shepherd is, that he has given also to his members; for Peter, too, was a shepherd, and Paul was a shepherd, and the rest of the Apostles were shepherds, and good bishops are shepherds. But no one of us says that he is the gate; this he himself has held for himself as his own, by which the sheep

13. 1 Tm 2.5.

may go in. Indeed, Paul the Apostle fulfilled the function of a good shepherd when he preached Christ, because he was going in through the gate. But when unruly sheep began to make schisms and to put up other gates for themselves, not by which they might go in to be assembled but by which they might wander to be separated, saying, some of them, "I belong to Paul," others, "I belong to Cephas," others, "I to Apollos," and others, "I to Christ," he was very much afraid for those who said, "I belong to Paul," and, as if shouting to the sheep: Wretches, where are you going? I am not the gate, he said, "Was it Paul who was crucified for you? Or was it in Paul's name that you were baptized?"[14] But those who were saying, "I belong to Christ," had found the gate.

4. Now, indeed, you are accustomed to hear constantly about one sheepfold and one shepherd; for we have often mentioned one sheepfold, preaching unity, that all the sheep might enter through Christ and none follow Donatus.[15] Nevertheless, in what regard the Lord said this by its proper signification[16] is sufficiently clear. For he was speaking among the Jews; but he had been sent to these very Jews, not for the sake of the ones unyielding in cruel hatred and persisting in darkness, but for the sake of the ones of that race who he says are his sheep. And about these he said, "I was sent only to the sheep which have been lost of the house of Israel."[17] He knew those, too, in the crowd of raging men and he foresaw them in the peace of those who believe. Therefore, what is, "I was sent only to the sheep which have been lost of the house of Israel," except that he showed his physical presence only to the people of Israel? To the Gentiles he did not go himself, but he sent; to

14. Cf. 1 Cor 1.12–13.
15. Donatus the Great, most likely the one from Casae Nigrae, is a somewhat obscure figure as scanty evidence for his biography survives. He was chosen at Carthage as the rival bishop to Caecilian (see *Tractate* 5.13, note 26) in A.D. 313 and remained as the schismatic bishop until he was deposed by imperial decree under the imperial legates Paulus and Macarius in A.D. 347. He was energetic and intelligent, and the schismatic movement took its name from him. See W. Frend, *The Donatist Church* (Oxford 1952) 11–21, 153–81.
16. Cf. *Tractate* 46.3, note 6.
17. Mt 15.24.

the people of Israel, in truth, he both sent and came himself so that those who were despising him would receive greater judgment because his presence was also shown to them.[18] The Lord himself was there, he chose a mother there, he wanted to be conceived there, to be born there, to pour out his blood there. His footprints are there; they are adored now where he last stood, at the place from which he ascended into heaven.[19] But he sent to the Gentiles.

5. But perhaps someone thinks that since he himself has not come to us, but has sent [others] to us, we have not heard his voice but the voice of those whom he sent. Perish the thought! Let that notion be expelled from your hearts. He himself was in those whom he sent. Hear Paul himself, whom he sent; for he especially sent Paul the Apostle to the Gentiles. And Paul, rousing fear not of himself but of him, said, "Can it be that you wish to receive a proof of the Christ who speaks in me?"[20] Hear also the Lord himself: "And I have other sheep," that is, among the Gentiles, "that do not belong to this fold," that is, to the people of Israel; "I must lead them, too." Therefore even through his own [he and] no one other leads them. Hear further: "They shall hear my voice." Look, he himself speaks through his own, and his voice is heard through those whom he sends. "That there may be one fold and one shepherd." To these two flocks, as if to two walls, he became the cornerstone.[21] Therefore, he is both the gate and the cornerstone; he is all these things through likeness, none of them properly speaking.[22]

6. For I have already said it and strongly asserted it, and those who grasp it understand; rather, those who understand

18. Cf. *Tractate* 31.11.

19. In Augustine's time and later, footprints were shown on the Mount of Olives as Christ's. See Jerome, *Liber Nominum Locorum ex Actis,* under *Mons Oliveti* (PL 23.1362), a passage which is repeated almost exactly by Bede, *Expositio De Nominibus Locorum vel Civitatum quae leguntur in Libro Actuum Apostolorum* (PL 92.1039); see also Sulpicius Severus, *Historia Sacra* 2.33 (PL 20.147–48), and the footnotes in PL 35.1733, Innes LNPF 7.261, and Browne LFC 29.626.

20. 2 Cor 13.3.

21. Cf. Eph 2.20; *Tractates* 9.17, 15.26, 17.9, and 20.7.

22. Cf. *Tractate* 46.3, note 6.

grasp it. And those who do not yet know with the understanding, let them hold with faith what they might not yet be able to understand. Through likeness Christ is many things which he is not through proper signification. Through likeness Christ is a rock, and Christ is a gate, and Christ is a cornerstone, and Christ is a shepherd, and Christ is a lamb, and Christ is a lion. How many things through likenesses, and other things which it would take too long to mention! However if you should investigate the proper significations of the things which you have been accustomed to see, he is not a rock, because he is not hard and without sensation; nor is he a gate, because a carpenter did not make him. And he is not a corner-stone, because he was not put together by a builder. He is not a shepherd, because he is not the guardian of four-footed sheep. And he is not a lion, because he is not a wild beast; nor is he a lamb, because he is not a domesticated animal. He is all these things, therefore, through likeness. What is he, then, by proper signification? "In the beginning was the Word, and the Word was with God, and the Word was God."[23] What about the human being who was seen? "And the Word became flesh and dwelt among us."[24]

7. Hear the rest also. "The Father loves me for this," he says, "that I lay down my life to take it up again." What does he say? "The father loves me for this," that I die to rise again.[25] For "I" was said with great emphasis "That I lay down," he said, "I lay down my life. I lay down." What is "I lay down"? *I* lay it down. Let the Jews not boast. They could rage, they could not have power; let them rage as much as they can. If I do not wish to lay down my life, what will they do by raging? By one answer they were laid low. When it was said to them, "Whom do you seek?" they said, "Jesus." And he said to them "'I am he.' They went backward and fell."[26] Those who fell at

23. Jn 1.1.
24. Jn 1.14.
25. Willems, following Migne, suggests that this abrupt sentence may be the result of a textual error, that it is superfluous, or that something is missing. Innes, LNPF 7.262, correctly disagrees.
26. Cf. Jn 18.4–6.

the one word of Christ who was about to die, what will they do when they will be judged, subjected to his voice? "I, I," I say, "lay down my life to take it up again." Let the Jews not boast as if they prevailed; he himself laid down his life.

(2) "I slept," he says. You know the psalm: "I slept and I took sleep; and I have risen up, for the Lord will take me up."[27] This psalm has just been read, we have just heard it. "I slept and I took sleep; and I have risen up, for the Lord will take me up." What is "I slept"? Because I wished it, I slept. What is "I slept"? I died. Did he not sleep who, when he wished it, rose up from the tomb as from a bed? But he loves to give glory to the Father, that he might build us up to give glory to our Creator. For what he added, "I have risen up, for the Lord will take me up"; do you think that here his courage, so to speak, failed him so that he could die through his own power but could not rise again through his own power? For so his words seem to declare when not more attentively understood. "I slept," that is, because I wished it, I slept. "And I have risen up." Why? "Because the Lord will take me up." Well now, would you not have the power to rise again by yourself? If you did not have the power, you would not say, "I have power to lay down my life and I have power to take it up again." Hear in another place in the Gospel that not only did the Father raise up the Son but the Son also raised up himself. "Destroy this temple," he said, "and in three days I will raise it up." And the Evangelist said, "But he spoke of the temple of his body."[28] For what died was raised up. For the Word did not die, that soul did not die. If not even yours dies, would the Lord's die?

8. How do I know, you say, if my soul does not die? If it is not killed by you, it does not die. How, you ask, can I kill my own soul? To pass over in silence, for the time being, other sins, "The mouth which lies kills the soul."[29] How, you say, am I assured that it does not die? Hear the Lord giving assurance to his servant: "Fear not those who kill the body and then can

27. Ps 3.6.
28. Jn 2.19, 21; see also *Tractate* 10.11.
29. Wis 1.11.

do no more." But what does he say clearly? "Fear him who has
the power to kill body and soul in Gehenna."[30] See that it dies,
see that it does not die. What is its dying? What is it for your
flesh to die? For your flesh to die is to lose its life; for your soul
to die is to lose its life. The life of your flesh is your soul; the
life of your soul is your God. As the flesh dies when its soul,
which is its life, has been lost, so the soul does when God, who
is its life, has been lost. Certainly then the soul is immortal.
Clearly it is immortal, because it lives even when dead. For
what the Apostle said about the widow given up to pleasure
can also be said about the soul if it has lost its God: "she is dead
while alive."[31]

9. How, therefore, does the Lord lay down his life?[32]
Brothers, let us search this out a little more attentively. The
hour does not limit us as is usual on the Lord's day; we have
leisure.[33] Let them have this profit who come together for the
word of God even on this day. "I lay down," he says, "my life."
Who lays it down? What [life] does he lay down? What is
Christ? Word and man. Yet he is not a man in such a way that
he is only flesh; but because he is a man, he consists of flesh
and soul. And, moreover, there is the whole man in Christ.
For he would not have taken on a worse part and foregone the
better part since, of course, the soul is a better part of the
human being than the body. Therefore, because there is
the whole man in Christ, what is Christ? The Word, I say, and
man. What is the Word and man? The Word, soul, and flesh.

(2) Hold fast to this because there have not been lacking
heretics also of this opinion, driven out indeed already long

30. A conflation of Mt 10.28 and Lk 12.4–5.
31. 1 Tm 5.6.
32. In the previous section the word for life was *vita* and *anima* meant
soul. Here Augustine uses *anima*, as in the Scripture citation, Jn 10.17–18, for
life as well as soul. This double connotation poses a continual translation
problem since English has no equivalent carrying the same range of meaning.
33. The older editions put *die dominico* with *vacat* rather than *solet*. This is
erroneous because the previous sermon was given on the Lord's Day and that
one was shortened because of the longer service. This one, on a weekday, can
therefore be longer; the subsequent sentence and the Tractate's opening
sentences also strongly support this as a weekday sermon. See CCL 36.409
and Browne LFC 29.629.

ago from the Catholic truth; but nevertheless like thieves and robbers not going in through the gate, they cease not plotting against the sheepfold. They are the heretics called the Apollinarists,[34] who dared to teach as doctrine that Christ is only Word and flesh; they assert that he did not take on a human soul. However some of them could not deny that there was *a* soul in Christ.[35] See the ridiculousness and madness not to be endured. They wanted him to have an irrational soul; they denied that he had a rational soul; they gave him the soul of a brute animal, took away that of a human being. But, not retaining their own reason, they took reason away from Christ. Let this be far removed from us who have been nourished and grounded in the Catholic faith. Therefore, on this occasion I would advise you, my beloved people, just as in the earlier readings we adequately informed you against the Sabellians[36] and the Arians[37] (the Sabellians who say: "The Father is he who the Son is," the Arians who say, "The Father is one thing, the Son another," as if the Father and the Son are not of the same substance)—we also informed you, as you remember and ought to remember, against the Photinian heretics[38] who

34. See *Tractate* 23.6, note 18.

35. There is disagreement among scholars as to whether the Apollinarists were dichotomists and held that the Logos replaced the soul and assumed only the body in Jesus' human nature or were trichotomists and held that the Logos replaced the rational soul (the mind) or both the rational soul and the irrational soul (the animating principle) in Jesus' human nature. Apollinaris was concerned partly on Scriptural grounds, e.g., that the Son had assumed the "flesh," and partly on logical grounds, e.g., that if Jesus were a complete human being, his rational soul would have been fallible and corruptible and the fallible and corruptible could not in any way become completely divine and therefore Christ could not have saved us. The Scripture under discussion, of course, Augustine would assert, immediately refutes this position since Jesus says he can lay down his *anima*, soul. A more extensive refutation of this position can be found in *DDQ* 80. See also C. Raven, *Apollinarianism* (Cambridge 1923) 169–232; J. Quasten, *Patrology* 3 (Westminster, Maryland, 1960) 381–82; J. Kelly, *Early Christian Doctrines*, 289–95; and, for a differing view, H. Wolfson, *The Philosophy of The Church Fathers* 1, 3rd ed. (Cambridge, Mass., 1956) 433–44, who maintains that Appollinaris held that Jesus did have the irrational animal soul but that the Logos nature so predominated that the animal soul was rendered a mere property or quality and not a nature.

36. See *Tractate* 29.7, note 17.   37. See *Tractate* 1.11, note 27.

38. See *Tractate* 26.5, note 18.

said that Christ was only human without his divinity and against the Manichees[39] who said that he was God alone without his humanity. On this occasion let us also inform you against the Apollinarists who say that our Lord Jesus Christ did not have a human soul, that is, a rational soul, an intelligent soul, a soul, I say, in which we differ from a brute animal because we are human beings.

10. How, therefore, did the Lord say here, "I have power to lay down my life"? Who lays down his life and takes it up again? Does Christ, from the fact that he is the Word, lay down his life and take it up again? Can it be from the fact that it is a human soul, that that soul lays itself[40] down and takes itself up again? Can it be from the fact that he is flesh that the flesh lays down its life and takes it up again? I have proposed three things; let us examine carefully all of them and choose the one which agrees with the measure of truth.

(2) For if we say that the Word of God has laid down his life and taken it up again, one must fear that a perverse thought may steal its way [into our minds], and it may be said to us, Therefore at some time that soul was separated from the Word and at some time that Word, after the time when he took up that soul, was without a soul. For I see that the Word was without a human soul, but at the time when "in the beginning was the Word, and the Word was with God, and the Word was God."[41] For from the time when the Word became flesh that he might dwell among us[42] and the man was taken up by the Word, that is, the whole man, soul and flesh, what did the passion do, what did death do if it did not separate the body from the soul? Truly, it did not separate the soul from the Word. For if the Lord died, rather, because the Lord died (for he died for us on the cross), without doubt his flesh

---

39. See *Tractate* 34.2, note 1. For the Manichaeans' docetic view of Christ, see Augustine, *De Haeresibus* 46.15 (CCL 46.317–18); G. Widengren, *Mani and Manichaeism*, 124; L. Koenen, "Augustine and Manicheism," 191–92; and S. Hopper, "The Anti-Manichaean Writings," *A Companion to the Study of St. Augustine*, ed. R. Battenhouse (New York 1955) 152–53.

40. See note 32.

41. Jn 1.1.

42. Cf. Jn 1.14.

breathed out[43] his soul; for a short time his soul abandoned his flesh, but that it might arise again when the soul returned. But I do not say that the soul was separated from the Word. To the soul of the robber he said, "This day you will be with me in paradise."[44] He did not abandon the believing soul of the robber; did he abandon his own? Perish the thought! But as the Lord kept that man's soul under his guardianship, truly he kept his own inseparably.

(3) But if we say that his soul laid itself down and took itself up again, the meaning is most ridiculous; for what was not separated from the Word could not be separated from itself.

11. Let us say, therefore, both what is true and what can be easily understood. Look, here is some man, not consisting of Word and soul and flesh, but of soul and flesh. Let us ask, as regards this man, how any man lays down his life.[45] Can it be, perhaps, that no man lays down his life? You can say to me: No man has power to lay down his life and take it up again. If a man could not lay down his life, the Apostle John would not say, "As Christ laid down his life for us, so, too, we ought to lay down our lives for the brethren."[46] Therefore, it is also allowed to us (if we, too, should be filled with his virtue, because we can do nothing without him) to lay down our lives for the brethren. When some holy martyr laid down his life for the brethren, who laid it down and what [life] did he lay down? If we have understood this, then we shall see how it was said by Christ, "I have power to lay down my life." O man, are you prepared to die for Christ? I am prepared, he says. I shall say this in other words. Are you prepared to lay down your life for Christ? And to these words he answers me: I am prepared—just as he had answered me when I asked, Are you prepared to die? Therefore, to lay down one's life is the same as to die. But for whom is the striving therein? For all men,

43. *Caro ipsius exspiravit animam.* Augustine probably has in mind, or at least uses the traditional language for, the ancient notion that the life-giving principle (the *anima*) is the breath, and that when the breath completely leaves the fleshy body (the *caro*), death occurs.

44. Lk 23.43.   45. *animam.* See note 32.

46. 1 Jn 3.16.

when they die, lay down their life, but not all lay it down for Christ. And no one has power to take up what he has laid down; but Christ both laid it down for us, and he laid it down when he wanted, and he took it up when he wanted. Therefore, to lay down one's life is to die. So also the Apostle Peter said to the Lord, "I will lay down my life for you,"[47] that is, I will die for you.

(2) Attribute this to the flesh; the flesh lays down its life, and the flesh takes it again. And yet the flesh does not do so by its own power, but by the power of him who dwells in the flesh; therefore, the flesh lays down its life by breathing it out. See the Lord himself on the cross. "I am thirsty," he said. Those who were there soaked a sponge in vinegar, tied it to a reed, and put it to his face. And when he had taken it, he said, "It is finished." What is "It is finished"? All things which were foretold about me, that they would be before my death, have been fulfilled. And because he had power to lay down his life when he wanted, after he said, "It is finished," what did the Evangelist say? "And he bowed his head and delivered over his spirit."[48] This is to lay down his life.

(3) Now pay attention here, my beloved people. "He bowed his head and delivered up his spirit." Who delivered up? What did he deliver up? He delivered up the spirit; the flesh delivered it up. What is, the flesh delivered it up? The flesh sent it out, the flesh breathed it out. And thus it is said to *ex-spire*, the spirit comes to be *extra*, [on the outside]. Just as *ex-sile*, one comes to be outside his land, and *ex-orbit*, one comes to be outside the normal path—so *ex-spire*, spirit comes to be on the outside. And this spirit is the soul. Therefore when the soul goes out from the flesh and the flesh remains without the soul, then a man is said to lay down his life. When did Christ lay down his life? When the Word willed it. For in the Word there

47. Jn 13.37.
48. Cf. Jn 19.28–30. A problem similar to that for the word *anima* exists in translating and interpreting the word *spiritus* (in Greek πνεῦμα). Here Augustine identifies the *spiritus* with the *anima* in the sense of soul rather than breath. See W. Schumacher, *Spiritus and Spiritualis,* 57–58. Cf. also *Tractate* 12.5, 7, notes 17 and 23 where *spiritus* is used for either the wind or the Holy Spirit.

was sovereignty; therein was the power when the flesh might lay down life and when it might take it up.

12. Therefore, if the flesh laid down its life, how did Christ lay down his life? For is not the flesh Christ? Yes, certainly, the flesh is Christ, and the soul is Christ, and the Word is Christ; and yet these three things are not three Christs, but one Christ.

(2) Examine the human being, and from yourself make a step to those things which are above you, and if these things are not yet understandable, at least they ought to be believed. For as one human being is soul and body, so one Christ is the Word and a human being. See and understand what I have said. Soul and body are two things, but there is one human being; the Word and the human being are two things, but there is one Christ.

(3) Therefore, inquire about the human being. Where is the Apostle Paul now? If someone should answer, At rest with Christ, he speaks the truth. Likewise if someone should answer, At Rome in his tomb, he also speaks the truth. He answers the former to me about his soul, the latter about his flesh. And yet we do not, therefore, say that there are two Apostles Paul, one who rests in Christ, another who had been placed in the tomb, although we say the Apostle Paul lives in Christ and we say the same Apostle Paul lies dead in the tomb. Someone dies. We say, A good man, a faithful man, he is at peace with the Lord. And immediately, Let us go to his last rites and bury him. You are going to bury him whom you had already said was at peace with God since the soul which flourishes immortally is one thing and the body which lies in corruptibility is another. But each of the two things from which the union of flesh and soul took the name of human being, now also single and separate, has kept the name of human being.

13. Therefore, let no one waver when he hears that the Lord said, "I lay down my life and I take it up again." The flesh lays it down, but by the power of the Word; the flesh takes it, but by the power of the Word. And the Lord Christ himself was called the flesh alone.

(2) How, he says, do you prove that? I dare to say that Christ was called the flesh of Christ alone. Surely we believe not in God the Father only, but also in Jesus Christ, his only Son, our Lord. Now I have said the whole—in Jesus Christ, his only Son, our Lord. Understand there the whole, Word and soul and flesh. And certainly you also profess that which the same faith holds, that you believe in that Christ who was crucified and buried. Therefore, you do not deny that Christ was also buried; and yet the flesh alone was buried. For if the soul was there, he was not dead; but if his death was real so that his resurrection may be real, he had been in the tomb without his soul. And yet *Christ* was buried.

(3) Learn this also in the Apostle's words: "Have this attitude in you," he says, "which was also in Christ Jesus who, though he was in the form of God, thought it not robbery to be equal to God."[49] Who, except Christ Jesus, as pertains to that which is the Word, God with God? But see what follows: "But he emptied himself, taking the form of a servant, made in the likeness of men and in habit found as a man."[50] And who [did] this except the same Christ Jesus himself? But here already are all things, both the Word in the form of God, which took the form of a servant, and the soul and flesh in the form of a servant which was taken by the form of God. "He humbled himself, becoming obedient even to death."[51] Now in death, the flesh alone was killed by the Jews. For if he said to his disciples, "Do not fear those who kill the body but cannot kill the soul,"[52] could they kill more than the body in him? And, nevertheless, when the flesh was killed, Christ was killed. Thus, when the flesh laid down its life, Christ laid down his life; and when the flesh, that it might arise, took up its life, Christ took up his life. And yet this was not done by the power of the flesh, but by the power of him who assumed both soul and flesh, whereby these things might be fulfilled.

14. "This commandment," he said, "I received from my Father." The Word did not receive the commandment by a

---

49. Phil 2.5–6.   50. Phil 2.7.
51. Phil 2.8.   52. Mt 10.28.

word, but in the only-begotten Word of the Father every commandment exists. But when the Son is said to receive what he
has substantially from the Father, as it was said, "As the Father
has life in himself, so he has given to the Son to have life in
himself,"[53] since the Son himself is life, his power is not lessened, but his generation is shown. For the Father did not, as it
were, add something to that Son who was born imperfect; but
in his begetting, he gave all things to him whom he begot as a
perfect being. Thus, he gave him his equality, whom he begot
not unequal. But when the Lord said these things, because the
light was shining in darkness and the darkness did not grasp
it,[54] "There again arose a dissension among the Jews because
of these words. And many of them were saying, 'He has a devil
and is out of his mind. Why do you listen to him?'" This was
the thickest darkness! "Others were saying, 'These are not the
words of one who has a devil. Can a devil open the eyes of the
blind?'" Already these men's eyes had begun to be opened.

53. Jn 5.26.
54. Cf. Jn 1.5.

TRACTATE 48

On John 10.22–42

S I HAVE already shown you, my dear people, you ought to keep it firmly in mind that the holy Evangelist John wishes us not to be always nourished with milk but to feed upon solid food. But whoever is still less fit for taking the solid food of God's word, let him be nourished with the milk of faith and let him not hesitate to believe the word which he cannot understand. For faith is a meritorious act, understanding a prize. In the very effort of concentration our mind's eye works hard to remove the stains of human mistiness and to be made clear for the word of God. Therefore, let no effort be refused if love is present; for you know that he who loves does not feel burdened by his effort. For all effort is burdensome to those who do not love. If lust supports such great efforts among the greedy, does love not support them among us?

2. Turn your attention to the Gospel. "Now the feast of the Dedication took place in Jerusalem." The Encaenia (feast of the Dedication[1]) was a celebration of the dedication of the temple. For in Greek καινόν[2] means new. Whenever something new was dedicated, the name *Encaenia* was given. Now, too, common usage employs this term; if anyone is dressed in

1. This is the feast of Hanukkah held in mid-December to celebrate the building of a new altar and the rededication of the Temple in 165 B.C. after Judas Maccabeus drove the Syrians, who had profaned the altar of holocausts, out of Jerusalem. See R. E. Brown, *The Anchor Bible* 29.401; B. Vawter, JBC 2.445.

2. In the Latin text the feast is called the *Encaenia*, a transliteration of the Greek ἐνκαίνια, from the prepositional prefix ἐν and the root καιν-, meaning renovation or renewal, used in the Sepuagint to translate Hanukkah which means dedication and as the common term for the dedication of temples. See R. E. Brown, *The Anchor Bible*, 29.402.

a new tunic, he is said *encaeniare*—to consecrate it. For the Jews were solemnly celebrating that day on which the temple was dedicated. That very feast day was being held when the Lord said the words which were read.

3. "It was winter. And Jesus was walking in the temple, in Solomon's portico. The Jews, therefore, gathered around him and were saying to him, 'How long do you keep our soul in suspense? If you are the Christ, tell us plainly.'" They did not desire the truth but were getting ready a slander. "It was winter" and they were cold; for they were slow to approach that divine fire. But to approach is to believe; he who believes approaches, he who denies withdraws. The soul is moved not by feet, but by feelings.[3] They had grown cold apart from the affection of loving, and they were hot with a lust for harming. They were far away and yet they were there. They did not approach by believing but pressed close by persecuting.

(2) They were seeking to hear from the Lord, I am the Christ, and perhaps they understood about Christ as regards the man. The prophets preached Christ. But not even the heretics understand the divinity of Christ preached both in the prophets and in the Gospel itself; how much less the Jews, as long as the veil is over their heart?[4]

(3) Accordingly, in a certain place the Lord Jesus, knowing that they understand about Christ as regards the man, but not as regards God, as regards the fact that he was man, but not as regards the fact that he remained God even when the man was assumed, said to them, "What think you of Christ? Whose Son is he?"[5] They answered according to their opinion, "David's." For so they had read, and they were holding to this alone, because they read of his divinity but did not understand it. But in order that he might keep them in suspense that they might seek the divinity of him whose weakness they despised, the Lord answered them, "Then how does David in spirit call him Lord, saying, 'The Lord said to my Lord, "Sit on my right hand, until I put your enemies under your feet"'? If David

3. Cf. *Tractate* 26.3.   4. Cf. 2 Cor 3.15.
5. Mt 22.42.

then in spirit calls him Lord, how is he his son?"[6] He did not deny, but he asked. Let no one, when he has heard this, think that the Lord Jesus denied that he is the son of David.

(4) If the Lord Christ would deny that he is the son of David, he would not enlighten the blind so invoking him. For one time he was passing by and two blind men, sitting beside the road, shouted, "Pity us, son of David."[7] And when he heard this word, he pitied them. He stopped, he healed, he gave light because he acknowledged the name. The Apostle Paul, too, says, "who was made to him of the seed of David according to the flesh."[8] And to Timothy, "Be mindful that Jesus Christ rose from the dead, of the seed of David, according to my gospel."[9] Because the virgin Mary traced her origin from the seed of David, from that source the Lord is of the seed of David.[10]

4. The Jews were seeking this from Christ as an important matter, so that if he were to say, I am the Christ, as far as they understood [him] to be only of the seed of David, they would falsely accuse him of claiming royal power for himself. What he answered them is more; they wanted to accuse him as the son of David. He answered that he was the Son of God. And how? Listen. "Jesus answered them, 'I speak to you and you do not believe. The works which I do in my Father's name, these give testimony concerning me. But you do not believe because you are not of my sheep.'" You have already earlier learned who the sheep are.[11] Be sheep! By believing they are sheep, by following the Shepherd they are sheep, by not despising the Redeemer they are sheep, by going in through the gate they are sheep, by going out and finding pasture they are sheep, by enjoying eternal life they are sheep. How then did he say to these, "You are not of my sheep"? Because he saw that they were predestined for eternal destruction, not purchased at the price of his blood for eternal life.[12]

6. Mt 22.43–45, quoting Ps 109 (110).1.
7. Cf. Mt 20.30–34.   8. Rom 1.3.
9. 2 Tm 2.8.   10. Cf. *Tractate* 8.9.
11. Cf. *Tractate* 45.9–13.
12. That God foreknows that some are condemned poses a theological problem in view of the orthodox teaching that Christ died for all and by his death and resurrection redeemed all. As in all matters touching predestina-

5. "My sheep hear my voice, and I know them, and they follow me. And I give them eternal life." Look, there are the pastures. If you recollect, he had said earlier, "He will go in and go out, and shall find pastures."[13] We went in by believing, we go out by dying. But as we went in through the gate by faith, so let us go out of the body, faithful. For so we go out through the gate itself that we may be able to find pastures. Life eternal is called the good pastures; there no grass dries up, all is green, all flourishes. There is a certain herb which is ordinarily called "always living";[14] there only is it found to live. "I shall give them," he says, "eternal life"—to my sheep. You seek malicious accusations precisely because you are thinking about the present life.

6. "And they shall not perish forever." You hear the implication, as if he said to them, You will perish forever because you are not of my sheep. "No one shall snatch them out of my hand." Receive it more attentively. "What my Father has given me is greater than all."[15] What can the wolf do? What can the thief and the robber do? They only destroy those predestined

---

tion, Augustine's view is complex, difficult, and somewhat obscure. It would appear that he holds that God does will the salvation of all men and in a general sense he does so by providing all with the power and the means for salvation. But he also, for his own reasons, gives men the freedom to choose or refuse salvation and then he foreknows that some will choose salvation and some damnation. He *could* intervene, but wills not to do so; were he to intervene freedom of will would be meaningless. Since he foreknows that some will refuse redemption and does not intervene, then in an absolute sense he wills the damnation of some. Why he chooses this kind of world over the many possible dispositions of creation is a mystery. See Browne, 29.1238–46, and E. Portalie, *A Guide to the Thought of Saint Augustine,* 215–23. But the situation is probably more complex than this, as all men's acts are the results of freely given, unmerited graces. Why are some not given graces to enable their perseverance? Augustine, then, would seem to take a rather rigid view of predestination: that God, for his own reasons, in fact *wills* the damnation of some. This tractate seems to support such a view. See J. Kelly, *Early Christian Doctrine,* 366–69, for a good, brief account of the latter position.

13. Jn 10.9.

14. Pliny in his *Natural History,* 18.159, 25.160, and 26.111, identifies this plant with the Latin *sedum* or *digitellum,* although there is another variety, and he says that it is called *semper vivum* because it is always green. The plant then is the English houseleek.

15. There are variant readings for Jn 10.29; see J. Birdsall, JThS 11 (1960) 342–44.

to destruction. But from those sheep about whom the Apostle says, "The Lord knows who are his,"[16] and "Those whom he foreknew he also predestined. And those he predestined he also called; and those he called he also justified; and those he justified he also glorified,"[17]—from those sheep neither does the wolf seize nor the robber kill. He who knows what he gave for them is sure about their number. And this is what he said: "No one shall snatch them out of my hand," and likewise, in regard to the Father, "What my Father has given me is greater than all."

(2) What did the Father give the Son greater than all? That he might be his only-begotten Son. What is "has given"? Did he to whom he was to give already exist or did he give by begetting? For if he to whom he gave that he should be Son existed, he existed at some time and was not Son. Perish the thought that the Lord Christ existed at some time and was not Son! This can be said about us; for at some time we were sons of men, but we were not sons of God. For he has made us sons of God by grace, him by nature, because he was born so. And you may not say, He did not exist before he was born. For he who is coeternal with the Father was never not born. He who understands, let him grasp it; he who does not grasp it, let him believe, let him be nourished and he will grasp it. The Word of God is always with the Father and is always the Word and because he is the Word, therefore he is the Son. Therefore, he is always the Son and always equal. For he was equal not by growing but by being born, who was always born Son from the Father, God from God, coeternal from eternal. But the Father is not God from the Son; the Son is God from the Father. Therefore, the Father, by begetting, gave to the Son that he be God; by begetting, he gave that he be coeternal to himself; by begetting, he gave that he was equal. This is what is greater than all.

(3) How is the Son life, and how is the Son one having life? He is what he has. You are one thing, you have another thing.

16. 2 Tm 2.19.
17. Rom 8.29–30.

For instance, you have wisdom. Are you wisdom itself? Accordingly, because you yourself are not what you have, if you lose what you have, you go back to the state of not having. And sometimes you take, sometimes you lose. As our eye does not have light inseparably in itself, it is open and takes the light; it is closed and loses it. Not so is God, the Son of God, not so is the Word of the Father. Not so is the Word, because he does not pass away in sounding, but abides in being born. He has wisdom in such a way that he himself is Wisdom and makes [men] wise; he has life in such a way that he himself is life and makes [men] alive. This is what is greater than all.

(4) John the Evangelist himself observed heaven and earth, wishing to speak about the Son of God; he observed them, and he passed beyond. He thought of the thousands of the army of angels above the heaven; he thought of and passed beyond the universe, as an eagle does the clouds, so with his mind, beyond creation. He passed beyond all great things; he reached that which is greater than all, and said, "In the beginning was the Word."[18] But because he of whom the Word is is not from the Word, but the Word is from him of whom the Word is, therefore he said, "What the Father gave me," that is, that I be his Word, that I be his only-begotten Son, that I be the splendor of his light, "is greater than all." Therefore, "no one shall snatch," he says, "My sheep out of my hand. No one is able to snatch out of my Father's hand."

7. "Out of my hand" and "out of my Father's hand." What is this: "No one snatches out of my hand" and "No one snatches out of my Father's hand"? Is there one hand of the Father and Son, or, perhaps, is the Son himself the hand of the Father? If we should understand hand as power,[19] the power of the Father and the Son is one, because their divinity is one; but if we should understand hand as it was said through the prophet, "And to whom has the arm of the Lord

18. Jn 1.1.
19. The Latin word *manus* is fertile in connotations, as Augustine shows in this section; the meaning whereby it designates persons in relation to other persons was not an uncommon metaphor in Latin authors, both secular and Christian. See TLL 8.357–58.

been revealed?,"[20] the hand of the Father is the Son himself. And this was not so said as if God has a human shape and, as it were, limbs of a body, but because all things were made through him. For men are accustomed to say that other men are their hands, through whom they do what they wish. Sometimes even the work of the man itself, because it is made through the hand, is called the man's hand, as someone is said to recognize his hand when he recognizes that which he wrote. Therefore since the hand of a man, who properly has a hand among the limbs of his body, is spoken of in many ways, how much more ought it not be understood in one way when one reads of the hand of God, who has no bodily form. And for this reason, in this passage it is better that we understand the hand of the Father and the Son as the power of the Father and the Son, lest, perhaps, when we have taken here the hand of the Father as said of the Son himself, carnal thought should begin to seek even a Son of the Son himself, whom it may similarly believe to be the hand of Christ. Therefore, "no one snatches from my Father's hand," that is, no one snatches from me.

8. But lest, perhaps, you still waver, hear what follows. "I and the Father, we are one thing."[21] Up to this point, the Jews could bear it. They heard, "I and the Father, we are one thing," and they did not endure it; but hard, as is their character, they ran to stones. "They took up stones to stone him." The Lord, because he would not suffer what he did not wish to suffer, and suffered only what he wished to suffer, speaks to them who still desire to stone him. "The Jews took up stones to stone him. Jesus answered them, 'Many good works I have shown you from my Father; for which of those works do you stone me?' And they answered, "It is not for a good work that we stone you, but for blasphemy, and because, although you are a man, you make yourself God.'" They gave this answer in reply to what he had said: "I and the Father, we are one thing." Look, the Jews understood what the Arians do not. They were angered precisely because they perceived that

20. Is 53.1.
21. See *Tractate* 36.9, note 28.

"I and the Father, we are one thing," could not be said except where there is equality of the Father and the Son.

9. See, however, what the Lord answered to the slow. He saw that they were not enduring the splendor of truth, and he softened it in his words: "Is it not written in your law," that is, in the law given to you, "that I said, 'You are gods'?" God says to men through a prophet in the psalm, "I said: You are gods."[22] And the Lord called all those Scriptures in general the law, although, elsewhere he uses "the law" in a particular sense, distinguishing it from the prophets, as "the law and the prophets up until John,"[23] and, "On these two commandments the whole law and the prophets depend."[24] Sometimes, however, he divided the same Scriptures into three, where he says, "All things which were written in the law and the prophets and the psalms about me had to be fulfilled."[25] But now he also called the psalms by the name of the law where it has been written, "I said: You are gods." "If it called those men gods to whom God's speech[26] was made—and Scripture cannot be broken—do you say to him whom the Father has sanctified and sent into the world, 'You blaspheme,' because I said, 'I am the Son of God'?" If God's speech was made to men, that they might be called gods, how is the Word of God himself, who[27] is with God, not God? If through God's speech men become gods, if they become gods by participation, is not he in whom they participate God? If enlightened lights are gods, is not the Light that enlightens God? If those warmed, in a way, by saving fire are made gods, is not he by whom they are warmed God? You approach the Light and you are enlightened and you are numbered among the sons of God; if you withdraw from the Light, you are darkened and you are accounted among the shadows. Yet, that Light does not approach itself, because it does not withdraw from itself. There-

22. Ps 81 (82).6.   23. Lk 16.16.
24. Mt 22.40.   25. Lk 24.44.
26. The Latin text has *sermo* and not *verbum* for the Greek λόγος.

27. The Latin has the neuter "which" to agree with the neuter *Verbum;* so too in the next sentence "He in whom" would be "That in which" by strict Latin syntax.

fore, if God's speech makes you gods, how is the Word of God not God?

(2) Therefore, "the Father sanctified his Son and sent him into the world." Perhaps someone may say, If the Father sanctified him, then was there sometime when he was not holy? As he begot, so he sanctified. For in begetting him, he gave to him that he be holy, because he begot him holy. For if what is sanctified was not holy before, how do we say to God the Father, "Hallowed by thy name"?[28]

10. "If I do not do my Father's works, do not believe me. But if I do and if you are unwilling to believe me, believe the works, so that you may know and believe that the Father is in me and I in him." The Son does not so say, "the Father is in me and I in him," as men can say it. For if we should think well, we are in God; and if we should live well, God is in us: as believers, participating in his grace, enlightened by him, we are in him and he in us. But not so the only-begotten Son; he is in the Father and the Father in him, as an equal is in him to whom he is equal. Of course, we can sometimes say, "We are in God and God is in us." Can we ever say, "I and God, we are one thing"? You are in God because God sustains you;[29] God is in you because you were made a temple of God.[30] But because you are in God and God is in you, can you ever say, "He who sees me sees God," as the only-begotten said, "He who has seen me has seen the Father,"[31] and "I and the Father, we are one thing"? Acknowledge the proper mark of the Lord and the gift of the servant. The proper mark of the Lord is equality with the Father, the gift of the servant is participation in the Savior.

11. "They sought, therefore, to seize him." Would that they had seized him, but by believing and understanding, not by being violent and by murdering. For now, my brothers, when I say such things, a weak man saying strong things, a small man saying great things, a fragile man saying solid things,

28. Mt 6.9.
29. That is, God preserves you in being. The verb is *continet* and might also be translated: "contains you."
30. Cf. 1 Cor 6.19 and 2 Cor 6.16.
31. Jn 14.9.

both you, as if from the same stuff from which I also am, and I, who speak to you, together we all wish to seize Christ. What is "to seize"? You understood, you seized. But not so the Jews. You seized that you may have; they wished to seize that they might not have. And because they want to seize in such a way, what did he do to them? "He went forth from their hands." They did not seize him because they did not have the hands of faith. The Word was made flesh, but it was not a great thing for the Word to free his flesh from hands of flesh. To seize the Word with the mind, this is to seize Christ rightly.

12. "And he went again across the Jordan into the place where John was at first baptizing and stayed there. And many came to him and they were saying, 'John indeed did no sign.'" You remember what was said to you about John, that he was a lamp and was giving witness to the day?[32] What, therefore, did they say about him? "John did no sign." John, they say, showed no miracle; he did not cause demons to flee, he did not drive out a fever, he did not enlighten the blind, he did not raise the dead, he did not feed so many thousands of men from five or seven loaves, he did not walk upon the sea, he did not command winds and waves. John did none of these things; and yet everything that he said gave testimony to this one. Let us come through the lamp to the day. "John did no sign, but all things whatsoever John said about this man were true." Look, these are they who seized him, but not as the Jews did! The Jews wished to seize him while he was departing; these seized him while he remained. Finally, what follows? "And many believed in him."

32. See Jn 1.6–8, 5.33–35; *Tractates* 2.5–6, 23.3.

TRACTATE 49

On John 11.1–54

MONG ALL the miracles which our Lord Jesus Christ performed, the resurrection of Lazarus is especially proclaimed. But if we should observe who did it, we ought to be delighted, rather than struck with wonder. He who made the man raised a man; for he is the only one of the Father through whom, as you know, all things were made.[1] If, therefore, all things were made through him, what wonder is it if one person arose through him since so many are born through him every day? It is a greater thing to create persons than to resurrect them. Yet, he deemed it good both to create and to resurrect—to create all, to resurrect some.

(2) For although the Lord Jesus performed many miracles, not all were written, as the same holy John the Evangelist himself attests that the Lord Christ both said and did many things which were not written; but those things were chosen for writing which seemed to meet the need of the salvation of believers.[2] For you heard that the Lord Jesus raised a dead man; this is enough for you, so that you may know that, if he wished, he would raise all the dead. And, indeed, he has kept this for himself until the end of the world. For you heard that, by a great miracle, he raised from his tomb one who was dead for four days; yet, as he himself said, "The hour will come when all who are in their tombs shall hear" his "voice and come forth."[3] He raised up a man already stinking, but nevertheless, in the stinking corpse there was still the shape of the limbs; on the last day, at one word, he will restore ashes into flesh. But it is necessary that he now do some things by which,

1. Cf. Jn 1.3. 2. See Jn 20.30–31.
3. Jn 5.28–29.

given as signs of his power, we may believe in him and be prepared for that resurrection which will be to life, not to judgment. And so, indeed, he says, "The hour will come when all who are in their tombs shall hear" his "voice, and those who have done well shall come forth to the resurrection of life; those who have behaved evilly, to the resurrection of judgment."[4]

2. Nevertheless, we read in the Gospel that three dead men were raised by the Lord, and, perhaps, not without purpose. For the deeds of the Lord are not only deeds but also signs.[5] If, therefore, they are signs, besides the fact that they are wonders, they assuredly signify something; and to find the signification of these deeds is considerably more laborious than to read or hear them.

(2) We heard in wonder, as though a vision of the great miracle had been placed before our very eyes when the Gospel was read, how Lazarus came back to life. If we should observe the more wondrous works of Christ, everyone who believes rises again; if all of us should observe and understand the more execrable deaths, everyone who sins dies.[6] But every person fears the death of the flesh, few fear the death of the soul. As for the death of the flesh, which will one day come without a doubt, all take care that it not come; this is the goal of their efforts. Man, destined to die, exerts effort not to die, and man, destined to live forever, does not exert effort not to sin. And when he exerts effort not to die, he exerts effort without good reason; for he does it in order to put off death for a long while, not to escape it. But if he does not wish to sin, he will exert no effort, and yet he will live forever. Oh, if we could stir up men and be equally stirred up with them that we might be such lovers of the life that abides as men are the lovers of the life that flees! What does a man, faced with the danger of death, not do? With a sword hanging over their necks, men have given up whatever they were keeping back

4. Jn 5.28–29.
5. Cf. *Tractates* 24.2; 25.2, 5; 44.1.
6. See *DDQ* 65 where Augustine also allegorically interprets the death of Lazarus as the death of the soul by sin.

for themselves with which they might live. Who has not immediately given it up to escape being struck? And perhaps after giving it up, he was struck. Who did not wish, in order to live, straightway to lose that by which he might live, choosing a beggar's life over swift death? To whom was it said, Sail that you may not die, and he put it off? To whom was it said, Work that you may not die, and he was lazy? God orders slight things that we may live forever, and we neglect to obey.

(3) God does not say to you, Lose whatever you have that you may live for a short time, harassed by work, but, Give to the poor from what you have that you may live forever, free of care, without work. The lovers of temporal life, which they have neither when they wish nor as long as they wish, reproach us; and we in turn do not reproach ourselves, so sluggish, so lukewarm to take eternal life which we shall have if we will and shall not lose when we have it. But this death which we fear, we shall have it even if we do not will it.

3. If, therefore, the Lord, by his great grace and his great mercy, raises up souls that we may not die forever, we understand well that those three dead persons, whom he raised up in their bodies, signify and represent something about the resurrection of souls which happens through faith. He raised up the daughter of the synagogue official while she was still lying in the house;[7] he raised up the widow's young son after he had been carried beyond the gates of the city;[8] he raised up Lazarus, who had been buried for four days.

(2) Let each one look into his own soul. If it sins, it dies; sin is the death of the soul. But sometimes one sins in thought. What is evil has delighted; you consented, you sinned. That consent killed you. But the death is internal, because the evil thought has not yet proceeded into deed. The Lord, signifying that he raises up such a soul, raised up that girl who had not yet been carried out, but was lying dead in the house, as if the sin was hidden.

(3) But if you not only consented to the evil delight but also did the evil deed itself, you have, as it were, carried the dead

7. Cf. Mt 9.18–25.
8. Cf. Lk 7.11–15.

beyond the gate; you are now outside, you have been carried out, dead. And yet the Lord also raised him up and returned him to his mother, the widow. If you have sinned, repent! The Lord raises you up, too, and will return you to your mother, the Church.

(4) The third dead person is Lazarus. There is a monstrous kind of death; it is called bad habit. For it is one thing to sin, it is another to make a habit of sinning. He who sins and is immediately corrected quickly returns to life; because he has not yet been ensnared by habit, he has not yet been buried. But he who sins habitually has been buried and it is well said of him, "He stinks." For he begins to have the worst reputation, like the foulest odor. Such are all who are accustomed to crimes, abandoned in character. You say to him, Do not do it. When does he listen to you, he whom the earth so presses and who is moldering in putrefaction and weighted down by the massive block of habit? And yet, no less was the power of Christ for raising him up. We know, we have seen, everyday we see men live better, after the worst habit has been changed, than they who were reproaching them live. You despised the man. Look, the very sister of Lazarus (if, perhaps, she is the same one who anointed the feet of the Lord with perfume and wiped with her hair what she has washed with her tears) was better raised up than her brother; she was freed from a huge mass of bad habit. For she was an infamous sinner, and about her it was said, "Many sins are forgiven her, because she has loved much."[9] We see many, we know many; but let no one

---

9. See Lk 7.36–50; the quotation is Lk 7.47. Innes LNPF 7.271, points out that the woman sinner in Lk is not specifically named and is erroneously identified with Mary, the sister of Lazarus. The Eastern Fathers did not make such an identification but the Western Fathers sometimes did. Hence John Chysostom, *In Ioannem Homiliae* 62.1 (PG 59.342 or FOTC 41.165) explicitly denies that this Mary was the sinner in Lk. Ambrose, *Expositio Evangelii Secundum Lucam* 6.14 (CCL 14.179) distinguishes the sinful woman of Lk from the woman in Mt 26.6–7 but doesn't mention Jn11.2. Jerome, *Commentariorum in Matheum* 4.1008–17 (CCL 77.246) denies that the woman in Mt 26.7 is the same as the one in Lk 7.37 but identifies her with Jn 12.3. Bede, *In Lucae Evangelium Expositio* 3 on Lk 7.6–7 (CCL 120.166–67) and *In Marci Evangelium Exposito* 4 on Mk 14.3 (CCL 120.606), identifies Mary, the sister of Lazarus, with this sinful woman and with Mary Magdalene and says that there

despair, let no one presume about himself. It is evil both to despair and to presume about oneself. So do not despair, in order that you may choose the one about whom you ought to presume.

4. And so the Lord raised up Lazarus, too. You heard what sort of person he was, that is, what the resurrection of Lazarus signifies. Now then, let us read, and because many things in this reading are clear, let us not seek an explanation about each point so that we may discuss thoroughly the necessary ones. "Now there was a certain sick man, Lazarus of Bethany, of the village of Mary and Martha, his sisters." In the previous reading you remember that the Lord eluded the hands of those who had wanted to stone him and went across the Jordan where John was baptizing. When the Lord, then, had come there, Lazarus became sick in Bethany, which was a village very near to Jerusalem.

5. "Now, Mary, whose brother Lazarus was sick, was she who anointed the Lord with ointment and wiped his feet with her hair. Therefore his sisters sent to him, saying." We already understand to what place they sent—where the Lord was, because he was away, across the Jordan, of course. They sent to the Lord, reporting that their brother was ill, so that, if he deigned, he might come and free him from the illness. He put off healing that he might be able to raise up.

(2) What then did his sisters report? "Lord, behold, the one you love is sick." They did not say, Come. For to one who loves there is only the need to tell. They did not dare to say, Come and heal. They did not dare to say, Order there and it will happen here. Now why would these women not also say this, if the faith of that centurion is praised for this very thing? For he said, "Lord, I am not worthy to have you come under my

---

were two incidents of anointing Jesus' feet. See J. Fitzmeyer, *The Gospel According to Luke* (I–IX), in *The Anchor Bible* 28 (Garden City, 1981) 688. Modern commentators vary in their approach to this problem as the JBC illustrates. B. Vawter (2.446–48), J. McKenzie (2.108), and C. Stuhlmueller (2.137) all see the same story but refashioned in four different ways, whereas, E. Mally (2.53) sees Lk as a different incident from the other three Gospels.

roof, but only say the word and my boy will be healed."[10] These women said none of these things, but only, "Lord, behold, the one you love is sick." It is enough that you know; for you do not love and abandon.

(3) Someone asks, How was a sinner signified through Lazarus and yet he was so loved by the Lord? Let him hear him speaking, "I have not come to call the just, but sinners."[11] If God does not love sinners, he would not come down to earth from heaven.

6. "But upon hearing this, Jesus said to them, 'This sickness is not unto death, but for the glory of God, that the Son of God may be glorified.'" Such glorification of him did not magnify him, but benefitted us. Therefore, he said this: "It is not unto death," because even the death itself was not unto death but rather for a miracle, by the performance of which men might believe in Christ and avoid true death.

(2) Indeed, see how, albeit indirectly, the Lord said that he was God because of certain ones who deny that the Son is God. For there are heretics who deny that the Son of God is God.[12] Look, let them hear: "This sickness," he said, "is not unto death, but for the glory of God." For what glory? Of what God? Hear what follows: "that the Son of God may be glorified." Therefore "this sickness," he said, "is not unto death, but for the glory of God, that the Son of God may be glorified by it." By what? By that sickness.

7. "Now Jesus loved Martha and her sister Mary and Lazarus." He was sick, they were sad, all were beloved; but he loved them, the Healer[13] of the sick, or rather, actually, the Raiser of the dead and the Comforter of the sad.

10. Mt 8.8.
11. Mt 9.13.
12. Especially the Arians and the Photinians.
13. *Salvator*. In Christian Latin the word primarily carries the connotation Savior. The word in fact is a Christian Latin creation as Augustine himself asserts in *Sermo* 299.6 (PL 38.1371), and the few instances cited in secular Latin writings all belong to the Christian period. See C. Mohrmann, *Die Altchristliche Sondersprache*, 145–46; A. Ernout and A. Meillet, *Dictionnaire étymologique de la langue latine* (Paris 1967) 592; and J. Krebs and J. Schmalz, *Antibarbarus der Lateinischen Sprache* 2 (Basel 1907) 530–31.

(2) "Therefore, when he heard that he was sick, even then he stayed in the same place for two days." Therefore, they reported to him; he remained there. So long a time was extended until four days were completed. Not without purpose, unless because, perchance—no, rather, because surely that very number of days suggests some mystery.

(3) "Then, after this he says again to his disciples, 'Let us go into Judea,'" where he had almost been stoned, and it seemed that he had departed from there precisely that he might not be stoned. He departed as a human being; but in returning, as though having forgotten his weakness, he showed his power. "Let us go," he said, "into Judea."

8. Then, after he said this, see how frightened the disciples were. "The disciples say to him, 'Rabbi, just now the Jews were seeking to stone you and are you going there again?' Jesus answered, 'Are there not twelve hours of day?'" What does this answer mean? They said, "Just now the Jews wanted to stone you and are you going there again" that they may stone you? And the Lord said, "Are there not twelve hours of the day? If a man goes walking by day, he does not stumble, because he sees the light of this world; but if he goes walking by night, he stumbles, because the light is not in him." He indeed speaks about the day, but in our understanding it is, as it were, still night. Let us call upon the Day that it drive out the night and illuminate the heart with its light. For what did the Lord intend to say? As far as it appears to me, as far as the depth and profundity of his meaning give forth a slight light, he intended to impugn their hesitation and lack of faith.

(2) They wanted to advise the Lord that he not die, and he had come to die that they themselves might not die! So, too, in a certain other place,[14] the holy Peter, loving the Lord, but still not fully understanding why he had come, feared that he might die; and he was displeasing to Life, that is, to the Lord himself. For when he was revealing to the disciples what he would suffer at Jerusalem from the Jews, among the others, Peter answered and said, "Far be it from you, Lord; be pro-

14. For this whole section see Mt 16.13–23.

pitious to yourself; this will not happen."[15] And immediately
the Lord said, "Go behind me, Satan, for you do not savor the
things that are of God, but the things that are of men." And a
little before, professing the Son of God, he had deserved
praise; for he had heard, "Blessed are you, Simon Bar-Jona;
for flesh and blood has not revealed it to you, but my Father
who is in heaven." To that one to whom he had said, "Blessed
are you," he says, "Go behind, Satan," because he was not
blessed by him. But by whom? "For flesh and blood has not
revealed this to you, but my Father who is in heaven." Look at
the source of your blessing, not from what is yours but from
what is mine. Not because I am the Father, but because all
things which the Father has are mine.[16] If he is blessed from
what is of the Lord himself, from what of whom is he satan?
He says it there; for he gave an accounting of the blessedness
so that he said, "Flesh and blood has not revealed" this "to
you, but my Father who is in heaven." This is the source of
your blessedness. But what I said, "Go behind me, satan," hear
also the cause of this thing. "For you do not savor the things
that are of God, but the things that are of men." Therefore, let
no one flatter himself; from his own, he is satan; from that
which is of God, he is blessed. For what is "from his own"
except from his own sin? Take away sin; what is yours? Justice,
he says, is from that which is mine. For what do you have that
you have not received?[17]

(3) Therefore, when men wanted to give advice to God, the
disciples to the Teacher, the servants to the Lord, the sick to
the Physician, he reproached them and said, "Are there not
twelve hours of the day? If a man goes walking by day, he does

15. Mt 16.22. Augustine's Latin version seems to contain a tautology; the
Greek ἵλεώς σοι κύριε is given twice, first in its interpreted form, *absit a te,
Domine,* and then in a literal translation, *propitius tibi esto.* Parallel texts dem-
onstrate that the Greek is probably equivalent to the first Latin phrase, as the
Vulgate has it; see E. Schweizer, *The Good News According to Matthew,* trans.
D. Green (Atlanta 1975) 345, and A. Schlatter, *Der Evangelist Mathaiis* (Stutt-
gart 1963) 516–17. Augustine has the same text in *En in Ps* 34.1.8, 39.25,
62.17, 68.2.5, 126.4 (CCL 38.306, 442–43; 39.805, 921; 40.1860) but in 34.2.6
(CCL 38.317) he leaves out *propitius tibi esto.*
    16. Cf. Jn 16.15.
    17. Cf. 1 Cor 4.7.

not stumble." Follow me, if you do not want to stumble. Do not give me advice, for you ought to receive advice from me. To what does this have reference: "Are there not twelve hours of the day?" Because, that he might show that he was the day, he chose twelve disciples. If I am the day, he said, and you are the hours, do the hours give advice to the day? The hours follow the day, not the day the hours. If, therefore, those men were the hours, what was Judas there? Was not he, too, among the twelve hours? If he was an hour, he was shining. If he was shining, how did he hand the day over to death? But the Lord in this expression had in view not Judas himself but already his successor. For when Judas fell, Matthias succeeded him and the number twelve remained.[18] Therefore, not without purpose did the Lord choose twelve disciples, but because he himself was the spiritual day. Therefore, let the hours follow the day, let the hours preach the day, let the hours be enlightened by the day, let the hours be illumined by the day, and through the preaching of the hours let the world believe in the day. Therefore, in summary, he said this: Follow me, if you do not want to stumble.

9. "And after this he says to them. 'Lazarus, our friend, is sleeping; but I am going that I may awaken him from sleep.'" He spoke the truth. To the sisters he was dead, to the Lord he was sleeping. He was dead to men who were unable to raise him up; for the Lord roused him from the tomb with such ease as you would not rouse a sleeping person from his bed. Therefore, as regards his own power he spoke of him as sleeping; for other dead men, too, are often referred to in the Scriptures as sleeping, as the Apostle says, "But I will not have you, brothers, ignorant about those who are asleep, so that you may not grieve, even as others who have no hope."[19] And so he, too, called them sleeping, because he foretold that they would rise again.

(2) Therefore, every dead man sleeps, both the good and the evil. But just as, among those who daily sleep and rise up,

18. See Acts 1.15–26. On Judas as one of the chosen twelve see also *Tractate* 27.10.
19. 1 Thes 4.13 (Douay 4.12).

what each one sees in dreams makes a difference (some perceive pleasant dreams, others tormenting ones, so that, wak-
ing, he fears to sleep lest he return again to them), so each
man sleeps with his own condition and rises with his own
condition. And it makes a difference for each one who is later
to be brought before the judge with what kind of guard he is
taken. For, in fact, detentions under guard are exercised in
accordance with the merits of the cases. Lictors are ordered to
guard some, a human and mild duty and appropriate to a
citizen; others are handed over to adjutants.[20] Others are sent
into prison; and in the prison itself not all, but in accordance
with the merits of more serious cases, [some] are thrust into
the lowest parts of the prison. Therefore, as there are various
guards for those performing an office, so there are various
guards for the dead and various merits for those rising again.
The poor man was taken, the rich man was taken, but the
former to the bosom of Abraham, the latter where he would
thirst and find not a drop.[21]

10. Therefore all souls have, that I may use this opportunity to instruct you, my beloved people, all souls have, when
they go out of the world, their own various receptions. Good
souls have joy, evil ones torments. But when the resurrection
has occurred, both the joy of the good will be greater and the
torments of the evil more severe, when they will be tortured
with the body. Received in peace were the holy partiarchs,
prophets, apostles, martyrs, the good faithful; nevertheless, in
the end all will still receive what God promised. For there has
been promised resurrection even of the flesh, the destruction of death, eternal life with the angels. We all will receive
this at the same time; for each person, when he dies, if he is
worthy of it, receives the rest which is given immediately after

20. The official called the *optio* was originally an assistant to a centurion or
other officer; see A. Jones, *History of the Later Roman Empire* (Oxford 1964)
459, 626–27, 665, and 673. Later it had a more extended signification, "overseer." See CCL 36.425; Innes LNPF 7.273, and Browne LFC 29.656. The
phrase *optio carceris* is perhaps a Roman legal term and is used not infre-
quently in the *Itala* and early Christian writings; hence one might translate
optio here "jailers," as Willems suggests. See TLL 9.823.49–75.
21. See Lk 16.19–24.

death.[22] In former times the patriarchs received it; see for how long they are at rest. Later the prophets, more recently the apostles, much more recently the holy martyrs, every day the good faithful. And some have been for a long time in this rest, others not so long, others for fewer years, and others not even yet for a short time.[23] But when they will awake from this sleep, all will receive at the same time what was promised.

11. "'Lazarus, our friend, is sleeping; but I am going that I may awaken him from sleep.' His disciples therefore said," as they understood, so they answered, "'Lord, if he is asleep, he will be well.'" For the sleep of the sick is usually a sign of health. "But Jesus had been speaking about his death; but they thought that he was speaking about sleeping in the sense of slumber. So then Jesus said to them plainly." For he had said somewhat obscurely, "He is sleeping." Therefore, he said plainly, "Lazarus is dead. And for your sakes I am glad I was not there, that you may believe." I both know that he is dead and I was not there; for he has been reported to be sick, not dead. But what could be hidden from him who had created and to whose hands the soul of the dying man had gone? This is what he said: "For your sakes I rejoice that I was not there that you may believe," so that now they might begin to wonder that the Lord could call him dead—something which he had neither seen nor heard.

(2) And here, indeed, we ought to remember that the faith even of the disciples themselves who had already believed in him was still being built up by miracles, not that that faith which was not might begin to be, but that that which had already begun to be might grow, although he used such a word as if they were at that time beginning to believe. For he did not say, "For your sakes I am glad," that your faith may be increased or strengthened; but he said, "that you may believe," which must be understood, that you may believe more fully and strongly.

22. Cf. *Tractate* 26.16.
23. This follows the CCL text. Some editors substitute *in* for *nec* and some simply omit *nec*. The text then says: "and others in recent time."

12. "'But let us go to him.' Then Thomas, who is called the Twin, said to his fellow disciples. 'Let us also go, and[24] let us die with him.' Jesus, therefore, came and found him already in the tomb four days." Concerning the four days, many things indeed can be said, as the obscurities of the Scriptures present themselves in such a way as to bear many senses according to the diversity of those who understand them. Let us, too, say what the man dead four days seems to us to signify. For as in that blind man we understand, in a way, the human race,[25] so, perhaps, also in this dead man we are going to understand many men; for one thing can be signified in various ways.

(2) When a human being is born, he is already born with death, because he contracts sin from Adam. For this reason the Apostle says, "Through one man sin entered the world and through sin death, and thus it has passed to all men, in whom all have sinned."[26] Look, you have one day of death, because man contracts it from the scion of death.

(3) Then he grows, he approaches the rational years so that he knows the natural law which all have fixed in their hearts: What you do not wish to be done to you, do not do to another.[27] Is this learned from the pages [of books] and is not read, in a way, in nature itself? Are you willing to suffer a theft? Of course you are not. Look, there is the law in your

24. Both the Vulgate and the Greek texts have a subordinate purpose clause here, "in order that we may die with him."

25. Cf. *Tractate* 44.1.

26. Rom 5.12. Augustine's Latin text creates as ambiguity. He does not give an expressed subject for *pertransiit*, "has passed," although both the Greek text and the Vulgate have an expressed "death" as its subject. Augustine takes "sin" to be the subject; this creates a problem with *in quo* which grammatically can refer to "sin" but could not do so to "death" in Latin because of the genders involved. Yet the sense becomes difficult if this is done. Augustine refers it to "one man," as he does everywhere in the many, many references to this quotation, as, e.g., in the *Contra Duas Epistulas Pelagianorum* 4.7 (PL 44.614); this is syntactically difficult. The Greek text has ἐφ' ᾧ which is a conjunctive phrase meaning "since," "inasmuch as," without strict relative force; the Latin *in quo* is a very strange equivalent (although *in quo* is also found in the Vulgate). Even the Greek ἐφ' ᾧ presents problems; see J. Fitzmeyer, JBC 2.307.

27. Cf. Mt 7.12, Lk 6.31, Tb 4.16.

heart: What you are not willing to suffer, do not do. And men transgress this law. Look, a second day of death!

(4) The Law has also been given divinely through Moses, the servant of God. There it was said: You shall not kill. You shall not commit adultery. You shall not utter false witness. Honor your father and mother. You shall not covet your neighbor's property. You shall not covet your neighbor's wife.[28] Look, the Law was written and it is disregarded. Look, the third day of death!

(5) What remains? The Gospel also comes, the kingdom of Heaven is preached, Christ is proclaimed everywhere. He threatens Hell; he promises eternal life. Even this is disregarded. Men transgress the Gospel. Look, the fourth day of death! Rightly does he now stink! And ought mercy be denied to such men? Perish the thought! The Lord does not disdain to approach even to raise up such men.

13. "Now many of the Jewish people had come to Martha and Mary to console them over their brother. Therefore, when Martha heard that Jesus was coming, she went to meet him. But Mary sat at home. Therefore, Martha said to Jesus, 'Lord, if you had been here, my brother would not have died. But even now I know that God will give you whatever you ask of God.'" She did not say: But even now I ask you to raise up my brother. For how did she know if it were beneficial for her brother to raise up? She only said this: I know that you can; if you wish, you will do it. For whether you should do it belongs to your judgment, not my presumption. "But even now I know that God will give you whatever you ask of God."

14. "Jesus says to her, 'Your brother will rise again.'" This was ambiguous. He did not say: I am now raising up your brother, but "'Your brother will rise again.' Martha says to him, 'I know that he will rise again in the resurrection on the last day.'" About that resurrection I am sure, about this one I am uncertain. "Jesus says to her, 'I am the resurrection.'" You say: My brother will rise again on the last day. It is true! But through him through whom he will then rise again he can also

28. Cf. Ex 20.12–17.

rise now, because, he says, "I am the resurrection and the life."
Hear, brothers, hear what he says. Surely, the whole expectation of those standing about was that Lazarus would come
back to life, a man dead four days. Let us hear and let us rise!
How many there are among this people whom the massive-
ness of habit weighs down! Perhaps there are some hearing
me to whom it is said, "Be not drunk with wine, for in that is
debauchery."[29] They say: We cannot [give it up]. Perhaps
some impure persons befouled by lusts and crimes hear me, to
whom it is said: Do not do this that you may not perish. And
they answer: We cannot be rid of our habit. O Lord, resurrect
them. "I am," he says, "the resurrection and the life." Because
he is the life, therefore he is the resurrection.

15. "He who believes in me, even if he should die, shall live;
and everyone who lives and believes in me shall not die forever." What is this? "He who believes in me, even if he should
die," as Lazarus died, "shall live," because he is not God of the
dead, but of the living. About the fathers who died long ago,
that is, about Abraham and Isaac and Jacob, he gave the Jews
this answer: "'I am the God of Abraham and the God of Isaac
and the God of Jacob.' He is not the God of the dead but of the
living. For all live to him."[30] Therefore, believe; and if you
should die, you will live. But if you do not believe, even when
you are alive, you are dead.

(2) Let us also prove that if you do not believe, even if you
are alive, you are dead. To a certain man who was putting off
following him and saying, "Let me go first to bury my father,"
the Lord said, "Let the dead bury their dead; you, come,
follow me."[31] There a dead man needed to be buried; there,
too, the dead were going to bury the dead. He was dead in the
flesh; they, in the soul. Why is there death in the soul? Because
there is not faith. Why is there death in the body? Because the
soul is not there. Therefore, faith is the soul of your soul.[32]

29. Eph 5.18.
30. Lk 20.37–38; cf. Mt 22.32, referring to Ex 3.6, 15.
31. Mt. 8.21–22 (the quotation is influenced by Lk 9.60).
32. or "life of your soul" or "life of your life." The word *anima* can mean
both "life" and "soul" and Augustine often plays on this double connotation.
See *Tractate* 47.10, note 32.

"He who believes in me," he said, "even if he should die," in the flesh, "shall live" in the soul until the flesh also rises again, never afterwards to die. That is, "He who believes in me," although he dies, "shall live."

(3) "And everyone who lives" in the flesh "and believes in me," even if he dies for a time because of the death of the flesh, "he shall not die forever" because of the life of the spirit and the immortality of the resurrection. This is what he said, "'And everyone who lives and believes in me shall not die forever. Do you believe this?' She said to him, 'Yes, Lord, I have believed that you are the Christ, the Son of God, who have come into the world.'" When I believed this, I believed that you are the resurrection, I believed that you are the life. I believed that he who believes in you, even if he dies, shall live, and he who lives and believes in you shall not die forever.

16. "And when she had said these things, she went back and silently called her sister Mary, saying, 'The Teacher is here and is calling for you.'" It should be noticed how [the Evangelist] called a restrained voice silence. For how was she silent who said, "The Teacher is here and is calling for you,"? It should be noticed also that the Evangelist did not say where or when or how the Lord called for Mary so that this must be understood from Martha's words instead, thus preserving the brevity of the narrative.

17. "When she heard this, she got up quickly and came to him. (For Jesus had not yet come into the village, but was still in that place where Martha had met him.) Therefore when the Jews, who were with her in the house and were consoling her, saw that Mary got up quickly and went out, they followed her, saying, 'She is going to the tomb, to weep there.'" Why was it a concern of the Evangelist to relate this? That we may see how it happened that there were many people there when Lazarus was raised up. For the Jews, thinking that she was hurrying for the very reason that she sought comfort for her grief in tears, followed her so that so grand a miracle—the raising up of a man dead four days—might find very many witnesses.

18. "Now when Mary had come to the place where Jesus was, seeing him, she fell at his feet and said to him, 'Lord, if

you had been here, my brother would not have died.' When, therefore, Jesus saw her weeping and the Jews who were with her weeping, he groaned in the spirit and troubled himself, and said, 'Where have you laid him?'" He has implied something to us by his groaning in the spirit and his troubling himself. For who could cause him trouble, except himself? So, my brothers, first observe here his power and so seek its signification.

(2) You are troubled against your will; Christ was troubled because he willed it. Jesus was hungry—it is true!—but because he willed it. Jesus slept—it is true!—but because he willed it. Jesus was sad—it is true!—but because he willed it. Jesus died—it is true!—but because he willed it. It was in his power to be affected in such and such a way, or not to be affected. For the Word took soul and flesh, joining to himself the nature of the whole man in the unity of person. For the soul of the apostle also was enlightened by the Word; the soul of Peter was enlightened by the Word; the soul of Paul, the souls of the other Apostles, of the holy Prophets, were enlightened by the Word. But about none of these was it said, "The Word was made flesh."[33] About none of these was it said, "I and the Father, we are one thing."[34] The soul and flesh of Christ together with the Word of God is one person, is one Christ. And through this [word] wherein there is the highest power, at the nodding of his will, weakness is manipulated, that is, "He troubled himself."

19. I have mentioned the power; attend to the signification. Very guilty is the one whom the four days of death and that burial signify. Therefore, what does it mean that Christ troubled himself, except that it signifies to you how you ought to be troubled when you are weighted down and oppressed by so great a mass of sin?

(2) For you observed yourself, you saw yourself guilty, you summed up for yourself: I did that, and God spared me; I committed that, and he held back. I heard the Gospel and I despised it; I was baptized and I have gone back again to the

33. Jn 1.14.
34. Jn 10.30.

same things. What am I to do? Where am I to go? In what way am I to escape? When you say these things, then Christ growls in complaint, because faith growls. In the voice of the one growling in complaint appears the hope of the one arising. If there is faith within, Christ is there, growling in complaint; if faith is in us, Christ is in us. For what else did the Apostle say: "to have Christ dwell through faith in your hearts"?[35] Therefore, your faith concerning Christ is Christ in your heart.

(3) Related to this is that account of when he was sleeping in a boat; and when the disciples were endangered, with shipwreck already threatening, they approached him and awoke him. Christ arose, gave orders to the winds and the waves; and a great calm came.[36] So it is with you. Winds enter your heart where, of course, you are sailing, where you are crossing this life as a storm-filled and dangerous sea; the winds enter, they stir up the waves, they trouble the ship. What are the winds? You heard an insult; you are angered. The insult is a wind; anger is a wave. You are endangered, you purpose to reply, you purpose to return abuse for abuse; now the ship is close to wrecking. Wake the sleeping Christ! For this is why you waver and get ready to return evils for evils—because Christ is sleeping in the boat. In your heart the sleeping of Christ is the forgetting of faith.

(4) For if you were to awaken Christ, that is, recall your faith, what does Christ, as if awakening in your heart, say to you? I heard, "You have a devil,"[37] and I prayed for them. The Lord hears and endures; the servant hears and is indignant! But you want to be avenged. Well now, have I then been avenged? When your faith says these things to you, orders are given as it were, to the winds and the waves, and a great calm comes. Therefore, just as to arouse Christ in the boat is to arouse faith, so in the heart of the person whom the great weight and habit of sin oppresses, in the heart of the man, the transgressor even of the holy Gospel, the despiser of eternal punishments, let Christ growl in complaint, let the man reproach himself.

35. Eph 3.17.   36. Mt 8.23–26.
37. Jn 7.20.

(5) Hear further: Christ wept; let the man weep for himself.
For why did Christ weep except to teach man to weep? Why
did he growl and trouble himself, except that the faith of a
man justly displeased with himself ought in some way to growl
in accusation of his evil works in order that the habit of sinning may give way to the vehemence of penitance?

20. "And he said, 'Where have you laid him?'" You knew
that he was dead and did you not know where he was buried?
And this is a signification that even God, in a way, does not
know the lost man. I did not dare to say, he does not know; for
what does he not know? But in a way, he does not know. How
can we prove this? Hear the Lord as he is going to speak in
judgment: "I do not know you, depart from me."[38] What is "I
do not know you"? I do not see you in my light, I do not see
you in that justice which I know. So also here, as if not knowing such a sinner, he said, "Where have you laid him?" Such is
the voice of God in paradise after man sinned: "Adam where
are you?"[39] "They say to him 'Lord, come and see.'" What is
"see"? Have mercy. For when he has mercy the Lord sees. For
this reason it is said to him, "See my lowliness and toil and take
away all my sins."[40]

21. "Jesus wept. The Jews, therefore, said, 'See how he
loved him.'" What is "He loved him"? "I have not come to call
the just, but sinners to repentance."[41] "But some of them said,
'Could not this man who opened the eyes of the blind man
have caused that even this man should not die?'" He was
unwilling to bring it about that he should not die; what he was
going to do is more, that the dead man should rise.

22. "Jesus therefore, again groaning in himself, comes to
the tomb." Let him also groan in you if you purpose to live
again. To every man who is overwhelmed by the worst habit it
is said, "He comes to the tomb. Now it was a cave and a stone
was laid across it." The dead man is under a stone, the guilty

38. Mt. 7.23.
39. Gn 3.9.
40. Ps 24 (25).18 (LXX). In *DDQ* 65 Augustine specifically applies Jn 11.34
to predestination; the Lord's question is a signification of our secret and
predestined calling, as if he were ignorant of it although in fact we are.
41. Lk 5.32; cf. Mt 9.13 and Mk 2.17.

man is under the law. For you know that the law that was given to the Jews was written on a stone.[42] But all the guilty are under the law; those who live well are with the law. The law has not been laid down for the just.[43]

(2) What then is "Take away the stone"? Preach grace. For the Apostle Paul says that he is the minister of the New Testament, not of the letter but of the spirit. "For the letter," he says, "kills; the spirit gives life."[44] The letter killing is as a stone pressing down. "Take away," he says, "the stone." Take away the weight of the law; preach grace. "For if there had been a law given which could give life, justice would be altogether from the law. But Scripture had shut all things in under sin that by the faith of Jesus Christ the promise might be given to those who believe."[45] Therefore, "take away the stone."[46]

23. "Martha, the sister of him who was dead, says to him, 'Lord, by now he stinks, for he has been dead four days.' Jesus says to her, 'Did I not say to you that if you believe, you will see the glory of God"? What is "You will see the glory of God"? That he raises up even one who stinks and is four days dead. "For all have sinned and lack the glory of God"[47] and "where sin has abounded, grace has abounded far more."[48]

24. "They then took away the stone. And Jesus, raising his eyes upward, said, 'Father, I thank you for having heard me; yet I knew that you always hear me. But I have said this because of the people who stand round that they may believe that you have sent me. When he had said these things, he cried with a loud voice." He groaned, he wept, he cried with a loud voice. With what difficulty does he whom the weight of bad habit presses down rise up! But nevertheless he rises up; he is given life by the grace hidden within, he rises up after a loud voice. What happened? "He cried with a loud voice, 'Lazarus, come out.' And immediately he who had been dead

---

42. See Ex 31.18.
43. Cf. 1 Tm 1.9.
44. 2 Cor 3.6.
45. Gal 3.21–22.
46. See *DDQ* 65 where he interprets the stone either as those who wished Christians to be circumcised or those who live evilly in the Church and cause those who wish to believe to stumble.
47. Rom 3.23.
48. Rom 5.20.

came forth, bound hands and feet with strips of cloth, and his face was bound with a cloth." Do you wonder how he came forth with his feet bound and not wonder that a man four days dead has risen? In each instance there was the power of God, not the strength of the dead men. He came forth and he was still bound; still wrapped, yet he now came out. What does it signify? When you despise, you lie dead; and if you despise such things as I have mentioned, you lie buried. When you confess, you come forth. For what is to come forth, except by going out, as it were, from hidden places to be shown openly? But that you may confess, God acts by crying with a loud voice, that is, by calling with great grace.

(2) Therefore, when the dead man had come forth still bound, confessing but still guilty, in order that his sins might be loosed, the Lord said this to his ministers: "Free him and let him go." What is "Free him and let him go"? Whatever you shall loose on earth shall be loosed in heaven.[49]

25. "Therefore many of the Jews who had come to Mary, and had seen what Jesus did, believed in him. Some of them, however, went to the Pharisees and told them what Jesus did." Not all of the Jews who had come to Mary believed, yet many did. "But some of them," either of the Jews who had come together or of those who had believed, "went to the Pharisees and told them what Jesus did," either for proclaiming it so that they themselves also might believe, or rather for betraying him so that they might rage. But howsoever and by whomever, these things were conveyed to the Pharisees.

26. "The priests and the Pharisees gathered a council and said, 'What are we to do?'" And yet they were not saying, Let us believe. For ruined men were giving more thought to how they might harm him in order to destroy him than to how they might counsel themselves that they might not perish. And yet they were afraid and, in a way, were taking counsel. "They

49. Cf. Mt 18.18. In *DDQ* 65 Augustine interprets the bindings as vexations of the flesh from which we can never be free as long as we have this present human body; the cloth over the face signifies that we can never have full knowledge in this life. The coming forth is the soul's rejection of carnal vices—yet the vexations and the incomplete knowledge are still with it.

said, 'What are we to do? For this man is performing many signs. If we let him go on like this, all will believe in him; and the Romans will come and take away our place and our nation.'" They were afraid of losing temporal possessions and gave no thought to eternal life, and so they lost each. For in fact the Romans, after the passion and glorification of the Lord, took away from them both their place and their nation, by assault and by removal; and that follows them which was said elsewhere: "But the children of this kingdom will go into the darkness outside."⁵⁰ But they feared this—that if all would believe in Christ, no one would remain who would defend the city and temple of God against the Romans; for they thought that the teaching of Christ was against the temple itself and against the laws of their fathers.

27. "But one of them, Caiphas, since he was the high priest of that year, said to them, 'You know nothing whatever; and you do not consider that it is expedient for us that one man die for the people and that the whole nation not perish.' (He did not say this on his own, but since he was the high priest of that year, he prophesied.)" Here we are taught that the spirit of prophecy foretells the future even through evil men; nevertheless, the Evangelist attributes this to divine mystery, because he was the high priest, that is, the highest priestly minister.

(2) It can, however, disturb us how he is called "the high priest of that year" since God established *one* as the highest priestly minister, and when he died, *one* would succeed him.⁵¹ But we must understand that because of ambitions and controversies among the Jews it was later established that there be

50. Mt 8.12.

51. In the Herodian-Roman period the high priesthood became a political office and ceased to be held by one person for life; the high priest could be appointed and removed from office at the will of authority. Hence in addition to the incumbent high priest, there were a number of former high priests who retained the title and held certain privileges and powers, e.g., membership in the Sanhedrin. Also the chief priests, priests of a rank below the high priest but, because of their pontifical office, above the less important priesthoods, would be involved in the term high priests. See J. Jeremias, *Jerusalem in the Time of Jesus*, trans. F. and C. Cave (Philadelphia 1969) 158–60 and 175–79; and *Encyclopedia Judaica* (Jerusalem 1971) 8.470–74 and 13.1086–88.

several and that they administer by turns in individual years. For this is also said about Zachary: "Now it happened, when he executed the priestly function before God in the course of his turn, according to the custom of the priestly office, that it fell to him by lot to offer incense, going into the temple of the Lord."[52] From this it is clear that there were more than one and that they took their turns; for it was allowed only to the highest priestly minister to offer incense.[53] And perhaps even during one year, more than one administered, to whom others would succeed in another year, from whom it fell by lot to some one to offer incense.

(3) What is it that Caiphas prophesied? "That Jesus would die for the nation, and not only for the nation but to gather in one the children of God who had been dispersed." This the Evangelist added; for Caiphas prophesied only for the nation of the Jews in which there were sheep concerning whom the Lord himself says, "I have been sent only to the sheep that are lost of the house of Israel."[54] But the Evangelist knew that there were other sheep who were not of this fold, who must be led in, that there be one fold and one shepherd.[55] These things, however, were said in regard to predestination. For they, who had not yet believed, were neither his sheep nor the children of God.

28. "From that day they planned to kill him. Jesus therefore no longer walked openly among the Jews, but went into the region near the desert, to a town which is called Ephrem; and there he stayed with his disciples." Not because his power had failed, in which of course, if he wanted, he might openly have dealings with the Jews and they would do nothing to him. But in the weakness of man, he showed an example of living to his disciples, in view of which it would be clear that there was no sin if his faithful, who are his members, should withdraw themselves from the eyes of persecutors and by hiding avoid the wrath of the impious rather than excite it more by offering themselves.

52. Lk 1.8–9.
53. Cf. Ex 30.7, Lv 10.1–2, Nm 16.
54. Mt 15.24.
55. Cf. Jn 10.16.

TRACTATE 50

On John 11.55–12.11

ODAY'S READING, about which we shall speak what the Lord will give, follows yesterday's reading of the holy Gospel, about which we spoke what the Lord gave. Certain sentences in the Scriptures are so evident that they ask for a listener rather than an exegete; we need not delay on these so that there is sufficient time for the ones on which we must necessarily spend time.

2. "Now the Jewish Passover was near." The Jews wished to have that feast day stained with the Lord's blood. On that feast day the Lamb was slaughtered, who by his blood has consecrated the same day as a feast for us. There was a plan among the Jews for slaughtering Jesus; he who had come from heaven to suffer wished to approach the place of his passion because the hour of the passion was imminent.

(2) "Therefore many from the country went up to Jerusalem before the Passover to purify themselves." The Jews did this according to the instruction of the Lord which had been enjoined in the law through the holy Moses, that all assemble from everywhere on the feast day which was the Passover and be purified by the celebration of that day.[1] But that celebra-

---

1. Originally the *Pascha*, the Passover, was an agricultural feast consisting of the slaughtering and eating of a paschal animal, often but not necessarily a lamb, and it was celebrated anywhere. With the cultic reforms of King Josiah (640–609 B.C.) this festival was centralized at the Temple in Jerusalem where all the paschal animals were ritually slaughtered; hence an annual pilgrimage became common. The Feast of Unlevened Bread was originally a separate feast that came to be combined with the Passover Festival at the time of the Exile. The *seder* meal was offered in private homes on the first night as part of the Passover Festival. See J. Jermias, *Jerusalem in the Time of Jesus*, 57, 75–77, and 101–03; "Passover," *Encyclopedia Judaica* (Jerusalem 1971) 13.163–73; G. McRae, "Feast of Passover," NCE 10.1068–70; and C. Pfeiffer, "Passover Lamb," NCE 10.1071.

tion was a shadowing of the future. What is a shadowing of the future? A prophecy of Christ, who is coming, a prophecy of him who was going to suffer for us on that day, so that the shadow might pass away and the light might come, so that signification might pass away and truth might be held. There-fore, the Jews held the Passover in shadow, we hold it in light.

(3) For why would the Lord instruct them to kill a sheep on this very feast day except that it was he about whom it was prophesied: "As a sheep led to the slaughter."[2] The doorposts of the Jews were marked with the blood of a slaughtered animal;[3] our foreheads are marked with the blood of Christ. And that sign, because it was a sign, was said to keep the destroyer away from the houses marked with the sign; the sign of Christ drives the destroyer away from us if our heart should receive the Savior. Why did I say this? Because many have doorposts marked with the sign and the Indweller does not remain inside; easily do they have the sign of Christ on the forehead and do not receive the word of Christ in the heart. And so I said, brothers, and I repeat it: the sign of Christ drives the destroyer away from us if our heart holds Christ as the Indweller. I have said these things in case anyone might be thinking about what these feasts of the Jews mean. Therefore, the Lord came in the place of a victim that we might have the true Passover when we celebrated his passion, as it were the sacrificing of a sheep.

3. "And they were seeking Jesus," but in an evil way. For blessed are they who are seeking Jesus, but in a good way. Those men were seeking Jesus that neither they nor we might have him; but we have received him who withdrew from them. They who are seeking are reproached, they who are seeking are praised; for it is the disposition of the seeker that finds either praise or condemnation. For you have this also in the psalms: "Let them be confounded and covered with shame who seek my life."[4] These are the ones who seek in an evil way. In another place, however, it says: "Flight has per-ished from me; and there is no one who seeks after my life."[5]

2. Is 53.7 (LXX).   3. Cf. Ex 12.7, 22.
4. Ps 39 (40).15.   5. Ps 141 (142).5.

They who seek are blamed; they who do not seek are blamed. Therefore let us seek Christ that we may have him; let us seek him that we may hold him, but not that we may kill him. For these men, too, were seeking him precisely in order that they might hold him but that soon they might not have him. "They were seeking, therefore, and they were saying to one another, 'What do you think, that he is not coming to the feast day?'"

4. "Now the high priests and the Pharisees had given an order that if anyone knew where he was, he should report it, so that they might apprehend him." Let us now report to the Jews where Christ is. May they wish to hear and to take hold of him, whoever are of the seed of those who had given the order that it be reported to them where Christ was. Let them come to the Church, let them hear where Christ is and apprehend him. Let them hear it from us, let them hear it from the Gospel. He was killed by their forefathers, he was buried, he rose again. He was recognized by the disciples and ascended into heaven before their eyes; there he sits at the right hand of the Father. He who was judged will come as the Judge. Let them hear and let them retain it!

(2) They answer: How shall I hold one who is not here? How shall I send my hand into heaven to hold him sitting there? Send your faith and you have held. Your forefathers hold with the flesh; you, hold with the heart because the absent Christ is also present. Unless he were present, he could not be held by us ourselves. But because what he said is true, "Behold, I am with you even to the consummation of the world,"[6] he both went away and yet is here; he both went back and yet does not abandon us. For he took his body to heaven, he did not take his majesty from the world.

5. "Therefore six days before the Passover Jesus came to Bethany, where Lazarus was whom Jesus raised from the dead. Now they made a banquet for him there, and Martha was serving. And Lazarus was one of those at table." That people might not think that a ghost had appeared, because a dead man arose, he was one of those at table. He was living,

6. Mt 28.20.

speaking, dining; truth was shown, the disbelief of the Jews
was being confounded. Therefore, the Lord reclined at table
with Lazarus and the others; Martha, one of Lazarus' sisters,
was serving.

6. But "Mary", the other sister of Lazarus, "took a pound of
perfume made from costly pistic aromatic nard; she anointed
Jesus' feet and wiped his feet with her hair, and the house was
filled with the ointment's fragrance." We have heard what
happened; let us search out the hidden meaning. You,
whoever wishes to be a faithful soul, together with Mary
anoint the Lord's feet with costly perfume. That perfume was
justice, and so it was a pound;[7] however it was a perfume made
from costly, *pistic,* aromatic nard. What does *pistic* mean? We
ought to believe it to be some place in which this was a costly
perfume; and yet this is not an idle phrase and is quite well
consonant with the mystery. The Greek word means faith.[8]
You were seeking to work justice: "the just man lives by
faith."[9] Anoint Jesus' feet: by living well, follow the Lord's
footsteps. Wipe with your hair: if you have more than enough,
give to the poor and you have wiped the Lord's feet. For hairs
seem to be the body's superfluity. For you they are superfluous, but for the Lord's feet, they are necessary. Perhaps on
earth the Lord's feet are in need. For about whom except

7. The Latin word for "pound," *libra,* also meant a balance or a pair of
scales, the symbol for justice.
8. The Greek adjective describing the perfume, πιστικός, is simply trans-
literated in the Latin text. Derived from the Greek verb, πίνω, it would mean
"liquid." Augustine gives the word two possible meanings. Following a common early Christian interpretation, he first of all traces the adjective to the
Greek noun πίστις, "faith," and gives it the meaning "faithful," that is,
"genuine" or "pure" in its literal application to perfume. Cf. Jerome, *Tractatus in Marci Evangelium* 10.82 (CCL 78.498) and Ambrose, *Expositio Evangelii Secundum Lucam* 10.137 (CCL 14.385). Secondly, Augustine suggests it
might refer to the name of the place from which the perfume came; Browne
LFC 29.672, points out that this derivation belongs to Augustine alone. Comeau, *Saint Augustin,* 65, sees the word as a loan word only. R. E. Brown, *The
Anchor Bible,* 29.448, suggests an overliteral translation of an Aramaic word
with a double meaning which is not reflected in the Greek equivalent; he also
suggests that it might be the corruption of another word similar in sound, τῆς
στακτῆς, an oil of the storax bush. B. Vawter, JBC 2.448, says that the word is
of uncertain meaning.
9. Rom 1.17, quoting Hb 2.4.

about his members will he say in the end, "When you did it for one of the least of mine, you did it for me"?[10] You spent your superfluity, but you gave service to my feet.

7. Now "the house was filled with the fragrance"; the world was filled with good report, for the good fragrance is good report. Those who live evilly and are called Christians do wrong to Christ; about such it was said that through them "the Lord's name is blasphemed."[11] If through such God's name is blasphemed, through the good the Lord's name is praised. Hear the Apostle; he says: "We are the good fragrance of Christ in every place."[12] It is also said in the *Song of Songs,* "Your name is perfume poured out."[13] Return your attention to the Apostle: "We are the good fragrance of Christ in every place, both among those who are saved and among those who are lost; to some we are the fragrance of life unto life, to others the fragrance of death unto death. And for these things who is suited?"[14]

(2) The present reading of the holy Gospel about this fragrance offers us an opportunity to speak in this way, so that it may both be sufficiently said by us and diligently heard by you, as the Apostle himself so says, "And for these things who is suited?" Therefore, that we may attempt to speak about this, are we at all suited and are you suited to hear these things? Indeed, we are not suited; but he is suited, who would deign through us to say what it would benefit you to hear. Look, the Apostle is "a good fragrance," as he himself says: but the good fragrance itself is "to some the fragrance of life unto life, but to others the fragrance of death unto death," but still a good fragrance. For does he say: for some we are the good fragrance unto life, for others the evil fragrance unto death? He said that he was a good fragrance, not an evil one; and he said that for some the same good fragrance was unto life, for others unto death. Happy are they who live by the good fragrance; but what is more unhappy than those who die by the good fragrance?

10. Mt 25.40.
11. Rom 2.24, quoting Is 52.5 and Ez 36.20.
12. 2 Cor 2.15, 14.　　　　13. Cant (Song) 1.3 (Douay 1.2).
14. 2 Cor 2.14–16.

8. And who is it, someone says, whom the good fragrance
kills? This is what the Apostle says: "And for these things who
is suited?" How God does these things wondrously, that both
the good may live and the evil die by the good fragrance; how
it may be, as far as God deigns to inspire (for perhaps a deeper
understanding may be hidden there which I cannot penetrate)—nevertheless in so far as I could penetrate it, it ought
not be refused by you. Everywhere his fame broadcast Paul
doing good things, living well, preaching justice in word,
showing it in deed, an admirable teacher, a faithful steward;
some loved him, some envied him. For he himself says in a
certain place about certain men, because they were proclaiming Christ not purely but from envy, "thinking," he says,
"to raise affliction for my chains." But what does he say?
"Whether by occasion or by truth, let Christ be proclaimed."[15]
They who love me proclaim; they who envy me proclaim. The
former live by the good fragrance; the latter die by the good
fragrance. Yet let Christ's name be proclaimed by the preaching of both; let the world be filled with the best fragrance. You
loved him doing good things, you lived by the good fragrance;
you envied him doing good things, you died by the good
fragrance. Because you wanted to die, did you for that reason
cause that fragrance to be evil? Do not envy and the good
fragrance will not kill you.

9. Finally, here also hear from this perfume how for some
it was a good fragrance unto life, for others it was a good
fragrance unto death. After the devout Mary did this in defer-
ence to the Lord, immediately "one of his disciples, Judas
Iscariot, who was about to betray him, said, 'Why was not this
perfume sold for three hundred pieces of silver,[16] and given to
the poor?'" Woe to you, unhappy man! The good fragrance
kills you. For the holy Evangelist made clear why he said this.
But we, too, would think that that man could have said this
from a concern for the poor if his intention were not related
to us by the Gospel. It is not so. But what? Hear the true
witness: "Now he said this, not because he was concerned for

the poor, but because he was a thief and, having the purse, he carried what was deposited [there]." He carried or carried off? He carried by his office, but he carried off by theft.[17]

10. Look, hear that this Judas did not go awry when he was seduced by the Jews and handed over the Lord. For very many who are careless about the Gospel think that Judas was lost then when he received money from the Jews to hand over the Lord. He was not lost then; he was already a thief, and he was following the Lord, he, a ruined man, because he followed not with the heart but with the body. He completed the number of Apostles at twelve, but he did not possess apostolic blessedness; he had been twelfth in point of form. And when he departed and another succeeded, both the apostolic truth was fulfilled and the complete number remained.

(2) What then, my brothers, did our Lord Jesus Christ want to teach his Church when he wanted to have one ruined man among the twelve, except that we should tolerate the evil and not divide Christ's body? Look, Judas is among holy men. Look, Judas is a thief; and, that you may not disdain this, a thief and a temple robber,[18] not any kind of thief at all—a thief of purses, but of the Lord's purses, of purses, but of sacred purses. If the crimes of theft and embezzlement, such as they are, are distinguished in court (for theft from the government is called embezzlement and theft of private property is not judged in the same way as that of public property), how much more severely ought a sacrilegious thief be judged who dared

17. In *Epistula* 108.3.8 (PL 33.409–10 or FOTC 18.221–22) Augustine gives the same interpretation of Jn 12.6, that Judas was stealing from the common treasury, although in the letter the point being made is that the goodness of the community is not affected by any evil that is intermingled within it.

18. The Latin word is *sacrilegus* which Augustine here uses in its legal technical sense of a temple robber; the word carried by his time a wide range of meanings, from one who stole an object from a religious place to any kind of descration of persons, places, objects, or ideas that were held sacred. Judas is considered guilty of a kind of peculation that was particularly offensive in Roman culture. For a very detailed discussion see C. Daremberg and E. Saglio, *Dictionnaire des antiquités grecques et romaines* (orig. Paris 1907, reprint Graz 1963), s. v. *sacrilegium*, 4.2.980–87; and W. Kroll, "*Sacrilegium*." *Pauly-Wissowa Realencyclopädie des classiches Altertumswissenschaft* (orig. Stuttgart 1920, reprint 1960) Series 2, 1.2. 1678–81.

to take not from anywhere but to take from the Church? He who steals something from the Church is put in the same category as the ruined Judas.

(3) Such was this Judas and yet he came and went with the eleven holy disciples. He approached equally to the very supper of the Lord. He could keep company with them; he could not corrupt them. From one bread both Peter and Judas received, and yet "what part has the faithful with the unfaithful?"[19] Peter received it for life, Judas for death. For as is that good fragrance, so is that good food. Therefore, just as the good fragrance gives life to the good and death to the evil, so also does the good food. "For he who eats and drinks unworthily, eats and drinks a judgment on himself,"[20] "a judgment on himself," not on you. If it is a judgment on himself and not on you, tolerate, good man, the evil man, that you may come to the rewards of the good, that you may not be sent to the punishment of the evil.

11. Learn from the example of the Lord while he dwelt on earth. Why did he to whom angels ministered have purses except that his Church was going to have its purses? Why did he admit a thief except that his Church may patiently endure thieves? But that man who had been accustomed to take money from purses did not hesitate, upon the reception of money, to sell the Lord himself.

(2) Let us see what the Lord answers to these words. See, brothers! He does not say to him, You say these things because of your thefts. He knew the thief, but he did not reveal him; rather, he endured him and pointed out to us an example of patience in enduring evil men in the Church. "Therefore, Jesus said to him, 'Leave her alone, that she may keep it for the day of my burial.'" He announced that he was going to die.

12. But what is this that follows? "For the poor you will always have with you, but me you will not always have." We do indeed understand, "the poor you will always have." These

19. 2 Cor 6.15.
20. 1 Cor 11.29.

words are true. When has the Church been without the poor? "But me you will not always have." What does he mean? How ought it to be understood: "But me you will not always have"?

(2) Fear not; it was said to Judas. Then why did he not say, thou will have, [in the singular], but said, ye will have [in the plural]? Because Judas is not one. One evil man signifies the body of evil men, just as Peter is the body of good men, nay, rather the body of the Church, but among good men.[21] For if the mystery of the Church were not in Peter, the Lord would not say to him, "I will give you the keys of the kingdom of heaven. Whatever things you shall loose on earth shall be loosed also in heaven, and whatever things you shall bind on earth shall be bound also in heaven."[22] If this was said only to Peter, the Church does not do this. But if it happens also in the Church, that the things which are bound on earth are bound in heaven and the things which are loosed on earth are loosed in heaven, since when the Church excommunicates, the excommunicated person is bound in heaven, [and] when one is reconciled by the Church, the one reconciled is loosed in heaven—if, then, this happens in the Church, when Peter received the keys, he signified the holy Church. If in the person of Peter the good men in the Church were signified, in the person of Judas the evil men in the Church were signified. It was said to the latter, "But me you will not always have."

(3) What is "not always"? And what is "always"? If you are good, if you belong to the body which Peter signifies, you have Christ both in the present and in the future; in the present through faith, in the present through a sign,[23] in the present through the sacrament of baptism, in the present through the food and drink of the altar. You have Christ in the present, but you will have him always. For when you have gone from here, you will come to him who said to the robber, "This day you will be with me in paradise."[24] But if you behave evilly, you will seem to have Christ in the present because you enter

21. There are some manuscript variations for this sentence, but all are of minor significance and do not affect the meaning.
22. Mt 16.19.   23. See section 2.
24. Lk 23.43.

the Church, you sign yourself with the sign of Christ, you mingle with the members of Christ, you approach the altar of Christ. You have Christ in the present, but by living evilly you will not have him always.

13. And so it can be understood: "The poor you will always have with you, but me you will not always have." Let the good also learn this, but let them be untroubled; for he was speaking about the presence of his body. For according to his majesty, his providence, his ineffable and unseen grace, there is fulfilled what was said by him, "Behold, I am with you until the consummation of the world."[25] But according to the flesh which the Word assumed, according to the fact that he was born from the Virgin, that he was seized by the Jews, was crucified on the wood, was taken down from the cross, was wrapped in linens, was hidden in the tomb, was made manifest in the resurrection, "you will not always have with you." Why? Because he associated, in accordance with the presence of his body, for forty days with his disciples; and, as they accompanied him by watching but not by following, he ascended into heaven, and he is not here.[26] For he is there, he sits at the right hand of the Father; and yet he is here, for the presence of his majesty has not departed. In other words, in accordance with the presence of his majesty we will always have Christ; in accordance with the presence of his flesh, it was rightly said to the disciples, "But me you will not always have." For the Church had him in accordance with the presence of his flesh for a few days; now it holds him by faith, it does not see him with the eyes. Therefore, whether it was thus said, "But me you will not always have," the question, as I think, no longer exists since it has been resolved in two days.

14. Let us hear the few other words which remain. "Then a great crowd of Jews discovered that he was there, and they came, not only because of Jesus, but to see Lazarus whom Jesus raised from the dead." It was curiosity that led them, not love; they came and they saw. Hear the amazing counsel of

25. Mt 28.20.
26. See Acts 1.3, 9–10.

vanity. When Lazarus, who had been raised up, was seen, because the news of so great a miracle of the Lord had been spread widely by its great obviousness, had been made known by so great a manifestation that they could neither hide what was done nor deny it, see what they contrived. "But the chief priests planned to kill Lazarus too because, on account of him, many of the Jews were going over and believing in Jesus." Oh, stupid plan! Oh, blind cruelty! The Lord Christ who could raise the dead, could he not raise one who had been killed? When you were bringing death to Lazarus, were you taking power away from the Lord? If a dead man seems one thing to you and a murdered man something else—look, the Lord did both—he raised up both Lazarus who was dead and himself after he had been murdered!

TRACTATE 51

On John 12.12–26

FTER THE Lord had raised up the man dead for four days to the astonishment of the Jews, some of them believing by seeing, and some perishing by envying, because of the good fragrance which is to some for life and to others for death;[1] after he had reclined at table in the house together with Lazarus who was resuming his place at the table, the one who had been raised up from the dead; after the perfume was poured over his feet and the house was filled with its fragrance; after the Jews in their corrupt heart conceived a vain cruelty and the most stupid and insane crime of killing Lazarus also—about all of these things, as far as we were able, we spoke in previous homilies what the Lord granted. Now, my beloved people, direct your thoughts to how much fruitfulness appeared from his preaching before the Lord's passion and to how great a flock of sheep of the house of Israel, from those who had been lost, heard the voice of the shepherd.

2. For thus says the Gospel which you just heard as it was being read, "Now, on the next day the great crowd that had come for the feast day, when they heard that Jesus was coming to Jerusalem, took palm branches and went out to meet him. And they kept shouting, 'Hosanna! Blessed is he who comes in the name of the Lord, the king of Israel.'"[2] The palm branches are praises, signifying victory; for the Lord was about to overcome death by dying and by the trophy of the cross was about to triumph over the devil, the prince of death.

1. Cf. 2 Cor 2.15–16.
2. Partly quoting Ps 117 (118).26.

271

(2) "Hosanna", however, is the word of one supplicating, as
some say who know the Hebrew language, more declaring a
feeling than signifying something.[3] Just as in the Latin language there are words which we call interjections, as when in
sorrow we say, *Heu!* Or when we are delighted, we say, *Vah!*
Or when we are amazed, we say, *Oh*, what a great thing! For
then *Oh* signifies nothing except the feeling of the one who is
amazed. And therefore one must believe that this is so, because neither the Greek nor the Latin could interpret this
word, as also this one: "Whoever shall say to his brother,
Racha."[4] For this also is thought to be an interjection which
shows the feeling of one who is indignant.

3. Now the verse, "Blessed is he who comes in the name of
the Lord, the king of Israel," must be so taken that "in the
name of the Lord" should be understood as in the name of
God the Father, although it can also be understood as in his
own name since he is himself also the Lord. And so elsewhere

3. Augustine also interprets Hosanna as an interjection in *DDC* 2.16
where, however, he says that it is the expression of a person rejoicing; and in a
sermon from the edition of A. Caillau and B. Saint-Yves, *Supplementum* 1
(Paris 1936), *Sermo* 33.5 (PL *Supplementum* 2.972) he defines it as meaning, "O
Lord, save me." The latter keeps the interjectional character and at the same
time gives the actual meaning of the Hebraic original, *hosha na*, linked into a
single word, *hoshana*, transcribed into Greek as *hosanna*; this was used as a
recurrent response in psalms and prayers and literally meant, "Save, I pray."
It was especially used with a group of psalms, 112(113)–117(118), sung at
various festivals. It was both a cry for continued help after a victory and
joyous shout of homage to God; hence Augustine's interpretations are all
correct. See "Hoshanat," *Encyclopedia Judaica* (Jerusalem 1971) 8.1028–30 or
M. Masterman, "Hosanna," NCE 7.153. Jerome, *Epistula* 20 (PL 22.375–79
and ACW 33.104–108) discusses the word in detail, deciding that it is an
imperative, "save," followed by an interjection of entreaty, "I beg," its actual,
literal meaning.

4. Mt 5.22. The NAB translators chose to interpret the Hebrew word,
supplying an English equivalent. Augustine's commentary requires the
Hebraic form of the word. In *DDC* 2.16, as here, he takes the word to be an
expression of indignation; so too in *De Sermone Domini in Monte* 1.9.23 (CCL
35.24, ACW 5.32, and FOTC 11.41–42) he says that it is not equivalent to the
Greek ῥάκος, a ragged person, but that a Hebrew man whom he asked had
said that it did not signify anything precise but expressed the feelings of an
indignant person. Jerome, *Liber Interpretationis Hebraicorum Nominum*, on
Matthew, s. v. *racha* (CCL 72.138) defines it as *vacuus*, empty, i.e., empty-
headed. Modern scholarship concurs with both fathers in both derivation and
interpretation.

it has also been written: "The Lord rained from the Lord."[5] But the words of him who said, "I have come in my Father's name, and you have not received me. Another will come in his own name; him you will receive,"[6] guide our understanding better.

(2) For the master of humility is Christ who humbled himself and became obedient even to death, even the death of the cross.[7] Thus, he does not lose his divinity when he teaches us humility; in the former he is equal to the Father, in the latter he is like us. By reason of the fact that he is equal to the Father, he created us so that we might be; by reason of the fact that he is like us, he redeemed us so that we might not perish.

4. The crowd was saying these praises to him: "Hosanna! Blessed is he who comes in the name of the Lord, the king of Israel!" What a crucifixion of the mind the envy of the leaders of the Jews could suffer when so great a crowd was shouting that its king was Christ! But what was it for the Lord to be the king of Israel? What great thing was it to the king of the ages to become the king of men? For Christ was not the king of Israel so that he might exact a tax or equip an army with weaponry and visibly vanquish an enemy; but he was the king of Israel in that he rules minds, in that he gives counsel for eternity, in that he leads into the kingdom of Heaven those who believe, hope, and love. Therefore, the Son of God is equal to the Father, he is the Word through whom all things were made;[8] the fact that he wanted to be king of Israel is a condescension, not an advancement. It is an indication of pity, not an increase in power. For he who was called king of the Jews on earth is the Lord of angels in heaven.

5. "And Jesus found a donkey and sat upon it." Here it was said briefly; for how it happened is read most fully in the other evangelists.[9] Moreover, the testimony of the prophets is applied to this event so that it was clear that the evil leaders of the Jews did not understand that it was he in whom what they read was being fulfilled.

5. Gn 19.24.   6. Jn 5.43.
7. Cf. Phil 2.8.   8. Cf. Jn 1.3.
9. Cf. Mt 21.1–7, Mk 11.1–7, Lk 19.29–35.

(2) Therefore "Jesus found a donkey and sat up upon it, as it was written: 'Fear not, daughter of Sion! Behold, your king comes sitting on a donkey's colt.'"[10] In that people, therefore, was the "daughter of Sion." Jerusalem is herself the same as Sion. In that wicked and blind people, I say, nevertheless was the "daughter of Sion" to whom it should be said: "Fear not! Behold your king comes sitting on a donkey's colt." This "daughter of Sion" to whom these things are divinely said was among those sheep who were hearing the voice of the shepherd; she was in that crowd which was praising the Lord with such great devotion as he came and was leading him in so great a column. To her it was said: "Fear not!" Recognize him who is praised by you and tremble not when he suffers; for the blood through which your depravity is to be demolished and life returned is poured out.

(3) But the donkey's colt upon which no one had sat (for this fact is found in the other evangelists) we understand as the people of the nations which had not received the Lord's law. However the donkey (because both beasts were led to the Lord) is his community which came from the people of Israel, clearly not unbroken, but which recognized the Master's manger.[11]

6. "At first his disciples did not understand these things, but when Jesus was glorified," that is, when he showed the power of his resurrection, "then they recalled that these things had been written about him and that they had done these things to him," that is, they did not do other things to him than those which had been written about him. For recalling, in accord with Scripture, of course, what things were fulfilled before the Lord's passion, or in the Lord's passion, there also they found the fact that he sat on a donkey's colt in accord with the statements of the prophets.

7. "Therefore the crowd which was with him when he called Lazarus out of the tomb and raised him from the dead gave testimony. For this reason also the crowd came to meet him because they heard that he had performed this sign.

10. Zec 9.9.
11. Cf. Is 1.3.

Therefore, the Pharisees said to one another, 'Do you see that we accomplish nothing? Look, the whole world has gone after him.'" A throng threw a throng into confusion.[12] But why are you envious, blind crowd, because the world has gone after him through whom the world was made?

8. "Now there were certain Gentiles among those who had come up to worship at the feast. These, therefore, approached Philip, who was from Bethsaida in Galilee, and asked him, saying, 'Sir, we wish to see Jesus.' Philip comes and tells Andrew; Andrew and Philip in turn tell Jesus." Let us hear what the Lord answered to these things. Look, the Jews want to kill him, the Gentiles to see him; but there were also those of the Jews who were shouting, "Blessed is he who comes in the name of the Lord, the king of Israel." Look, these from the circumcised, those from the uncircumcised,[13] coming like two walls from different directions and meeting with the kiss of peace in the one faith of Christ. Therefore, let us hear the voice of the Cornerstone.

(2) "Now Jesus," [the text] says, "answered them, saying, 'The hour has come for the Son of Man to be glorified.'" Here perhaps someone thinks that he said he was glorified for the reason that the Gentiles wanted to see him. It is not so. But he saw that after his passion and resurrection the Gentiles themselves in all the nations would believe; for, as the Apostle says, "Blindness in part has happened in Israel until the fullness of the nations should enter in."[14] Thus from the occasion of these Gentiles who desired to see him he announces the coming fullness of the nations. And he promises that at this precise moment the hour of his glorification is at hand; and when this has happened in heaven, the nations would have believed. Concerning this it has been foretold: "Be exalted above the

---

12. There is a difficult to translate play on words here: *turba turbavit turbam*, literally, "a crowd disturbed a crowd." Innes LNPF 7.284, has: Mob set mob in motion. Browne LFC 29.683, has: The people put them in sore perturbation.

13. Literally, from the circumcision . . . from the uncircumcision. For the terminology see, e.g., Rom 2.25–29.

14. Rom 11.25.

heavens, O God, and above all the earth your glory."[15] This is the fullness of the nations about which the Apostle says, "Blindness in part has happened in Israel until the fullness of the nations should enter in."

9. But the lowliness of the passion had to precede the loftiness of glorification. And so he continued and added, "Amen, amen, I say to you, unless the grain of wheat falling into the earth dies, it remains alone. But if it dies, it produces much fruit." Now, he was talking about himself. He was the grain that had to meet death and be multiplied, to meet death by the lack of faith of the Jews, to be multiplied by the faith of the peoples.

10. Now urging us to follow in the steps of his passion, he says, "He who loves his life will lose it." This can be understood in two ways. "He who loves will lose," that is, if you love, lose; if you desire to keep life in Christ, fear not death for Christ. Likewise, in another way. "He who loves his life will lose it." Do not love that you may not lose; do not love [it] in this life that you may not lose [it] in eternal life. But the sense of the Gospel seems more to have the second meaning which I stated. For it continues: "And he who hates his life in this world will keep it to life eternal." Therefore, to what was said above, "He who loves," it is implicitly understood, in this world; this very one certainly will lose. "But he who hates," in this world, of course, he himself will keep it to life eternal. A great and wondrous expression: how a man's love for his life should be that it perish, his hatred that it not perish! If you have loved badly, then you have hated; if you have hated well, then you have loved. Happy are they who have hated it in keeping it that they may not destroy it in loving it.

(2) But watch out that a wish to destroy yourself not creep upon you unawares, by so understanding that you ought to hate your life in this world. For, from this, certain evil and wicked men, in themselves crueler and more criminal murderers, give themselves to flames, suffocate in water, smash themselves by leaping from a height, and perish.[16] Christ did

15. Ps 107 (108).6.
16. Namely, Donatist martyrs; see *Tractate* 11.15.

not teach this; rather, to the devil suggesting such a leap, he even answered, "Get behind, Satan; it has been written, 'You shall not tempt the Lord your God.'"[17] Moreover, he said to Peter, signifying by what death he would glorify God, "When you were younger, you fastened your own belt and went where you would; but when you are older, another will fasten your belt and carry you off where you would not."[18] And there he made it sufficiently clear that he who follows Christ's steps ought to be killed not by himself but by another.

(3) Therefore, when the critical juncture is reached, that this condition is proposed, either that one must act contrary to God's teaching or depart from this life, and a man is forced to choose one of these two, with the persecutor threatening death, then let him choose to die with love for God rather than to live with hatred of God; there let him hate his life in this world so that he may keep it for life eternal.

11. "If anyone serves me, let him follow me." What is "let him follow me" except, let him imitate me? "For Christ suffered for us," the Apostle Peter said, "leaving us an example that we should follow in his footsteps."[19] Look at what has been said: "If anyone serves me, let him follow me." With what benefit? With what recompense? With what reward? "And where I am," he says, "there also will my servant be." Let him be loved freely that the reward for the work with which he is served may be to be with him. For where will there be good without him, or where can it be bad with him? Hear it more clearly. "If anyone serves me, my Father will honor him." With what honor except that he be with his Son? For what he said previously, "Where I am, there also will my servant be," we understand that he explicated this when he says, "My Father will honor him." For what greater honor could the adopted son receive than that he be where the only one is, not made an equal to his divinity but a cosharer in his eternity?

12. We ought, however, rather to investigate what it is to serve Christ, the work for which so great a recompense is

17. Mt 4.7, 10, quoting Dt 6.16; cf. Lk 4.12.
18. Jn 21.18.
19. 1 Pt 2.21.

proposed. For if we think that to serve Christ is this: to prepare the things which are necessary for the body, or to cook, or to put food before a diner, or to give him a cup or mix the drink[20]—they who were able to have him present in body did this, such as Martha and Mary when Lazarus was also one of those reclining at table. But in this way even the lost Judas served Christ; for it was he who held the purse. And although he most wickedly stole from the things which were deposited, nevertheless necessities were also acquired through him. As a result of this fact, when the Lord said to him, "What you do, do quickly," some thought that he ordered him to prepare the necessities for the feast day or to give something to the indigent.[21] Therefore, in no way would the Lord say about servants of this sort, "Where I am, there also will my servant be. If anyone serves me, my Father will honor him." For we see that Judas who was performing such services was condemned rather than honored. Why, therefore, do we seek elsewhere what it is to serve Christ and not rather recognize it in these very words.

(2) For when he said, "If anyone serves me, let him follow me," he intended this to be understood as if he were to say, If anyone does not follow me, he does not deserve me. Therefore, they serve Jesus Christ who seek not the things that are their own but those that are Jesus Christ's.[22] For "let him follow me" means this: let him walk in my ways, not his own, as it was written elsewhere, "He who says that he abides in Christ ought himself also to walk even as he walked."[23] He ought, also, if he offers bread to a hungry man, to do it from mercy, not from display, not to seek there anything else than a good work, with the left hand not knowing what the right is doing,[24] that is, that the aim of desire be kept far from the work of love. He who serves in this way serves Christ, and rightly it will be said to him, "As often as you did it for one of the least of mine, you did it for me."[25] Doing for Christ's sake not only the things

20. A reference to the ancient practice of mixing water with wine.
21. Cf. Jn 13.27–29.   22. Cf. Phil 2.21.
23. 1 Jn 2.6.   24. See Mt 6.3.
25. Mt 25.40.

which pertain to corporal mercy but all good works (for then they will be good works because "Christ is the end of the law, to justice for everyone who believes"[26]), he is the servant of Christ even to that work of great love which is to lay down his life for his brothers; for this is also to lay it down for Christ. For he will also say this on behalf of his own members: when you did it for these, you did it for me. For with regard to such a work he also deigned to make and call himself a servant, when he said, "Even as the Son of Man has come not to be served, but to serve, and to lay down his own life for many."[27] Therefore, each one is a servant of Christ in the same way as Christ also is a servant. So his Father will honor the one who serves Christ with that great honor that he be with his Son and his happiness never cease.

13. Therefore, brothers, when you hear the Lord saying, "Where I am, there also will my servant be," do not think only of good bishops and clerics. Do you too, in your measure, serve Christ by living well, by giving alms, by preaching his name and his teaching to whomever you can, so that each head of a family also acknowledges in this name that he owes paternal affection to his family. Let each one admonish all his own people for Christ's sake and for eternal life; let him teach, encourage, correct, employ good will, exercise discipline. In this way, in his own house he will fulfill in a way a churchly and episcopal function, serving Christ so that he may be with him forever. For many of your number have also given that greatest service, the service of suffering. Many who were neither bishops nor clerics, young men and women, older men and women as well as younger, many married men and women, many mothers and fathers, heads of families, serving Christ, have also laid down their lives in witness of him;[28] and the Father has honored them, and they have received the most glorious crowns.

26. Rom 10.4.
27. Mt 20.28.
28. I.e., by martyrdom. One might translate: "in martyrdom for him."

TRACTATE 52

On John 12.27–36

FTER THE Lord Jesus Christ in the words of yesterday's reading encouraged his servants to follow him
when he had predicted his passion in these words,
"Unless the grain of wheat, falling into the earth, dies, it remains alone. But if it dies, it produces much fruit,"[1] wherein
he stirred up those who wished to follow him to the kingdom
of heaven to hate their life[2] in this world if they were thinking
of keeping it to eternal life, he again tempered his feeling to
our weakness and he said—the point where today's reading
begins—"My soul is troubled now." Why is your soul troubled,
Lord? Surely you said a little before, "He who hates his life in
this world keeps it to life eternal."[3] Is your soul then loved in
this world and for that reason is it troubled by the coming
hour in which it is to go out of this world? Who would dare to
assert this about the Lord's soul? But he has carried us over
into himself; he, our head, has taken us into himself. He has
taken on the emotional disposition of his members; and therefore his troubled state did not arise from someone else but, as
was said about him when he raised up Lazarus, "He troubled
himself."[4] For it was necessary that the one mediator of God
and men, the man Christ Jesus,[5] as he stirred us to the highest
things, so suffer with us also the lowest things.[6]

---

1. Jn 12.24–25.
2. Again the translation problem for the Latin word *anima* which means
both soul and life, and *vita* which means only life: "hate their *soul* . . . to
eternal *life*." See *Tractate* 47.10, note 32, and Innes, 287, note 1.
3. Jn 12.25.   4. Jn 11.33.
5. Cf. 1 Tm 2.5.
6. Most of the codices read here: suffer with us also weaknesses. But the
text reading is probably preferable in view of Augustine's frequent emphasis

2. I hear him saying earlier, "The hour has come for the Son of Man to be glorified; if the grain of wheat dies, it produces much fruit."[7] I hear, "The man who hates his life in this world keeps it to life eternal."[8] And not only I am allowed to wonder, but I am directed to imitate. Then in the following words, "If anyone serves me, let him follow me; and where I am, there also will my servant be."[9] I am set afire to despise the world, and all the vain fervor of this life, however long it has lasted, is in my sight nothing. For me, all things temporal become worthless in comparison with the love of the eternal. And again I hear my Lord himself, who by those words has wrested me away from my weakness to his strength, saying, "My soul is troubled now."

(2) What is the meaning of this? How do you order my soul to follow if I see your soul to be troubled? How am I to endure what such great strength feels to be heavy? What foundation am I to seek if the Rock gives way? But I seem to hear in my thought my Lord answering me and in a way saying: You will follow me even more because I set myself among you in this way so that you may endure; you heard the voice of my strength [speaking] to you. Hear the voice of your weakness in me. I supply strength for you to run and I do not restrain your speeding up, but I transfer to myself your alarm, and I lay down the roadbed whereby you may proceed. O Lord, mediator, God above us, man because of us, I acknowledge your mercy! For, because you, as great as you are, are troubled by the will of your love, you comfort many in your body who are troubled by the necessity of their weakness that they may not perish by despair.

3. Well then, let the person who wishes to follow hear how he should follow. Perhaps a terrible hour has come; a choice is put forward either of committing some wrong or of undergo-

---

on the God on high lowering himself to share our humanness, although the next sections do make a contrast between Christ's divine strength and human weakness. One might also suggest that it is more likely that *infima*, the *lectio difficilior*, be changed to *infirma* than the other way around.

7. Jn 12.23–24.   8. Jn 12.25.
9. Jn 12.26.

ing some suffering. The weak soul is troubled, and on its
account the unconquerable soul is troubled of its own accord.
Put God's will before your will. Pay attention to what your
Creator and your Master who made you adds on next; and he
was even himself made what he made that he might teach you.
For he who made man was made a man; but the unchangeable
God remained and changed man for the better. Therefore,
hear what he adds on next when he said, "My soul is troubled
now." "And what shall I say?" he said. "Father, save me from
this hour. But for this I came to this hour. Father, glorify your
name." He taught you what you should think, he taught you
what you should say, whom you should call upon, in whom
you should hope, whose will, certain and divine, you should
put before your will, human and weak.

(2) Therefore, let him not seem to you to be demoted from
his high estate because he wishes you to be promoted from
your lowly estate. For he deigned even to be tempted by the
devil, by whom assuredly, if he were unwilling, he would not
be tempted, just as if he were unwilling, he would not suffer.
And he gave to the devil those answers which you ought to
give amid temptations.[10] He was indeed tempted, but he was
not endangered, that he might teach you, when you are endangered by temptation, to answer the tempter and not to go
following after him, but to go away from the danger of temptation. However, as he said here, "My soul is troubled now," so
also where he says, "My soul is sad, even to death" and "Father, if it is possible, let this cup pass me by,"[11] he has taken up
man's weakness that he may teach him, saddened and troubled in the same way, to say what follows: "Nevertheless not
what I will, but what you will, Father." For in this way man is
guided from human things to the divine when the divine will
is put before the human will.

(3) But what is, "Glorify your name," except in his passion
and resurrection? For what else is it except that the Father
may glorify the Son who glorifies his own name also in the
similar sufferings of his servants? Hence it has been written

10. See Mt 4.1–11, Lk 4.1–13.
11. Mt 26.38–39.

about Peter that he said, "Another will fasten your belt and carry you off where you would not," about him, for the very reason that he wished to signify "by what death he was to glorify God."[12] Therefore, God also glorified his name in him because so in his members he also glorifies Christ.

4. "Then a voice came from the sky: 'I have glorified it and will glorify it again.'" "I have glorified it," before I made the world; "and will glorify it again," when he will arise from the dead and ascend into heaven. And "I have glorified it" can be understood in another way: when he was born of a virgin, when he exercised his powers, when he was adored by the Magi with the sky showing the way by a star, when he was acknowledged by holy ones filled with the Holy Spirit, when at the descent of the Spirit in the appearance of a dove he was proclaimed, when he was pointed out by the voice sounding from the sky, when he was transfigured on the mountain, when he performed many miracles, when he healed and cleansed many, when he fed so great a crowd from a very few loaves, when he gave orders to winds and waves, when he raised up the dead. "And I will glorify it again," when he will rise up from the dead, when death will have no further dominion over him,[13] when God will be exalted above the heavens and his glory above all the earth.[14]

5. "Then the crowd which was standing about and had heard said it had thundered. Others said, 'An angel spoke to him.' Jesus answered and said, 'This voice did not come for my sake, but for yours.'" Here he showed that by that voice what he already knew was not revealed to him but to those to whom it needed to be revealed. Moreover, as that voice was uttered by divinity not for his sake, but for the sake of others, so his soul was troubled by his will not for his sake, but for the sake of others.

6. Pay attention to the rest. "Now," he says, "is the judgment of the world." What, therefore, ought to be looked for at the end of this age? But the judgment which is looked for in the end will be the one for the judging of the living and the dead;

12. Jn 21.18–19.   13. Cf. Rom 6.9.
14. Cf. Ps 107 (108).6.

it will be a judgment of eternal rewards and punishments. What kind of judgment, therefore, is there now? Already in earlier readings, as best as I was able, I informed you, my beloved people, that a judgment not of damnation, but of distinction, was being spoken of;[15] about this it has been written, "Judge me, O God, and distinguish my cause from an unholy people."[16] There are, however, many judgments of God. Hence it is said in the psalm, "Your judgments [are] a great deep."[17] Also, the Apostle says, "Oh, the depth of the riches of the wisdom and the knowledge of God! How inscrutable are his judgments!"[18]

(2) And of these judgments also is this one which the Lord mentions here: "Now is the judgment of the world." And that judgment has been reserved for the end wherein finally the living and the dead must be judged. Therefore, the devil was in possession of the human race and was holding them guilty of capital crimes by the signature of their sins. He was ruling in the hearts of the unbelieving; he was dragging them, deceived and captive, to worship the creature since they had abandoned the Creator. However, through the faith of Christ, which was affirmed by his death and resurrection, through his blood, which was poured out for the remission of sins, thousands of believers were freed from the domination of the devil, were joined to Christ's body, and under so great a head, by his one Spirit, his fruitful members were enlivened. This he called judgment—this distinction, this expulsion of the devil from his own redeemed ones.

7. Pay attention, then, to what he says. As if we were searching after the meaning of his words, "Now is the judgment of the world," he continued and explained. For he said, "Now will the prince of this world be cast out." We have heard what sort of judgment he said it was. Not, therefore, that which will come in the end, when the living and the dead are to be judged, with some separated on the right, some on the left,

---

15. See *Tractates* 19.8, 22.5, 43.9, and 44.17.
16. Ps 42 (43).1 (LXX).
17. Ps 35 (36).7.
18. Rom 11.33. The Greek text has "the depth of the riches *and* the wisdom and the knowledge" with a textual variant omitting the first "and."

but the judgment by which "the prince of this world will be cast out."

(2) How then was he within and whither did he say he ought to be cast out? Is it this: that he was in the world and has been sent away from the world? For if he were speaking about that judgment which will come in the end, someone could think of eternal fire where the devil is to be sent with his angels and all who are of his party, not by nature but by fault, not because he created and begot but because he persuaded and controlled. Someone could, therefore, think that eternal fire was outside the world and that this is what "he will be cast out" meant. However, because he said, "Now is the judgment of the world," and, explaining what he meant, he said, "Now will the prince of this world be cast out," this must be understood as what happens now, not what will be so much later on the last day. Therefore, the Lord was preaching what he knew, that after his passion and glorification many peoples throughout the whole world within whose hearts the devil was would believe. And when they renounce him from their faith, he is cast out.

8. But someone says, "Was he not cast out of the hearts of the patriarchs and prophets and the just men of old?" Certainly he was cast out. How then was it said, "Now he will be cast out"? How do we think, except that what then happened among a very few persons has been foretold to happen very soon among many great peoples? So also in regard to that which was said, "However the Spirit had not yet been given since Jesus had not yet been glorified,"[19] one can use a similar question and a similar solution. For the prophets did not foretell future events without the Holy Spirit; or else the old man Simeon and the widow Anna did not recognize the infant Lord in the Holy Spirit,[20] and so too Zachary and Elizabeth who foresaid through the Holy Spirit such great things about him when he was not yet born but already conceived.[21] But "the Spirit had not yet been given," that is, that abundance of

19. Jn 7.39. See *Tractate* 33.6.
20. See Lk 2.25–38.
21. See Lk 1.39–45 and 67–79. The last part of this sentence is an anacoluthon.

spiritual grace by which, assembled together, they would speak in the tongues of all, and so the future Church would be foretold in the tongues of all nations, by which spiritual grace peoples were to be gathered together, by which sins were to be forgiven far and wide and thousands of thousands be reconciled to God.

9. Well, then, someone asks, because the devil will be cast out of the hearts of those who believe, does he thereafter tempt no one of the faithful? Rather he does not cease tempting them. But it is one thing to rule within, another to assail from without; for sometimes an enemy assails a very well fortified city and yet does not prevail. And if some of his missiles penetrate, the Apostle reminds us how it is that they may do no harm; he recalls to our mind the breastplate and shield of faith.[22] And if sometimes the enemy inflicts a wound, he who heals is at hand. For it was said as to those who were fighting, "I am writing these things to you that you may not sin." So those who are wounded hear what follows: "And if anyone has sinned, we have an advocate with the Father: Jesus Christ, the just. He is the propitiation for our sins."[23] For what do we pray when we say, "Forgive us our debts," except that our wounds be healed? And what else do we seek when we say, "Lead us not into temptation,"[24] except that he who plots or contends from the outside may not break in from any side, may not be able to overcome us by any deceit, by any strength? And yet however huge the siege machines he erects against us, since he does not hold the place in the heart where faith dwells, he has been cast out. But unless the Lord guards the city, he who guards will watch in vain.[25] Therefore, presume not about yourselves if you wish not to call the devil who has been cast out inside again.

10. But perish the thought that we consider that the devil was called the prince of the world in such a way that we believe him able to be lord over heaven and earth. But *world* is used as a designation for evil men who are scattered over the whole globe, as *house* is used for those by whom it is lived in: and in

22. Cf. 1 Thes 5.8 and Eph 6.16.   23. 1 Jn 2.1–2.
24. Mt 6.12, 13; cf. Lk 11.4.   25. Ps 126 (127).1.

this regard we say, "It is a good house," or "It is a bad house," not when we blame or praise the construction of walls and roofs, but when we blame or praise the character of good or evil men.[26] So therefore was it said, the prince of the world, that is, the prince of all the evil ones who live in the world. *World* is also used as a designation for the good who are similarly scattered over the whole globe. Hence the Apostle says, "God was in Christ, reconciling the world to himself."[27] These are the ones from whose hearts the prince of this world is cast out.

11. Therefore, when he said, "Now will the prince of this world be cast out, and I," he says, "if I am lifted up from the earth, will draw all things after me." What are "all things" except those from which he is cast out?[28] He did not, however, say all men but "all things", for not all men have the faith.[29] And so he did not refer this to the totality of mankind, but to the wholeness of the creature, that is, spirit, soul and body, that by which we understand, that by which we live, and that by which we are visible and touchable. For he who said, "Not a hair of your head shall perish,"[30] draws all things after him.

(2) Or if men themselves are to be understood as "all things", we can say all things predestined for salvation; for from these "all things" he said that nothing would perish when he was speaking previously about his sheep.[31] Or certainly all kinds of men, whether in all languages, or in all ages, or in all degrees of honor, or in all diversities of abilities, or in all professions of lawful and useful arts, and whatever else can

26. Cf. *Tractates* 2.11 and 3.5.
27. 2 Cor 5.19.
28. This involved exegesis of "all things" results from the reading of the neuter in the Latin text. For while some Greek manuscripts have neuter, most read "all men" as the NAB translates; this masculine renders exegesis easier. See Comeau, *Saint Augustin*, 67–68. R. E. Brown, *The Anchor Bible*, 29.468, mentions the neuter as an alternative reading in some manuscripts. F. Blass, A. Debrunner, and R. Funk, *A Greek Grammar of the New Testament and Other Early Christian Literature* (Chicago 1961) 76–77, indicate that the neuter is sometimes used with reference to persons when a general quality is emphasized and cite this verse as an example.
29. Cf. 2 Thes 3.2.
30. Cf. Lk 21.18.
31. See Jn 10.28; also *Tractate* 48.6.

be said about the innumerable differences by which men differ among themselves, except only for sins, from the highest
all the way to the lowliest, from the king all the way to the
beggar, "all things", he says, "I will draw after me," that he
may be their head and they his members.

(3) But "if I am lifted up," he says, "from the earth," that is,
when I am lifted up; for he has no doubt that that which he
comes to fulfill will be. This is connected to what he said earlier, "But if the grain of wheat dies, it produces much fruit."[32]
For what else did he mean by his "lifting up" than the suffering on the cross? And not even the Evangelist kept this quiet;
for he continued and said, "Now he said this signifying by
what death he was to die."

12. "The crowd answered him, 'We have heard out of the
law that the Christ remains forever. And how do you say, The
Son of Man must be lifted up? And who is this Son of Man?'"
They kept in their memories that the Lord constantly was
saying that he was the Son of Man. For in this place he did
not say, If the Son of Man is lifted up from the earth, but he
had said previously, which was read and explained yesterday,
when those Gentiles who desired to see him were announced:
"The hour has come for the Son of Man to be glorified."[33]
And so, retaining this in their minds and understanding what
he says now, "when I am lifted up from the earth," to mean
the death of the cross, these men questioned him and said,
"We have heard out of the law that the Christ remains forever.
And how do you say, The Son of Man must be lifted up?" For
"Who is this Son of Man?" For if he is the Christ, they say, he
remains forever; if he remains forever, how will he be lifted
up from the earth, that is, how will he die by the passion of the
cross? For they understood that he had spoken of the very
thing which they were plotting to do. It was not an infusion of
wisdom, but the goad of conscience, that opened the obscurity
of these words to them.

13. "Therefore Jesus said to them, 'Yet a little light[34] is

32. Jn 12.25; see sections 1 and 2.
33. Jn 12.23; see *Tractate* 51.8.
34. An amphibology arises in the Latin text from the absence of a word for
time to go with *modicum;* the Greek text has μίϰϱον χϱόνον which should

among you.'" From this you can understand that the Christ remains forever. "Therefore walk while you have the light that darkness may not come over you." Walk, approach, understand wholly that the Christ will die and he will live forever and will pour out his blood by which he may redeem and will ascend on high whither he may lead the way. But darkness will come over you if you believe the eternity of Christ in such a way that you deny the humbleness of death in him. "And the man who walks in darkness does not know where he is going." So he can stumble against a stone of stumbling and a rock of scandal,[35] which the Lord was to the unseeing Jews, just as for believers the stone which the builders rejected was made the head of the corner.[36] For this reason they disdained to believe in Christ because their impiety despised [him] dead, it laughed at him slain; and it was itself the death of the grain that was to be multiplied and the exalting of him who draws all things after him. "While you have the light," he says, "believe in the light that you may be the children of light." When you have heard something true, believe in the Truth that you may be reborn in truth.

14. "Jesus spoke these things and went away and hid himself from them." Not from those who had begun to believe and love, not from those who had come to meet him with palm branches and praises, but from those who saw with their eyes and cast malicious looks,[37] because they did not see, but stumbled upon that stone in blindness. Now when Jesus hid himself from those who desired to kill him (a thing which you must often be reminded of, because of forgetfulness), he had regard for our weakness, he did not impair his own power.

---

produce *modicum tempus.* The Latin text has simply the adverb *modicum,* meaning "for a little while"; but this could also serve as an adjective modifying *lumen,* meaning "a little light" and so Augustine takes it. He then understands the text to mean that there is still in them only a partial understanding of the character of the Messiah. See *Tractate* 53.1.

35. Cf. Rom 9.32–33, quoting Is 8.14; also 1 Pt 2.8.
36. Cf. 1 Pt 2.7, quoting Ps 117 (118).22.
37. A difficult to translate play on words: *videbant et invidebant,* literally, "they saw with their eyes and they cast evil eyes."

TRACTATE 53

On John 12.37–43

FTER THE Lord Christ had foretold his passion and his fruitful death in the lifting up of the cross, where he said that he would draw all things after himself, since the Jews had understood that he had spoken about his death and had asked him how he could say that he would die since they heard from the Law that the Christ remains forever, he encouraged them that, while yet a little light was in them, by which they had learned that Christ was eternal, they might walk that they might learn the whole in order that they not be overcome by the darkness. And when he had said these things, he hid himself from them. You learned these things in the readings and words of the previous Lord's day.[1]

2. Then the Evangelist continued with the words from which today's brief passage was read, and he said, "Now, although he had done so many signs in their presence, they did not believe in him, so that the words of the prophet Isaiah in which he said, 'Lord, who has believed what has reached our ears? And to whom has the arm of the Lord been revealed?' might be fulfilled"[2] Here he shows well that the Son of God was himself called the arm of God, not because God the Father is limited by the shape of human flesh and the Son adheres to him as a limb of the body; but rather because all things were made through him, he was called, therefore, the arm of God. For just as it is your arm through which you work, so his word was called the arm of God, because through the Word he constructed the world. For why does a person, in

1. This refers to the readings and words of the last Lord's day (*Dominica dies*). Cf. *Tractate* 52.11–14.
2. Jn is quoting Is 53.1.

290

order to construct something, stretch out his arm except because what he said is not immediately done? If, however, he possessed superior capability from so great a power that, without any movement of his body, whatever he said would happen, his word would be his arm. But the Lord Jesus, the only-begotten Son of God the Father, just as he is not a limb of the Father's body, so he is not a conceptual or sounding and passing word; but when all things were made through him, he was God's Word.

3. Therefore, when we hear that the Son of God is the arm of God the Father, let ordinary ideas about bodies not impede us; but as far as we can, by his gift, let us think of the Power and Wisdom of God,[3] through which all things were made. Such an arm, to be sure, is neither stretched forth and extended, nor drawn in and pulled back.[4] For he himself is not he who is the Father, but he himself and the Father are one thing;[5] and equal to the Father, he is everywhere whole as the Father. Let no occasion provide an opening for the abominable error of those who say that there is only the Father, but that according to a difference of conditions,[6] he is called the Son, he is called the Holy Spirit. And in respect to these words may they not dare to say: Look, you see that there is only the Father if his arm is the Son; for a man and his arm are not two persons but one. They do not understand or observe how words are transferred from some things to other things be-

3. Cf. 1 Cor 1.24.
4. This probably has reference to the Sabellian heresy (see *Tractate* 29.7, note 17) and a particular notion of Sabellius that changes in the mode of being of the one God occur through self-extensions (πλατυσμοί) or (ἐκτάσεις) and self-contractions (συστολαί); see Browne LFC 29.699, and G. Bardy, "Monarchianisme," *Dictionnaire de théologie catholique* (Paris, 1929) 10.2.2205. For the terminology see Athanasius, *Contra Arianos* 4.9.50–15.91 (PG 26.479–88); the fourth oration against the Arians is probably spuriously attributed to Athanasius, but still provides a sound source for this information.
5. Cf. Jn 10.30.
6. Or perhaps "necessities" or "exigencies": *pro diversitate causarum.* Here *causa* seems to be Augustine's Latin word for the Greek χρεία, a technical term used by Sabellius to suggest the "cause" of a change in mode in God. See Browne LFC 29.700; and Athanasius, *contra Arianos* 4.12.73 (PG 26.483–84) and note 4 above.

cause of some likeness, even in everyday expressions about visible and well known things. How much more in order that things ineffable may be in some way expressed, things which cannot at all be expressed as they [really] are! For a man both calls another man, through whom he usually does whatever he does, his arm, and if he is taken from him, he says in grief, "I have lost my arm." And to the one who has taken him, he says, "You have taken my arm from me." Therefore, let them understand how the Son has been called the arm of the Father, through which the Father effected all his works, that they may not, by not understanding this and by remaining in the darkness of their error, be like the very Jews about whom it was said, "And to whom has the arm of the Lord been revealed?"

4. Here another question comes up, about which I think, in point of fact, that neither my strength, nor the shortness of time, nor your capability allows that anything be discussed properly and all its most hidden hollows be searched out and explored as is appropriate. Nevertheless, because, in your expectation, we are not allowed to pass over to other things if we should not say something about it, accept what we will be capable of; and where we are not up to your expectation, ask for growth from him who has appointed us to plant and to water because, as the Apostle says, "neither he who plants is anything, nor he who waters, but God who gives growth."[7]

(2) Therefore, some mutter to one another and at times shout out where they can and contend in stormy debate, saying, "What did the Jews do or what was their fault if it was necessary 'that the word of the prophet Isaiah which he said might be fulfilled: Lord, who has believed what has reached our ears? And to whom has the arm of the Lord been revealed?'" Now to these we answer that the Lord, foreknowing the future, had through the prophet foretold the lack of faith of the Jews; yet he had foretold it, not effected it. For God does not force anyone to sin because he already knows men's future sins. For he foreknew their sins, not his own, nor any-

7. 1 Cor 3.7.

one else's but theirs. Therefore, if those sins which he foreknew are not theirs, he did not truly foreknow; but because
his foreknowledge cannot be deceived, without a doubt no
one else but they themselves sin who God foreknew would sin.
Therefore, the Jews committed sin which he, whom sin does
not please, did not compel them to commit; but he from
whom nothing is hidden foretold that they would commit it.
And therefore, if they had not wanted to do an evil but a good,
they would not have been prevented; and it would be foreseen
that they would do this by him who knows what each one will
do and what return he will make to him for his work.

5. But the words of the Gospel which follow are more pressing and pose a deeper question. For he adds and says, "The
reason they could not believe was because Isaiah said again,
'He has blinded their eyes and hardened their heart that they
should not see with their eyes and understand with their heart
and be converted, and I should heal them.'"[8]

(2) For it is said to us: If they could not believe, what is the
sin of a man not doing what he cannot do? But if they sinned
by not believing, then they could believe and did not. Therefore if they could, how does the Gospel say, "The reason they
could not believe was because Isaiah says again, 'He has
blinded their eyes and hardened their heart,'" so that—what
is more serious—the cause by which they did not believe is
referred to God, inasmuch as he himself "blinded their eyes
and hardened their heart"? For surely this is not said about
the devil but about God as the prophetic Scripture itself attests. For if we think that this, "He blinded their eyes and
hardened their heart," was said about the devil, effort must be
exerted as to how we can show their fault because they did not
believe, about whom it is said, "they could not believe." Then
what will we answer about another testimony of the prophet
himself which the Apostle Paul cites, saying, "Israel did not
obtain what he was seeking, but the election did obtain it. The
rest indeed have been blinded, as it has been written, 'God
gave them a spirit of insensibility, eyes that they should not

8. Jn is quoting Is 6.10.

see, and ears that they should not hear until this present day.'"⁹

6. You have heard, brothers, the question proposed; you see, of course, how profound it is. But we answer as best we can. "They could not believe," because Isaiah the prophet foretold this. But the prophet foretold it because God fore-knew that it would be. Why they could not, however, if it should be asked of me, I quickly answer, because they were not willing: for God foresaw their evil will and he, from whom the future cannot be hidden, foretold it through the prophet.

(2) But, you say, the prophet states another cause, not of their will. What cause does the prophet state? That "God gave them a spirit of insensibility, eyes that they should not see and ears that they should not hear, and he blinded their eyes and hardened their heart." I answer that their will earned even this. For thus God blinds, thus God hardens by abandoning and not helping; and he can do this by a hidden judgment, but he cannot do it by an evil one. The piety of the religious ought altogether keep this unshaken and inviolate; as the Apostle says when he was discussing this very same, most difficult question: "What shall we say, then? Is there injustice with God? Not at all!"¹⁰ Therefore, if it is not at all the case that there is injustice with God, either when he helps, he acts mer-cifully, or when he does not help, he acts justly, because he does all things not with rashness but in judgment. Accord-ingly, if the judgments of the saints are just, how much more so those of the sanctifying and justifying God!¹¹ Therefore, they are just, but hidden.

(3) And so when questions of this sort present themselves, why one person thus but another thus, why that one is blinded, abandoned by God, yet this one is enlightened, aided by God, let us not appropriate judgment to ourselves about the judgment of so great a judge, but trembling, let us shout

9. Cf. Rom 11.7–8; the quotation is a loose conflation of Is 29.10 and Dt 29.3.
10. Rom 9.14.
11. See, e.g., 1 Cor 1.30; this is, of course, a major theme of Rom which is itself quoted three times in this section.

out with the Apostle, "Oh, the depth of the riches of the wisdom, and the knowledge of God! How inscrutable are his judgments and how unsearchable are his ways!"[12] And in regard to this it was said in the psalm, "Your judgments, like the great deep."[13]

7. Therefore, my beloved brothers, let your expectation not force me to penetrate this depth, to probe this deep abyss, to search out the inscrutable. I recognize my little measure [of ability]; I seem also to perceive your little measure. This is higher than my growth, and mightier than my strength—than yours too, I think! Therefore, let us together hear Scripture saying and warning us: "Things too high for you, seek not; into things beyond your strength, search not."[14] Not that these things have been denied to us, since God our teacher says, "Nothing is hidden which will not be revealed."[15] But if we should walk in what we have attained, as the Apostle says,[16] not only what we do not know and ought to know, but also if in anything we are otherwise minded, God will reveal that also to us.

(2) Now we have attained the path of faith; let us hold this with the uttermost perseverence. This will lead us to the King's chamber in whom are all the hidden treasures of wisdom and knowledge.[17] For the Lord Jesus Christ himself was not begrudging to those great and especially chosen disciples of his when he said, "I have many things to say to you, but you cannot bear them now."[18] We must walk, we must make progress, we must grow, that our hearts may be able to hold those things which we cannot now hold. But if the last day finds us making progress, we shall learn there what we could not here.

8. If, however, someone knows that he is able, and has the confidence, to expound this question more clearly or better, far be it from me not to be more ready to learn than to teach. Only let no one so dare to defend free will in such a way that

12. Rom 11.33.   13. Ps 35 (36).7.
14. Ecclus (Sir) 3.22.   15. Mt 10.26.
16. See Phil 3.15–16.   17. See Col 2.3.
18. Jn 16.12.

he try to take from us the prayer in which we say, "Lead us not into temptation."[19] Again, let no one deny freedom of the will and dare to excuse sin.

(2) But let us hear the Lord, both instructing and aiding, both ordering what we should do and helping us that we might be able to carry it out. For on the one hand, too much trust in their own will raised up certain ones into pride; on the other hand, too much distrust of their own will has cast down certain ones into slackness. The former say, Why do we ask God that we not be overcome by temptation—something that is in our power? The latter say, Why do we try to live well—something that is in God's power? O Lord, O Father who art in heaven, lead us not into any of these temptations, "but deliver us from evil!"[20]

(3) Let us hear the Lord saying, "I have prayed for you, Peter, that your faith not fail,"[21] that we may not think that our faith so lies in free will that there is no need of divine help. Let us hear also the Evangelist saying, "He gave them power to be made the children of God,"[22] that we not think at all that what we believe is not in our power. Nevertheless, let us acknowledge his benefits in both. For we must both give thanks because power has been granted and pray that our weakness not succumb. This is the faith which works through love,[23] as the Lord has portioned out his measure to each one[24] that he who glories glory not in himself, but in the Lord.[25]

9. Therefore, it is no wonder that they could not believe whose will was so proud that, ignoring God's justice, they wished to establish their own, as the Apostle said of them, "They did not subject themselves to the justice of God."[26] For they were swollen up not from faith, but, as it were, from works, and, blinded by this very self-inflation, they stumbled on the stone of stumbling. Thus, however, was it said "they could not," where it must be understood that they were un-

---

19. Mt 6.13; cf. Lk 11.4.   20. Mt 6.13.
21. Lk 22.32.   22. Jn 1.12.
23. Cf. Gal 5.6.   24. Cf. Rom 12.3.
25. Cf. 1 Cor 1.31, referring to Jer 9.23–24.
26. Cf. Rom 10.3.

willing, just as it was said about the Lord, our God: "If we do not believe, he remains faithful; he cannot deny himself."[27] Of the omnipotent it was said "He cannot." Therefore, the fact that the Lord "cannot deny himself" is praise of the divine will, just as that they "could not believe" is the fault of human will.

10. Look, I also say that they, who are so proud-minded that they think so much ought to be ascribed to the strength of their own will that they deny that divine help is necessary to them to live well,[28] cannot believe in Christ. For the syllables of Christ's name and the sacraments of Christ offer no profit when there is resistance to faith in Christ. Now faith in Christ is to believe in him who justifies the ungodly,[29] to believe in the Mediator without whose interposition we are not reconciled to God, to believe in the Savior who came to seek and to save what had been lost,[30] to believe in him who said, "Without me you can do nothing."[31] Therefore, because, ignoring God's justice by which the ungodly person is justified, he wishes to establish his own [justice] by which the proud person may be convicted, he cannot believe in him. For this reason those men too "could not believe," not because men cannot be changed for the better; but they cannot believe as long as they have such an idea. They are blinded by this and hardened because in denying divine help they are not helped. God foreknew this about the Jews who were blinded and hardened, and in his Spirit the prophet foretold it.

11. But in regard to what [the prophet] added, "and be converted and I should heal them," should a "not" be understood, that is "and not be converted," in close connection with the clause connected before where it was said, "that they may not see with their eyes and understand with the heart," be-

---

27. 2 Tm 2.13.
28. The Pelagians who denied that divine help was needed and asserted that the human will was in itself strong enough. See Comeau, 214; G. de Plinval, *Pélage* (Lausanne 1943) 234–38; and J. Ferguson, *Pelagius* (Cambridge 1956) 122–168.
29. Cf. Rom 4.5.   30. See Lk 19.10.
31. Jn 15.5.

cause this also, to be sure, was meant,[32] that they may not understand? For conversion itself is from his grace to whom it is said, "God of hosts, convert us."[33] Or perhaps must this also be understood as done out of the mercy of the heavenly medicine so that because they were of proud and wicked will and wanted to establish their own justice, they were abandoned for the purpose of being blinded, [and] they were blinded for the purpose of stumbling on the stone of stumbling and that their face might be filled with ignominy and thus humbled they might seek the name of the Lord and not their own justice by which the proud is puffed up, but God's justice by which the ungodly is justified? For this benefitted many of them for their good, who, pricked with remorse over their own wrongdoing, afterwards believed in Christ; and for these he had even prayed himself, saying, "Father, forgive them, for they know not what they do."[34] And about this ignorance of theirs the Apostle, too, said, "I bear them witness that they have a zeal for God, but not according to knowledge." For then he also added this and said, "For, not knowing God's justice and seeking to establish their own, they have not submitted themselves to the justice of God."[35]

12. "Isaiah said these things when he saw his glory and spoke of him." What Isaiah saw and how this pertains to the Lord Christ must be read and understood in his book. For he did not see just exactly as it is, but in a certain signifying manner as a prophet's vision ought to have been shaped. For

---

32. The Benedictine text, followed by PL and CCL, has a note concerning this sentence as follows: "Perhaps the reading should be 'was not stated,' unless the meaning is that the negative prefixed to the verb 'may see' is mentally conjoined to the verb 'may understand,' cf. Vulgate, 'and may not understand with their heart.' But in the ancient Biblical texts at Corbie, in agreement with the Greek, there is no repetition at this place." Now, this unnecessarily complicates the matter. In secular classical Latin *ut non* expresses result; in Christian Latin *ut non* sometimes replaces *ne* and expresses purpose, as in this quotation where the Greek text clearly makes the clause purpose. Augustine is indicating to his audience that *ut non* functions as *ne* which would make all four subordinate verbs, see, understand, be converted, and heal, negative.

33. Ps 79 (80).8.   34. Lk 23.34.
35. Rom 10.2–3.

Moses also saw, and yet he said to him whom he saw, "If I have found favor in your presence, show yourself to me that I may see you clearly."[36] For he did not see him as he is.

(2) Now when this will be for us, this same holy John the Evangelist says in his epistle, "Dearly beloved, we are God's children, and it has not yet appeared what we shall be. We know that when it appears, we shall be like him, for we shall see him as he is."[37] He could have said, "for we shall see him," and not have added, "as he is." But because he knew that he had been seen by certain fathers and prophets, but not as he is, when he had said, "we shall see him," he added, "as he is."

(3) Let no one, brothers, of those who say that the Father is invisible and the Son visible deceive you. For they who think that he is a creature claim this,[38] and do not understand him according to what was said: "The Father and I, we are one thing."[39] Accordingly, in the form of God in which he is equal with the Father, the Son, too, is invisible; but that he might be seen by men, he took the form of a servant, and made in the likeness of men,[40] he was made visible. Therefore, before he took on flesh, he also showed himself to the eyes of men, as he wished, in a creature subject to him, not as he is. Let us cleanse our hearts through faith that we may be made ready for that ineffable and, so to speak, invisible vision. For "blessed are the clean of heart, for they shall see God."[41]

13. "And yet, even among the chief men, many believed in him; but because of the Pharisees they did not admit it[42] so they would not be ejected from the synagogue. For they loved the glory of men more than the glory of God." See how the Evangelist noted and disapproved of certain ones whom nonetheless he said believed in him. For if in this entry to the faith they were to advance, they would also, in advancing,

36. Ex 33.13.(LXX).
37. 1 Jn 3.2. NAB, and some other translations, render "when he appears" for "when it appears." Neither the Latin nor the Greek text makes one or the other clearly preferable.
38. E.g., the Gnostics, the Manichaeans, the Arians, and the Photinians.
39. Jn 10.30.   40. See Phil 2.7.
41. Mt 5.8.
42. So NAB, CCD, and JBC; Douay has "they did not confess [him]."

overcome their love of human glory, which the Apostle had overcome, saying, "But as for me, far be it that I should glory except in the cross of our Lord Jesus Christ, by whom the world has been crucified to me and I to the world."[43] For this reason, in truth, the Lord himself also fixed on the foreheads of those who would believe in him his cross, whereon the madness of proud impiety mocked him, whereon there is, in a sense, the seat of shame, so that faith may not blush at his name and may love God's glory more than man's.

43. Gal. 6.14.

TRACTATE 54

On John 12.44–50

HEN OUR Lord Jesus Christ was speaking with the Jews and working such great, miraculous signs, some, predestined for eternal life, whom he called his sheep, believed; but some did not believe, nor could they believe because they had been blinded and hardened[1] by the hidden and yet not unjust judgment of God, since he who resists the proud but gives favor to the humble[2] abandoned them. Moreover, of those who believed, some confessed to such an extent that they took up branches of palm and met him as he came, rejoicing in the same confession of praise; but others among the chief men did not dare to confess so that they might not be ejected from the synagogue. And the Evangelist noted these, saying that "they loved the glory of men more than the glory of God."[3] Also, of those who did not believe, some were going to believe afterwards, whom he foresaw when he said, "When you have lifted up the Son of Man, then you will know that I am he."[4] But others were going to remain in the same lack of faith, whom even this nation of the Jews is imitating which later, utterly defeated in war, was dispersed through almost the whole world—for a witness of the prophecy which was written about Christ.

2. When matters were in this state and his passion was now drawing near, "Jesus cried out and said"—from this point today's reading begins: "He who believes in me believes not in me but in him who sent me, and he who sees me sees him who sent me."

1. Cf. Jn 12.37–40.
2. Cf. Jas 4.6, quoting Prv 3.34; also 1 Pt 5.5.
3. Jn 12.42–43; see *Tractate* 53.13.
4. Jn 8.28.

(2) In a certain place he had already said, "my doctrine is not my own but his who sent me."[5] There we understood that he had said that his doctrine was the Word of the Father, which he himself is, and that he had signified this by saying, "My doctrine is not my own but his who sent me," because he was not from himself but he had one from whom he was. For he is God from God, Son of the Father. But the Father is not God from God, but God, the Father of the Son.

(3) Now, however, how are we to understand his words, "He who believes in me believes not in me but in him who sent me," except that the man appeared to men while the God was hidden? And, that they might not think that only this which they were seeing was he, wishing that he be believed to be such and as great as the Father is, he says, "He who believes in me does not believe in me," that is, in this which he sees, "but in him who sent me," that is, in the Father. But he who believes in the Father must necessarily believe that he is the Father; but whoever believes that he is the Father must necessarily believe that he has a Son, and in this way he who believes in the Father must necessarily believe in the Son.

(4) But let no one believe about the only-begotten Son what he believes about those who were called the children of God according to grace, not nature, as the Evangelist said, "He gave them power to be made children of God."[6] On this same point, the Lord himself recalled what was said in the law: "I have said, 'You are gods, and all of you sons of the Most High.'"[7] He said, "He who believes in me believes not in me," for this reason: that not everything which is believed about Christ be believed according to his humanness. That man, therefore, he said, believes in me who does not believe in me according to that which he sees me [to be], but believes in him who sent me, so that when he believes in the Father, he may believe that he has a Son equal to himself and then he may truly believe in me. For if he thinks that he only has children

5. Cf. Jn 7.16; see *Tractate* 29.3–7.
6. Jn 1.12.
7. Jn 10.34, quoting Ps 81 (82).6; Augustine completes verse six of the psalm, only part of which is quoted in Jn.

according to grace, who are, of course, his creation, not his word, but made through the Word, and that he does not have a Son equal to and coeternal with himself, always born, equally unchangeable, unlike and unequal in no regard, he does not believe in the Father who sent him, because this is not the Father who sent him.

3. And so when he had said, "He who believes in me believes not in me but in him who sent me," that it might not be thought that he so wished the Father to be understood as the Father of the many children reborn through grace[8] and not of the only one, the Word equal to him, he immediately added, "and he who sees me sees him who sent me." Does he say, He who sees me sees not me but him who sent me, as he had said, "He who believes in me believes not in me but in him who sent me"? For he said the former in order that he might not be believed to be, as he seems, only the Son of Man; but he said the latter in order that he might be believed equal to the Father. He who believes in me, he said, believes not in this which he sees me to be but believes in him who sent me. Or when he believes in the Father who begot me equal to himself, not as he sees me, but so let him believe in me just as in him who sent me; for there is absolutely no difference between him and me so that he who sees me sees him who sent me.

(2) Surely the Lord Christ himself sent his apostles, a fact which their name even declares, for as those called angels in Greek are messengers in Latin, so those called apostles in Greek are the ones sent [i.e. missioners] in Latin. Yet no one of the apostles would ever dare to say, "He who believes in me believes not in me but in him who sent me." For he would not at all say, "He who believes in me." For we believe the apostle, but we do not believe *in* the apostle; for the apostle does not justify the ungodly. But for him who believes in him who justifies the ungodly, his faith is credited as justice.[9] The apostle could say, He who receives me receives him who sent me, or He who hears me hears him who sent me. For the Lord

8. *filiorum per gratiam regeneratorum:* the phrase perhaps stems from Ti 3.5–7 or 1 Pt 1.3–4.
9. Cf. Rom 4.5.

himself said this to them: "He who receives you receives me, and he who receives me receives him who sent me."[10] For the Lord is honored in his servant and the Father in the Son, but the Father as in the Son, the Lord as in the servant.

(3) But the only-begotten Son could rightly say, "Believe in God and believe in me,"[11] and what he says now, "He who believes in me believes not in me but in him who sent me." He did not remove the faith of the believer from himself, but he did not wish the believer to remain at the form of the servant; for when anyone believes in the Father who sent him, he immediately believes in the Son without whom he does not know that he is the Father. And he believes in such a way that he believes him equal because he continues, "and he who sees me sees him who sent me."

4. Pay attention to the rest; "I have come a light into the world that whoever believes in me may not remain in darkness." In a certain place he said to his disciples: "You are the light of the world. A city set on a mountain cannot be hidden. Neither do men light a lamp and put it under a bushel, but upon a lamp-stand that it may give light to all who are in the house. So let your light shine before men that they may see your good works and give glory to your Father who is in heaven."[12] Nevertheless, he did not say to them: You have come a light into the world that whoever believes in you may not remain in darkness. I declare that this can be read nowhere. All the saints are lights; but, in believing, they are enlightened by him from whom, if anyone withdraws, he will be darkened. But that Light by which they are enlightened cannot withdraw from itself because it is wholly unchangeable. Therefore we believe the enlightened light, as a prophet, as an apostle; but we believe him for this reason: not that we may believe in this [light] which is enlightened, but that we may believe together with him in that light by which he is enlightened so that we, too, may be enlightened not by him, but together with him by that one by whom he is enlightened.

10. Mt 10.40.   11. Jn 14.1.
12. Mt 5.14–16.

(2) Moreover when he says, "that whoever believes in me may not remain in darkness," he makes it quite clear that he found all in darkness; but that they may not remain in the darkness in which they were found, they ought to believe in the light which has come into the world because the world was made through it.

5. "And if anyone hears my words," he says, "and does not keep them, I do not judge him." Remember what I know you heard in earlier readings; and you who have perchance forgotten, recall. And you who were not present but are now, hear how the Son speaks. "I do not judge him," although he says in another place, "The Father judges no one but has given all judgment to the Son"[13]—except that this must be understood: I do not judge him *now*. Why does he not judge now? Pay attention to what follows. "For I did not come," he says, "to judge the world but to save the world," that is, to cause the world to be saved. Therefore, now is a time of mercy, afterwards will be a time of judgment; for, he says, "of mercy and judgment I will sing to you, Lord."[14]

6. But about the coming last judgment itself see also what he says: "He who despises me and does not accept my words has one who judges him. The word which I have spoken, *that* will judge him on the last day." He does not say, He who despises me and does not accept my words, I do not judge him on the last day. For if he had said this, I do not see how it could not be contradictory to that sentence which he said, "The Father judges no one but has given all judgment to the Son." But when he said, "He who despises me and does not accept my words has one who judges him," and to those looking for whoever that might be, he continued and said, "The word which I have spoken, that will judge him on the last day," he made it quite clear that he himself would judge on the last day. For indeed he spoke himself, he announced himself, he posited himself as the door by which he himself as the shepherd might enter to the sheep.[15]

13. Jn 5.22; see *Tractates* 21.11–13, 22.11, 24.13–15, and 36.12.
14. Ps 100 (101).1.
15. See Jn 10.7 and 9.

(2) And so they who have not heard will be judged in one way; they who have heard and scorned in another way. "For they who have sinned without the law," the Apostle says, "will perish also without the law; and they who have sinned in the law will be judged by the law."[16]

7. "For I," he says, "have not spoken of myself." He says that he has not spoken of himself for the reason that he is not of himself. We have already said this often; now we ought not to teach it, as it is very well known, but to recall it to mind. "But he who sent me, the Father, gave me commandment what I should say and what I should speak." We would not exert ourselves if we knew that we were speaking with those with whom we spoke earlier; not with all of those but with those retaining in memory what they heard. But now because perhaps there are some present who did not hear, and those like them who have forgotten what they heard, for their sakes, let those who remember what they heard endure our dallyings.

(2) How does the Father give a command to his only Son? With what word does he speak to the Word, since the Son himself is the only-begotten Word? Is it through an angel, even though angels were created through him?[17] Is it through a cloud, which, when it sounded forth to the Son, sounded forth not for his sake (as he himself also says elsewhere) but for the sake of others who needed to hear in such a way?[18] Is it through a sound sent from the lips [of one] who has no body, and the Son is separated from the Father by no interval of spaces so that there is no air midway between them by striking which the voice might be produced and come into the ear? Far be it that we suppose such things about that incorporeal and ineffable Substance! The only Son is the Word of the Father and the Wisdom of the Father; in that Wisdom are all the commands of the Father.

(3) Neither in truth did the Son ever not know the Father's command so that it would be necessary for him to have in time

16. Rom 2.12.
17. See Jn 12.28–29.
18. See Mt 17.5, Mk 9.6, and Lk 9.34–35.

what he did not have before. For he has received what he has from the Father in such a way that he received by being born and [the Father] gave it to him by begetting. For he is life and has received life by being born, of course, but not by existing before without life. For the Father has life and is what he has; yet he has not received it because he is not of anyone. The Son, however, has received life, and the Father from whom he is gave it; and he himself is what he has, for he has life and is life. Hear him speaking himself. "As the Father," he says, "has life in himself, so he has given it to the Son also to have life in himself."[19] Did he give it to one existing but not having? But he who begot Life gave it by the very act of begetting; and Life begot Life. And because he begot an equal not an unequal Life, therefore it was said, "As he" himself "has life in himself, so he has given it to the Son also to have life in himself." He gave life, because by begetting Life, what did he give except to be Life? And because the birth itself is eternal, the Son who is Life never was not; the Son was never without life. And as the birth is eternal, so he who was born is eternal Life.

(4) Thus also the Father did not give a command which the Son did not have; but, as I have said, in the Wisdom of the Father, which is the Word of the Father, are all the commands of the Father. The command, however, is said to have been given because he to whom it is said to have been given is not of himself. And to give to the Son that without which the Son never was is the same as to beget a Son who never was not.

8. Now, he continues: "And I know that his commandment is eternal life." Therefore, if the Son himself is eternal Life and the Father's commandment is eternal life, what else has he said but, I am the Father's commandment? Accordingly, that also which he adds and says, "The things that I say, even as the Father said to me, so do I speak." Let us not take "said to me" as if the Father spoke words to his only Word, or the Word of God would need the words of God. Therefore, the Father spoke to the Son as he gave life to the Son, not what he did not know or did not have, but what the Son himself was.

19. Jn 5.26.

(2) But what is "even as he said to me, so do I speak" except "I speak the truth"? Thus that one said as one who is true; thus this one[20] speaks as the Truth. The true one, moreover, begot the Truth. What then would he now say to the Truth? For the Truth was not imperfect so that something true might be added to it. Therefore he spoke to the Truth because he begot the Truth. Then the Truth itself so speaks as it was said to it, but to those understanding, whom it teaches, as it was born. In order that men, however, might believe what they are not yet able to understand, words sounded forth from the mouth of flesh and went away; the sounds, flying by, made their noise, lasting the short stay of their own timespans. But the realities themselves, of which the sounds are signs, having been cast in a way into the memory of those who heard, have reached us too through the letters which are visible signs. The Truth does not so speak: to understanding minds it speaks within, it instructs without sound, it floods with intelligible light.[21] Therefore, he who can see the eternity of its birth in this [Truth], himself so hears it speaking, as the Father said to it what it should say.

(3) It has stirred us up to a great longing for its interior sweetness; but we take hold of it by growing, we grow by moving ahead, we move ahead by improving that we may be able to attain.

20. Both CCL and the PL read *ista* here: He speaks these things. But clearly *iste* is required in correlation to *ille,* as I here translate. So reads the text in *Patres Ecclesiae* 123, *Augustinus* 16, ed. A. Caillau, et al. (Paris 1842) 94.
21. On the Interior Master, a frequent theme of Augustine, see *Tractate* 1.7, note 23.

INDICES

GENERAL INDEX

Numbers Refer to Tractate, Section, and Paragraph

Abraham, 28.3(2); 30.4; 41.2(1),
(3); 42.1–7, 15(2); 43.10, 13, 16–
18; 44.6(4); 45.9(5); 49.9(2),
15(1)
Adam, 30.3(4), 5(1); 34.9(1); 38.5;
41.5(1); 42.11(1), (3), 13(2);
43.9(3); 44.1(2); 49.12(2), 20
adoption: humans as sons of God,
29.8(3); 42.16(2)
adultery, 33.4–5; 45.2(2); 46.8(1)
aliens, Christians as: *See* peregrina-
tion
alms, 51.13
Amen, meaning of, 41.3
Amorite, 42.10(4)
analogy, 45.2(2); 46.3; 47.5–6
Andrew, 51.8(10)
angel(s), 30.7(2); 34.3; 36.1, 11–12;
38.4(2), 8(2), 10(1); 40.4(2);
42.10(5), 12; 43.11, 15(1);
44.6(1), (3); 48.6(4), 49.10;
50.11(1); 51.4; 52.5, 7(2); 54.3(2),
7(2)
anger, 32.3(1); 41.12(1); 43.10(1),
17; 44.11; 48.8; 49.19(3)
Anna, 32.6(2); 52.8
anointing, 44.8–9, 13, 15
Antichrist, 29.8(1), (4)
Apocalypse, 36.5(2)
Apollinarists, 47.9(2)
apostle(s), 29.6(3); 37.6(3); 38.5;
40.4(2); 42.1(2); 44.5(2); 46.7(1);
47.3(4); 49.10, 18(2); 50.10;
54.3(2), 4(1)
Apostolic Succession, 37.6(3)
Arianism, 29.5 n.; 36.9(3), (4);
37.6–7; 39.2 n.; 40.7; 43.14(2),

15(2); 47.9(2); 48.8; 49.6(2) n.;
53.3 n., 12(3) n.
Arius, 45.5(3)

baptism, 28.9(2); 38.6(1); 41.5(1),
10(3); 42.5(2); 44.2; 45.9(3);
47.3(4); 49.19(2); 50.12(3)
beatific vision, 34.7(1), 9(2); 35.9;
43.12(4); 45.15(3); 53.12(3)
beauty, 32.3, 9(2); 39.6(2); 40.4(3),
8(2)
belief, 29.6; 31.9(1), 11(2); 32.6(1);
35.4(1), (3), 5, 9; 36.2(2), 3, 7,
11; 37.1(2), 3, 5, 8; 38.5–11;
39.1(1), 3(2), 5(1), 8(2); 40.2(2),
(3), 7–9, 11; 41.1(2), 2(1); 42.9,
15(1), 16(2), (3); 43.16(1); 44.2(2),
12, 15, 17(2); 45.7, 9, 15(3);
46.8(1); 47.4, 10(2), 13(1); 48.3(1),
4–6, 10–11; 49.1(2), 2(2), 6(1),
8(3), 11, 15, 22–26; 50.5, 14; 51.1,
4, 8(2); 52.6–7, 9, 13–14; 53.2, 5,
8(3), 9–11, 13; 54.1–4, 8(2)
bishop, 45.11(2), (4); 46 *passim;*
51.13
blasphemy, 43.18; 44.11; 45.12(2);
48.8–9; 50.7(1)
Blood of Christ, 31.9(1); 38.7(2);
40.2(2); 41.4(3), 6; 43.18; 47.2(1),
(2), 4; 48.4; 50.2(1), (3); 51.5(2);
52.6(2), 13
Body of Christ, 28.1(2), 2, 7(3), 9,
11; 29.6(3), 8(3); 31.11(1);
32.7(4), 8; 38.7(2); 39.5(1);
41.8(2); 46.7(1); 47.1–3; 49.28;
50.6, 10(2), 12–13; 51.12(2);
52.1–3, 6(2), 11(2)

311

bread: symbol of truth, 41.1(3)
brothers of Jesus, 28.3–5

Caesar, 40.9(2); 41.2(3)
Caiphas, 49.27(1), (3)
calf: symbol of Luke, 36.5(2)
catechumen, 44.2(2)
Catholic, 34.2(2), 10(2); 36.2(2), 6,
    8; 37.6(3); 39.2; 42.13(2); 45.5(5),
    11(4), (5); 47.9(2)
Cethaean, 42.10(4)
Charybdis, 36.9(2), (3)
chastity, 33.5(1); 39.6(2), 8(2), (3);
    45.12(2)
chrism, 33.3
Christ: the anointed, 33.3; ascen-
    sion of, 31.9; 32.6(3); 36.4(1), 12;
    39.5(1), 6(1); 40.2(2), 4(2);
    44.5(2); 45.9(2); 47.4; 50.4(1), 13;
    52.4, 13; as cornerstone, 47.5–6;
    as creator, 29.8; 30.3(2); 31.5(3),
    11(1); 34.2(2); 36.1, 4(4); 37.5(1),
    8(2), 9(2); 38.3(1), 5–6, 8, 10;
    40.6, 9(2); 42.8(2), 10, 15(3);
    43.1(1), 2(2), 16–17; 44.4; 48.7;
    49.1(1), 11(1); 51.3–4, 7; 52.3(1);
    53.2–3; 54.2(4), 4(2), 7(2); cruci-
    fied, 31.6; 36.4(4); 37.9–10;
    38.7(2); 40.2(3), 4(2); 41.1(2),
    5(4); 43.9(3); 45.10; 47.3(4), 10–
    11, 13(1); 50.13; 51.2(1), 3(2);
    52.11–12; 53.1; 54.1; as the Day,
    35.2(1), 6(2), 8; 44.4–6, 9(1), 16;
    45.2(1); 48.12; 49.8(1), (3); death
    of, 28.2, 6(3); 31.6(3), 9(1);
    36.4(4); 37.9; 38.1–3, 7(2); 40.2,
    4(2); 42.1(2), 2(1), 4, 6; 43.11;
    47.2(2), 4, 7–11, 13; 49.8(2), 27;
    50.2(1), 4(1), 11, 13; 51.2–3, 9–
    10, 12(2); 52.3(3), 6(2), 12–13;
    53.1; divinity of, 28.5(2) n.;
    30.3(2); 31.2(4), 3–5, 7; 33.1(2);
    34.4(2), 9(3); 36 passim; 37 pas-
    sim; 38.8, 10–11; 39 passim; 40.1,
    3–7, 9; 41.1(3), (4), 3; 42.1(1), 8;
    43.14–18; 44.4; 45.5; 46.2(2),
    3(3); 47.3, 9(2), 13(2); 48.3, 6(2),
    7–9; 49.5(3), 7(3); 50.13; 51.3(2),
    11; 52.3(1), 5; 53.7(1); 54.2–3, 5–
    8; as the door, 47.2(1); 54.6(1);

dual nature of, 28.1, 4, 6(3), 8(2);
    29.2, 8(2); 30.3(2); 31.1–5, 7,
    9(2); 33.1(2), 2; 34.6; 36 passim;
    37 passim; 38.2, 4, 8, 10–11; 39
    passim; 40.1–7, 9; 41.1(3), (4),
    5(4); 42.1(1), 4, 8; 43.9(3), (4),
    14–18; 44.2(1), 4, 15; 45.5, 8(2), 9,
    14; 46.3(3); 47.3–4, 6, 9–13;
    48.3, 6, 8–9, 11; 49.7(3), 18(2);
    50.13; 51.3(2), 11; 52.1–3;
    53.12(3); 54.2–3, 5–8; exaltation
    of, 40.2(3); as fire, 48.3(1), 9;
    foreknowledge of, 30.1(1); 38.2;
    40.2(2); 42.16; 45.12; 53.4(2);
    54.1; as fountain, 32.4; 34.4–5;
    35.6(1), 9; as the gate, 45.8–9,
    14–15; 46.1–4; 47.1, 3, 5–6, 9(2);
    48.4–5; as the gatekeeper, 46.1–
    4, 7(3); 47.1; gentleness of, 33.4–
    7; glory of, 28.5–6, 11; 31.8; 32.1,
    6, 9(3); 43.3, 8–9, 14; 45.5(5);
    46.6(4); 49.6, 26; 51.6, 8(2), 9;
    52.3(3), 7–8, 12; as Head, 28.1–
    2; 46.7(1); humility of, 28.1–2,
    5(2), 6(3); 29.8(2); 35.6(2), 7(2);
    36.2(1); 38.11(3); 40.2(3), 9(1);
    45.5(5), 8(2), 9(1); 51.3(2), 9;
    52.2–3, 13; immutability of,
    45.8(2); 46.2–3; 52.3(1); 54.4(1);
    incarnation of, 36.1–2, 7(3), 8;
    40.6; 42.8; 46.3(3); as inner
    teacher or master, 38.10(1);
    41.12(2); 44.1(2), 13; 45.15(2);
    47.5, 11(2); 49.19(2); 50.2(3);
    54.8(2); as judge, 28.6; 31.5(2),
    11(2); 33.4(2), 7–8; 34.8; 35.3(1),
    6(2); 36.3–5, 7, 9(1), 11; 39.6–7;
    40.4(2); 43.4, 8–9; 44.3(2), 17(2);
    45.1, 9(5); 47.7(1); 49.20; 50.4(1);
    53.6(1); 54.5–6; as Justice, 33.5–
    6; 52.9; kindness of, 33.4(2), 7;
    as king, 33.4(2); 51.4; 53.7(2); as
    the Lamb, 28.6(3); 35.7(2);
    46.3(2); 47.5; 50.2(1); as Life,
    34.9; 45.2(2); 48.6(3); 49.8(2), 14;
    as Light, 29.5; 30.2; 31.4; 33.2;
    34.2–5, 9(1); 35.1–3, 9; 36.3(2);
    39.1(2); 40.3(2); 43.16(1); 44.5;
    48.9; 50.2(2); 52.13; 54.4; as lion,
    46.3(2); 47.5; majesty of, 41.1(4);

6(2), 9; 36.5(2); 42.5(2); 48.9, 12;
49.4; as a lamp, 35.2–3, 6(2);
48.12
Joseph, 31.3; 41.2(2)
joy, 28.8(1); 43.16(1); 46.8(2); 49.10
Judas, 46.7(1); 49.8(3); 50.9–12;
51.12(1); as a wolf, 45.10
judgment, 28.6–7; 30.6–8; 33.8;
36.3, 4(6), 7–8, 10(2), 12; 37.2(2);
38.3; 39.6(1); 40.11; 43.3, 7–9,
15(2); 44.9(2), 14 n., 16–17; 45.1,
6(3) n.; 46.2(2); 47.4; 49.1(2), 13,
20; 50.4(1), 10(2), (3); 52.6–7;
53.6; 54.1, 5–6
justice, 28.6–7; 33.4–6; 35.3–4;
36.4(3); 40.4(3); 41.8–12; 43.7,
13; 45.15(4); 49.8(2), 20, 22(2);
50.6, 8; 53.6(2), 9–11; 54.1, 3(2)
justification, 44.13; 45.12(1);
48.6(1); 53.10 54.3(2)

kingdom of Heaven, 30.7(2); 51.4;
52.1
kiss of peace, 51.8(1)
knowledge, 32.5

Laban, 28.3(2)
lamb: symbol of Christ, 28.6(3);
35.7(2); 46.3(2); 47.5; 50.2(1)
lamp: John the Baptist as, 35.3(1),
(3), 3(1), 6(2); 48.11; prophets as,
35.2(1), 7(2), 8–9; scripture as,
35.9
Law, the, 29.2; 30.2, 4–6; 31.2(2);
33.1–2, 4–5; 36.10, 13; 41.6,
13(2); 45.2(2); 46.6(1); 48.9;
49.12(4), 22, 26; 50.2(2); 51.5(3);
52.12; 53.1; 54.2(4), 6(2)
Lazarus, 49 *passim;* 50.5–6, 14;
51.1, 7, 12(1); 52.1
Levite, 43.2(3)
life, 32.4, 6(3), 9(3); 34.4–5, 7–9;
35.4(1); 38.10(2); 43.10(1), 13;
45.2(2), 13(3), 15(3); 47 *passim;*
48.5–6; 49.1–3, 14–15, 22, 24(1);
50.7, 9–10; 51.1, 10, 12(2); 52.1–
2; 54.7–8
light, 30.2; 31.4; 34.2–7, 9(2); 35.3–
6, 8–9; 36.3; 38.5; 39.8(3);
40.3(2), 9(2); 44.2(2), 4–5, 16;

45.2(1); 47.3(2), 14; 48.3(4), 9;
49.8(1), 20; 50.2(2); 52.13; 53.1;
54.4, 8(2)
lion: symbol of Christ, 46.3(2);
47.6; symbol of Matthew, 36.5(2)
liturgy, 47.9(1)
Lord's Day, 47.9(1)
Lot, 28.3(2)
love, 29.4, 6(3); 30.8; 32.1–2,
8–9; 33.7; 34.9; 35.9; 36.8; 38.5;
39.5; 40.4(3), 9–10; 41.8, 10(3);
43.5, 7–8, 16(1); 44.6(2);
45.15(3); 46.6(4); 47.2(3); 48.1,
3(1); 49.2–3, 5(2), 7(1), 21; 50.8,
14; 51.4, 10–12; 52.1–2, 14;
53.8(3)
Luke, 36.5(2)
lust, 38.5; 41.8(2), 10(2), 12;
44.3(2); 48.1, 3(1); 49.14
lying, 29.1; 39.8(3); 41.2(3), 4(1);
42.11–15; 43.15(2); 44.9(2)

Magi, 31.2(2); 43.9(3); 52.4
magic, 35.8
man, symbol of Mark, 36.5(2)
Manichaeism, 34.2(2); 39.2 n.;
42.10, 12, 15(1); 43.15(1); 45.8(2)
n.; 47.9(2); 53.12(3) n.
Marcion, 43.15 (1) n.
Marcionites, 43.15(1)
Mark, 36.5(2)
Martha, sister of Lazarus, 49 *passim;* 50.5; 51.12(1)
martyr(s), 43.12; 47.11(1); 49.10;
51.10(2), 12–13
Mary: mother of Jesus, 28.3(2);
32.6(2); 33.2; 40.4(2); 41.1(3);
43.9(3); 47.4; 48.3(4); sister of
Lazarus, 49 *passim;* 50.6, 9;
51.12(1); Magdalene, 49.3(4) n.
Matthew, 36.5(2)
Matthias, 49.8(3)
memory, 40.4(1)
mercy, 32.6(1); 33.7–8; 34.3–4;
36.2(1), 4, 6(2); 41.10(3); 43.2(3);
44.13; 46.2; 49.3(1), 12(5), 20;
51.12(2); 52.2(2); 53.6(2), 11;
54.5
merit, 49.9(2)
mind, human. *See* intellect

GENERAL INDEX

Sion, 51.5(2)
slander, 48.3(1)
slavery, 40.11; 41.2–4, 7–8; 42.1(1); 43.7(1); 44.9(1)
sloth, 49.2(2), (3)
soul, 32.1–2, 5–6; 33.5(3); 34.10(3); 35.3(2); 36.2(2); 38.2; 39.5, 8(2), (3); 42.11(3), 15(3), 16(2); 43.12(3); 44.16; 46.8(2); 47.7–13; 48.3(1); 49.2–3, 10–11, 15(2); 52.1–3, 11(1)
spirit, 38.4(2); 41.10–11, 13(1); 42.10; 46.8(2); 47.11(2); 49.18(1), 22(2); 52.11(1). See also God; soul
stealing, 45.2(2), 6, 12(2), 15(3); 50.9–11; 51.12(1)
suffering, 28.5–6
suicide, 51.10(2)
Susanna, 36.10
symbol, 44.2(1). See also sign
synagogue, 44.9–10

temple of God: the body as, 47.7(2); humans as, 48.10; in Jerusalem, 49.26–27
temptation, 40.10(3); 41.9(2); 43.5–6, 8; 45.13(2); 51.10(2); 53.3(2), 8, 9
testimony, 51.7; 53.5(2)
Thomas, 49.12(1)
time, 31.5; 38.10–11; 40.6
Timothy, 46.5(3); 48.3(4)
Tobias, 35.3(2)
Trinity, 29.7; 36.6, 10; 39.2–5; 40.3–4; 46.4(2)
truth, 30.6–7; 33.7; 34.9; 35.3–4, 6(1); 36.2–3; 37.6–7; 38.10–11; 39.7–8; 40.4–5, 9, 11; 41.1–4, 6, 8(2), 10(3); 42.2(1), 4, 7–8, 11–13, 15; 43.15(2); 45.2(3), 7–8, 11(3), 13(2), (5); 46.4(2), 6(2), (4); 47.9–12; 48.3(1), 9, 12; 49.9(1), 14, 18(2); 50.2(2), 5, 9–10, 12(1); 52.13; 54.8(2)
type, 31.11(1). See also figure

understanding, 29.6; 34.1, 5, 7(2); 35.4(2); 36.1–7, 9(2); 37.1, 4–5,

7(1); 38.3–4, 8–11; 39.3–5, 8(5); 40.4–5, 9–10; 41.2(1), 6, 9(1), (3); 42.1(2), 9, 12–13, 15; 43.6–7, 13, 16–17; 44.3(3), 8, 16–17; 45 passim; 46.4–6; 47, 1–3, 6, 11(1), 13(1); 48.1, 3, 6–7, 9, 11; 49.2–3, 8, 11–12, 16; 50.8, 12–13; 51.3(1), 5(1), (3), 10, 12(2); 52.7, 11–13; 53 passim; 54.8(2)
unity, 32.7–8; 39.5; 47.4–5
universality, 32.7
uprightness, 28.7

vanity, 50.14
Vergil, 43.6(2)
victim, 41.6
victory, 51.2(1)
virgin birth, 30.7(3); 31.3. See also Christ
virtue, 47.11(1)
vocation, 40.10(3)

wasteland: symbol of this world, 28.9(4)
will, 37.8(3); 41.8(3), 12(3); 42.10(2) n.; 49.18(2); 52.3, 5; 53.6, 8–10
wisdom, 35.3–4; 40.4(3); 45.3–4; 48.6(3); 52.12; 53.7(2)
witness, 35.2–6, 9; 36.2–3, 10–11; 41.9(2); 45.2(2); 48.4, 12; 49.17; 50.9; 53.11; false witness, 45.2(2)
wolf: symbol of devil, 46.7–8; 47.1(2); 48.6(1); symbol of heretics and schismatics, 45.10, 12(2); 46 passim; symbol of Jews, 45.10, 12(2); symbol of Judas, 45.10, 12(2)
work, servile, 30.6(2)
world: metaphor for persons, 28.7(3), 8(1); 38.4–6; 39.6(1); 40.10(2); 52.10; end of, 52.6(1)
wrestlers, Christians as, 33.3

Zacharias, 32.6(2); 36.5(2)
Zachary, 49.27(2); 52.8

INDEX OF HOLY SCRIPTURE

(Books of the Old Testament)

(Books of the New Testament)

19.37: 36.12
20.22: 32.6(3) *bis*
20.29: 40.9(1)
20.30–31: 49.9(1)
21.15–17: 47.2(3)
21.18: 47.2(3);
   51.10(2)
21.18–19: 52.3(2)
21.19: 47.2(3)

Acts
1.3: 32.6(3); 50.13
1.5–26: 49.8(3)
1.9: 32.6(3)
1.9–10: 50.13
1.11: 36.12; 40.4
2.1–4: 32.6(3) *bis*
2.1–12: 44.5(2)
2.2–6: 39.5(1)
2.37: 31.9(1);
   40.2(3)
2.41: 40.2(2)
3.1–10: 44.5(2)
3.1–11: 39.5(1)
3.1–16: 31.9(1)
4.4: 40.2(2)
4.32: 39.5(1)
5.15: 44.5(2)
8.23: 42.16(3)
9.4: 28.1(2); 31.9(3)
9.23–25: 46.7(2)

Romans
1.3: 48.3(4)
1.7: 45.15(3)
1.17: 50.6
2.4: 50.7(1)
2.4–6: 33.7
2.12: 54.6(2)
2.25–29: 51.8(1)
3.4: 39.8(3)
3.23: 49.23
4.5: 29.6(3); 53.10;
   54.3(2)
5.5: 32.8(2); 39.5(2)
5.12: 30.5(1);
   49.12(2)
5.12–19: 44.1(2)
5.20: 49.23
6.9: 32.9(1); 45.14;

52.4
6.12–13: 41.12(1)
6.20: 41.8(3)
6.22: 41.8(3)
7.7: 41.12(4)
7.15: 41.10(2)
7.18: 41.12(3)
7.22: 41.10(3), 11(1)
7.23: 34.10(3);
   41.10(2), 11(1)
7.24–25: 34.10(3);
   41.11(2)
7.25: 41.11(2), 12(2)
8.3: 41.5(4); 42.1(1)
8.6: 28.4
8.17: 30.7(3)
8.29–30: 48.6(1)
8.29–32: 45.12(1)
8.33: 45.12(1)
9.14: 53.6(2)
9.32–33: 52.13
10.2–3: 53.11
10.3: 53.9
10.4: 28.9(1);
   51.12(2)
10.10: 36.4(1)
11.16–21: 42.5(1)
11.25: 51.8(2)
11.33: 52.6(1);
   53.6(2)
12.3: 53.8(6)
13.12–13: 35.8
15.8: 31.11(2)
15.9: 31.11(2)

1 Corinthians
1.12–13: 47.3(4)
1.24: 38.11(2); 53.3
1.30: 53.6(2)
1.31: 53.8(3)
2.9: 34.7(2); 35.9;
   40.9(1), 10(2)
2.11: 32.5(1);
   33.5(3)
3.1–3: 36.6
3.6–7: 29.6(1)
3.7: 53.4(1)
4.5: 35.9
4.7: 49.8(2)
5.3: 46.8(2)

6.3: 28.6(2)
6.19: 48.10
7.40: 37.3
10.1–4: 45.9(3)
10.4: 28.9(4);
   30.5(1); 45.9(4);
   46.3(2)
10.11: 28.9(1)
11.29: 50.10(3)
12.7–10: 32.8(1)
12.31: 32.8(2)
13: 32.8(2)
13.12: 34.9(2)
15.21: 30.5(1)
15.26: 34.10(4);
   41.13(1)
15.53: 34.10(4)
15.53–55: 41.13(1)

2 Corinthians
1.20: 28.9(1)
1.22: 32.5(2)
2.14–15: 50.7(1)
2.14–16: 50.7(2)
2.15: 31.11(2)
2.15–16: 51.1
3.6: 49.22(2)
3.15: 48.3(2)
4.13: 45.9(2)
5.5: 32.5(2)
5.6–7: 34.7(1), 10(1)
5.15: 41.13(1)
5.17: 30.7(3)
5.19: 52.10
5.20: 41.5(2), 13(2)
5.21: 41.5(4)
6.8: 29.1
6.15: 50.10(3)
6.16: 48.10
11.33: 46.7(2)
13.3: 47.5

Galatians
3.16: 42.5(1)
3.21: 49.22(2)
3.29: 42.5(1)
4.4: 28.5(1); 31.5(2)
5.6: 29.6(3);
   45.15(3); 53.8(3)
5.13: 41.8(3)